# ENGLISH STAGE COMEDY 1490–1990

English stage comedy has weathered centuries of social and theatrical change. How did it survive?

*English Stage Comedy 1490–1990* is a unique and beautifully written study of the comedy of the English stage from the Tudor period to the late twentieth century. Organized thematically, it shows how this remarkably enduring genre has dealt with the tensions of social life, using its conventions as tools for social inquiry.

Through an examination of comedy Alexander Leggatt demonstrates that an approach through genre, neglected in recent criticism, can have much to say about our current concerns with the relations between literature and society.

*English Stage Comedy 1490–1990* surveys five centuries of classic comic drama, focusing on major playwrights such as:

* Shakespeare
* Jonson
* Etherege
* Wycherley
* Congreve
* Vanbrugh
* Goldsmith
* Sheridan
* Wilde
* Shaw
* Coward
* Orton
* Ayckbourn
* and many lesser known figures

**Alexander Leggatt** is Professor of English at University College, University of Toronto, and is the author of *Shakespeare's Political Drama* (1988, Routledge) and *Jacobean Public Theatre* (1992, Routledge).

# ENGLISH STAGE COMEDY 1490–1990

## Five centuries of a genre

*Alexander Leggatt*

London and New York

First published 1998
by Routledge
11 New Fetter Lane, London EC4P 4EE

Simultaneously published in the USA and Canada
by Routledge
29 West 35th Street, New York, NY 10001

Typeset in Baskerville by Routledge
Printed and bound in Great Britain by
Clays Ltd, St. Ives PLC

*British Library Cataloguing in Publication Data*
A catalogue record for this book is available from the British Library

*Library of Congress Cataloging in Publication Data*
Leggatt, Alexander,
English Stage Comedy, 1490–1990: Five centuries of a genre / Alexander Leggatt.
p. cm.
Includes bibliographical references and index.
1. English drama (Comedy) – History and criticism. 2. Literary form. I. Title.
PR631.L44 1998
822`.052309–dc21                    98–12864

ISBN 0–415–18936–5 (hbk)
ISBN 0–415–18937–3 (pbk)

FOR MY STUDENTS

# CONTENTS

# ACKNOWLEDGEMENTS

As this project has developed over the years I have accumulated many debts. Some of the ideas were tried out in talks at the University of San Francisco, the University of Michigan at Ann Arbor, McMaster University's Stratford (Ontario) Seminars, the Arts and Letters Club of Toronto, the Department of English Colloquium at the University of Toronto, the Symposium on the 1890s at University College, and the lunchtime discussion group at University College. I am grateful to the organizers of these occasions, and to the audiences for their helpful and challenging responses. I am also grateful to the Work in Progress in English Group at the University of Toronto, who helped me think about the relations between literature and social history.

For particular responses to the talks in question, and for the sharing of questions and ideas over the years, I am indebted to Susan Akbari, Ronald Bryden, Eleanor Cook, Mira Friedlander, Linda Hutcheon, Robert Irish, Ejner Jensen, David Rayside and Giles Slade. Linda Hutcheon (again) and J.R. de J. Jackson provided especially valuable support and advice at a crucial stage. David Bevington, Brian Parker, Susan Snyder and John Velz have also provided essential support. At Routledge, Talia Rodgers, Jonathan Bate and Peter Thomson have been helpful and encouraging in their comments on the manuscript, and Talia Rodgers and Jason Arthur have coped resourcefully not just with the usual business of publication but with mysteriously disappearing faxes and chronic postal failures.

I am particulary grateful to Alan Bewell, Brian Corman and Alan Somerset, who read the entire manuscript with great care, and whose comments were invaluable. The imperfections that remain are my own responsibility. Another very special debt is to the students in my graduate seminar, Comic Form in English Drama, who over the years have contributed immeasurably to this project. My debt to them is part of a larger debt acknowledged in the dedication.

Finally, I am grateful to the Killam Program of the Canada Council for the Killam Research Fellowship that, with the cooperation of the University of Toronto, made possible the released time that allowed me to complete this project; without it, this book could not have been written.

# NOTE

Quotations from plays are taken from the editions listed in the Appendix. Quotations have been brought into line with modern British spelling and punctuation, except in the case of Bernard Shaw, whose typographical idiosyncrasies I have preserved, since they are as much a part of his text as the archaisms in Spenser. The presentation of speech headings and stage directions has been regularized. Line numbers are given where available; otherwise, page numbers. The Revels Plays system of decimal numbering for stage directions has been adopted.

The dates given for plays are the dates (sometimes approximate) of first production. The date is given on a play's first appearance in a chapter, and reiterated if it reappears after a significant interval.

# INTRODUCTION
## Five centuries of a genre

### A question of genre

Several lines intersect in the making of a play: the author, the culture, the theatre, actors and audience, and the genre. My concern is with the last of these. English stage comedy forms part of what has been called 'the longest, most continuous generic tradition in Western literature',[1] tracing its roots back to Aristophanes and Menander, appearing in many different national literatures, surviving centuries of cultural change with its basic conventions stubbornly intact. I am limiting the discussion to one island culture over a mere five centuries, in the hope of taking a closer look, under selected local conditions, at the ways in which this remarkably healthy organism has adapted and survived.

To think of comedy as an organism, a single living entity, is in a literal sense misleading. There is no such thing as comedy, an abstract transhistorical form; there are only comedies. But they accumulate to create a body of case law, a set of expectations within which writers and audiences operate. In a generally cautious and sceptical study of the problems of writing literary history, David Perkins declares: 'A sorting by genre is valid if the concept of genre was entertained by the writer and his contemporary readers. For in this case the expectations associated with the concept were effective in forming both the work and the responses to it.'[2] There are problematic cases (*Troilus and Cressida*, *The Cherry Orchard*) but in general if a play is called a comedy, by a writer or by his contemporaries, the expectations involved are clear and firm.

In the current state of criticism, however, genre has been neglected in favour of seeing a literary text as product and producer of the culture of its time, implicated (often with the connotations of guilt that word implies) in ideologies, structures of power, methods of production. This is an understandable reaction against an older habit of seeing literature as a timeless phenomenon, against those critics who contemplated the well-wrought urn but asked no questions about the working conditions or markets involved in its creation. Yet this reaction, necessary and useful though it has been, inevitably imposes its own set of blinkers. Thus one critic sees Crosswill, the demanding, arbitrary father of Richard Brome's comedy *The Weeding of Covent Garden* (c.1633), as part of Brome's analysis of Charles I's period

1

of personal rule; another sees the strong-willed heroines of Goldsmith's *The Good-Natured Man* (1768) and *She Stoops to Conquer* (1773), who exercise a firm control over their potential husbands, as a sign of Goldsmith's opposition to Lord Hardwicke's Marriage Act of 1753, which seemed to give excessive power to parents and guardians.[3] Neither reading can be ruled out; but what they ignore is that arbitrary fathers who give their children a hard time, and strong-minded heroines who control the terms of their own marriages, are part of the stock in trade of comedy for generations before, and for generations after, the plays in question. David Perkins's objection is harshly put but makes a valid point: 'historical context almost invariably means, in practice, the world that was contemporary with the text when it was produced. Since writers also derive impulses from works of former ages, this contextualizing practice is simpleminded.'[4] There is such a thing as literary context, and to get a full sense of how Brome's Crosswill and Goldsmith's heroines operate we need to remind ourselves that, while it does indeed matter that a play was written in the 1630s, or the 1770s, it also matters that it is a comedy. We need a sense of literature both as social process and as form, each factor feeding and modifying the other. Stage comedy, at once socially aware and highly formalized, is an ideal site for such a study.

Part of comedy's artifice is a tendency to the metatheatrical, bringing an awareness of comic tradition on to the stage. Thus, writers of Restoration comedy regularly quote Ben Jonson, with or without formal acknowledgement. In John Crowne's *The Married Beau* (1694) old Thorneback boasts of his continuing sexual prowess by quoting *Bartholomew Fair* (1614): 'I'm like Ben Jonson's Ursly, the Pig-Woman, / 'Gad, I roast pigs as well as e'er I did' (II.p.20). Thomas d'Urfey's *The Richmond Heiress* (1693) borrows from *Epicoene* (1609), without acknowledgement, a joke about a prolific family called De la Fool (II.ii.p.34). The habit persists in the twentieth century. Tom Stoppard's *The Real Thing* (1982) contains half-heard echoes of Noël Coward's *Private Lives* (1930): the playwright Henry tries to recall a hotel where the band, to his annoyance, kept coming back to the same tune: 'we were in some place like Bournemouth or Deauville' (I.ii.p.16). The situation is that of Act One of *Private Lives*, where the setting is Deauville. Coward's acid line, 'Very flat, Norfolk' (I.p.206) lurks just under Henry's mischievous references to a flat in the hills in Norfolk (I.ii.p.31). Echoes pass down the generations. In *She Stoops to Conquer* (1773), Kate Hardcastle, in the plain dress that makes Marlow take her for a barmaid, asks, 'Don't you think I look something like Cherry in *The Beaux' Stratagem*?' (III.i.230–31), and the dialogue in which Marlow and Hastings mistake Hardcastle for an innkeeper closely echoes an equivalent scene in Farquhar's play (1707). When in *She Stoops* Hardcastle declares, 'I love everything that's old: old friends, old times, old books, old wine; and I believe, Dorothy, *(taking her hand)* you'll own I have been pretty fond of an old wife' (I.i.20–23) he is setting up Clive Champion-Cheney in Somerset Maugham's *The Circle* (1921): 'I love old wine, old friends, and old books, but I like young women' (II.p.234).

Some of these allusions are, as it were, audibly footnoted. Others are left for the knowing members of the audience to pick up on their own, the slyness of the reference implying a compliment to their knowledge. In both cases, though more powerfully in the latter, the playwright bonds with the audience in a common awareness of the tradition of English comedy. This awareness is aided by the theatrical habit of keeping plays in repertory; one gets a very misleading impression of the theatre of any period if one studies only new plays. Following Hardcastle, audiences seem to like old comedies in particular. Late Restoration comedies continued to thrive on the London stage well into the eighteenth century,[5] and the audiences of Goldsmith and Sheridan could also see, among others, Shakespeare, Jonson, Fletcher, Congreve and Centlivre.[6] As manager of Drury Lane, Sheridan prepared the ground for *The School for Scandal* by staging revivals of Congreve.[7] The repertory system that lasted into the nineteenth century allowed an enormous number of plays to keep their place as living theatre; even now, when the number of plays on view is restricted by the custom of the long run and the relatively small repertoires of the subsidized companies, the theatre-goer in London and elsewhere has a choice of centuries. And the classic comedies are still widely available as literary texts. Joe Orton's diary records his reading of English comedy and his sometimes surprising judgments: he admired Congreve's style, but preferred Sheridan to what he called 'Restoration rubbish', and liked the Savoy operas.[8] Orton reacted, powerfully, to the society of his time; but in shaping that reaction he drew on his knowledge of what other comic writers had done before him. Even when he served a prison term for defacing library books, he was, he insisted, defending classic literature, revenging himself on a library in Islington that was stuffed with 'rubbish novels' but could not produce a copy of Gibbon.[9]

## The function of comedy

The continuing life that stage comedies have across the centuries, for both writers and audiences, justifies our study of the genre across a broad historical range. But if genre is expectation, what are the expectations of comedy? Theatre is a practical business, and it is best to start with a working playwright describing his job. Hugh Kelly, in the preface to his 1773 comedy *The School for Wives*, writes, 'the great business of comedy [consists] in making difficulties for the purpose of removing them; in distressing poor young lovers; and in rendering a happy marriage the object of every catastrophe' (p. iv). The value of this statement lies in its sheer ordinariness. It summarizes a set of stock expectations that audiences have brought to the theatre for centuries. Even the writers who play against such expectations (by refusing to end with marriage, for example) are conscious of doing so; they invoke the expectation by denying it. A comedy, then, is a problem-solving story, ending in resolution and order normally symbolized by marriage. The other distinctive feature of comedy is laughter. The prologue to Jonson's *Volpone* (1606), one of the grimmest of English comedies, promises to rub the audience's cheeks with salt 'till, red with laughter, / They shall look fresh a week after' (35–6). Goldsmith's 1772 essay comparing laughing and sentimental comedy, however misleading as an account of eighteenth-century drama, is a

3

compelling statement of conventional wisdom: comedy which denies laughter is betraying itself as comedy.

But the plays Goldsmith calls sentimental, though they did not eliminate laughter, restrained it in the interests of good feeling; and in Jonson's promise of laughter there is a clear edge of cruelty. As a student of mine, Dena Bain, once put it in class discussion, 'You never laugh at anything nice.' The classic statements about why we laugh see laughter as a way of coping with something uncomfortable. For William Hazlitt, laughter recognizes 'the difference between what things are, and what they ought to be'; 'The essence of the laughable then is the incongruous, the disconnecting one idea from another, or the jostling of one feeling against another'.[10] Incongruity, disconnection, jostling – all imply a discomfort that stands against the harmonious relationships of the ordered ending. According to Henri Bergson, we laugh at the disconcerting sight of a person losing the elasticity of humanity, becoming a mechanism, a thing, 'something mechanical encrusted on the the living'.[11] Salt is an ancient metaphor for wit. Jonson promises (or threatens) to make us laugh by rubbing our cheeks with it. Bergson writes of the bitterness that analysis uncovers in comedy: laughter 'is a froth with a saline base. Like froth, it sparkles. It is gaiety itself. But the philosopher who gathers a handful of it to taste may find that the substance is scanty, and the aftertaste bitter'.[12] Laughter may bring pleasure; but to trace the origins of laughter is to make uncomfortable discoveries. The comedy of starvation in *The Gold Rush*, in which a companion becomes an hallucinatory chicken and a shoe becomes a gourmet treat, was based on Chaplin's reading of the story of the Donner party, trapped and starving in the mountains on the way to Oregon: most died; some turned to cannibalism; others ate their moccasins.[13]

You never laugh at anything nice. A comedy that *ends* with a laugh is a comedy that ends not with a solution but with a fresh disaster. At the end of Gogol's *The Government Inspector* the real government inspector arrives; the trouble is just beginning. At the end of George F. Kaufman and Moss Hart's Broadway comedy *The Man Who Came to Dinner*, the eccentric Sheridan Whiteside, who has wrought havoc in the lives of the Middle American family in whose home he is stranded by a broken ankle, walks out the door to universal relief, slips on the front step, and breaks his ankle again. According to Arthur Koestler, laughter does not truly release tension because it does not solve the problem; it fritters away energy in purposeless physical reflexes that make action impossible.[14] Laughter is not a solution, it is a sign of the problem. As a number of writers have observed, there is a built-in contradiction between comedy's two purposes, laughter and the happy ending.[15] In its normal operation the function of comedy is to make the audience stop laughing.

## Comedy and society

According to George Meredith, the comic poet 'addresses . . . men's intellects, with reference to the operation of the social world upon their characters';

according to Bergson, we laugh not at immorality but at unsociability.[16] Comedy's focus on the social level of life is as common a feature as its use of laughter and the happy ending. As the order affirmed in the traditional ending is essentially social – marriage, the family, the rule of law – so the anxieties on which comic laughter plays are social anxieties: the need for money, security and social position, and the fear that such needs are dehumanizing. Some of the sharpest anxieties surround marriage and the family, institutions that are both comforting and oppressive. Characters want marriage, and fear it; they need to find their parents, and to escape from their parents. There is a pervasive double-edged quality in these anxieties that corresponds to comedy's built-in contradiction between laughter and the happy ending. The strong-minded heroines of comedy work to get their men on their own terms, knowing the ultimate price of getting them is to dwindle into wives, losing the freedom and authority they enjoy in courtship. And yet they want marriage. The thing you desire is inside the thing you fear; the thing you fear is inside the thing you desire. It is no wonder that comedy, pervasively aware of this dilemma, deals in anxiety.

Richard Napier, a seventeenth-century physician who treated many cases of mental disturbance, left a record of the anxieties that preyed on his patients: they centred on courtship, including lovers' quarrels and betrayals; and on marriage, with its worries about money, childbearing and the unkindness of spouses. Many of his patients were, like the principal characters of comedy, young; they were caught in the stress of moving from dependence on their parents to full responsibility for themselves as adults.[17] Their worries are the worries that comedy acts out; their case histories are like the salt that remains when the froth of comedy's laughter has dissipated. Michael MacDonald, in his study of Napier's work, is struck by the analogies with contemporary drama, with its 'profoundly sensitive treatment of youthful love and married life' and calls for an opening of the lines of communication between literary criticism and social history, to 'enable readers to negotiate beyond both the crude literalism that leads a Peter Laslett to repudiate literature and the stratospheric structuralism that prompts a Northrop Frye to neglect history'.[18] 'Stratospheric structuralism', as we have seen, hardly describes the present state of literary study; the need is rather to reintroduce literary scholars to literature. But MacDonald offers a valid warning against pure formalism. I have argued that the historical perspective needs to be complicated by an awareness of genre; equally, the generic perspective needs to be complicated by an awareness of history. The social institutions in which comedy deals are, like comedy itself, long-lasting and bound by tradition. But they are not timeless abstractions, any more than comedy is, and our study of the genre needs to include an awareness of the particular society in which it operates.

There are, however, certain cautions to issue about the relations between a play and its social period. Peter Laslett has acknowledged that 'the spontaneous assumptions in the literature of any age, the behaviour of the minor characters, the conventions against which irony and humour must be understood, reveal with great precision facts of considerable interest about the structure of society',

5

but he is reluctant to extrapolate from a literary work to the general characteristics of a whole era. We might, for example, imagine from Restoration comedy an age of licentiousness; but 'the demographic record' (illegitimate births as an index of illicit sex in an age of unreliable birth control) does not bear this out.[19] Drama does not provide simple mirror images of its society. In fact the illegitimacy curve, rising during the eighteenth century and reaching a peak in the early nineteenth,[20] might lead one to imagine that comedy mirrors society by reversing it: as the audience after a bawdy Restoration comedy went chastely home, the audience after a pure-minded eighteenth-century comedy, having had their moral uplift for the day, scattered to strange beds and alleyways. But there are far too many problems in drawing such a conclusion, beginning with the fact that the demographers sample a wide range of largely rural populations, and the segment of London society to which comedy played, and which it depicted, barely shows on the graphs.

The restriction of my study to stage comedy is another complication. My decision to exclude other forms, particularly the novel, is not just a pragmatic one intended to keep the scale manageable. The brevity and immediacy of the stage form create pressures that make its brand of social comedy distinctive. Jane Austen can take several weeks of action, and several hours of reading time, to get Emma and Mr Knightley together, and in the process she can allow a relaxed exploration of their mutual attraction and mutual misunderstanding. Men and women working toward marriage in stage comedy have minutes where Austen's characters have weeks. There is urgency, pressure, even at times panic, not just in particular moments (Austen allows that) but as a basic condition. Everything is broader, simpler, faster – and necessarily more conventionalized. By the same token, the society in which the central characters are embedded cannot be examined week by week as it goes about its business; it has to be rendered in shorthand. Fielding and Dickens can allow long journeys, digressions, inserted stories, lectures from the narrator on social questions. The action of a stage comedy has to be much tighter than that, the story more conventionalized, the formulas more obtrusive, the social insights embodied in action. (Lectures are allowed, but they have to be quick and simple.) In general, formal conventions loom much larger in stage comedy than in other media, and more of comedy's thinking is done through them.

These qualities of economy and stylization mark a sharp difference between stage comedy and social life. John Habakkuk's magisterial study of English landownership draws freely on literary evidence; but it draws on novels, Austen and Trollope in particular.[21] A novel, we might say, has time to tell the truth; a play, not always. Lawrence Stone has reported some fascinating case histories showing what a shadowy business it could be, given the state of the law before the Marriage Act of 1753, to determine whether a couple was actually married or not.[22] In Jonson's *Epicoene* the question of whether or not Morose is married to the title character is solved at a stroke when Dauphine whips off Epicoene's peruke and announces, 'here is your release, sir; you have married a boy' (V.iv.204–5). It was never that simple in the courts, or the lawyers would have starved. But if drama had tried to emulate the complexity of actual cases the audience would have gone home long before the end.

Stage comedy, however, does not stylize so much as to lose contact with the social world it draws on. There is even a sense in which its very stylization reflects the means by which society itself is constructed. Comedy deals, notoriously, in type-characters: the heavy father, the young lovers, the fop. This is one of its oldest traditions: writing in the fourth century, Donatus specifies a clothing code: white for old men, twisted cloaks for parasites, and so on.[23] Peter L. Berger and Thomas Luckmann have argued that this is just what we do in everyday life, dealing with other people by type-casting them: ' "a man", "a European", "a buyer", "a jovial type", and so on'.[24] As the worries of Richard Napier's patients were the worries of characters in comedy, the comic process of character typing is one of the processes of everyday social life. Comedy may be treacherous evidence for social history, and social history a problematic guide to comedy. But they are not two solitudes. The discussion that follows is essentially and deliberately literary; the degree to which social history impinges on it will vary from topic to topic, and will sometimes be found more in the footnotes than in the text. It will try to show that comedy has its own distinctive ways of thinking about the way people live in society. But it will not do so in formalist isolation: the lines of communication to social history will be left open.

## The problems of literary history

In a wide-ranging survey of comedy, Robert Bechtold Heilman takes what he calls 'the way of timelessness', seeing the great comic writers of all periods as 'contemporaries of each other'.[25] But comedy itself does not take the way of timelessness. It is acutely aware of social change, and often highlights it: the dialogue on the disappearance of wigs that opens Sheridan's *The Rivals* (1775), the onstage appearance of a motorcar in Shaw's *Man and Superman* (1905). Seen from a distance, English comedy changes its character as it moves through history: learned and scatological in the Tudor period, romantic in Shakespeare and his Elizabethan predecessors, satiric from Jonson (with an emphasis on money) to the Restoration (with an emphasis on manners and sex), genteel and sentimental through the eighteenth and nineteenth centuries, ironic in the twentieth. This pattern can be related to changes in English society, notably the turn to gentler manners in the eighteenth and nineteenth centuries.[26] But on closer inspection the pattern breaks down.[27] Many Jacobean comedies are as sentimental as anything the Victorians could have written; on the Restoration stage, broad physical comedy flourishes as readily as verbal wit and polished manners; and the twentieth century did not invent irony. The narrative of historical change also depends on classifying plays according to type, and given the internal eclecticism that characterizes English drama in all periods, individual plays can be formidably difficult to label. Romance, manners, sentiment, laughter – in play after play these features dance around each other. They are useful terms for describing a particular effect, a particular moment; but as terms to describe a whole play or a whole period they are problematic.

The narrative form also falls into what David Perkins calls 'the drearily familiar figures of the birth, maturity, decline, and end of a form, genre, national literature, and so on'. He objects, 'the literary series is not a plant or an animal'.[28] By this model, English stage comedy is born in the Renaissance, flourishes in the Restoration, becomes attenuated in the eighteenth century, brain-dead in the nineteenth (with brilliant but brief revivals under Goldsmith, Sheridan and Wilde) and is only a memory in the twentieth. In practice, however, words like 'flourish' and 'decline' describe not what a genre does but how far it satisfies the taste of the writer who is describing it; unless, of course, one is using them as purely quantitative measurements, in which case comedy flourished mightily in the eighteenth century. The view that the tradition is dead in the modern world is particularly widespread: T.G.A. Nelson calls *The Importance of Being Earnest* 'perhaps the last important exemplar of the Menandrian tradition in European comedy'; Eric Bentley pronounces comedy extinct or senile; J.L. Styan declares that to revive the old tradition now would be 'an affront to the dignity of the atomic-age audience'.[29] As I hope to show, these reports of comedy's death are greatly exaggerated. They prevent us from noticing how much fresh life writers as diverse as Coward, Orton, Stoppard and Churchill have found in the old conventions.

Another common historical generalization I hope to question is that since mainstream English comedy is satiric and urban it springs essentially from Jonson, and Shakespeare stands apart from it.[30] This generalization could easily be turned another way: since comedy concerns itself with courtship, marriage and the family, Shakespeare is right in the mainstream, and Jonson, with his relative lack of interest in such matters, is the isolated figure. For all the respect later comic writers pay to him, they draw much less from him than we might expect, and their affinities with Shakespeare, about which they are largely silent, are actually stronger.

All this is by way of explaining why this book is not a chronological survey: the generalizations such a survey would demand break down too easily. And it would have to be tied to a narrative of history of the sort that historians themselves are starting to question. The story of change in English society, in social practice and social attitudes, depends on a set of vulnerable generalizations. The real story, according to many historians, is continuity. Ralph A. Houlbrooke has argued that the structure and function of the family changed very little between the fifteenth and eighteenth centuries.[31] According to Linda A. Pollock, the notion that eighteenth century people had a greater capacity for emotion than their Renaissance forebears is a myth that does not survive a study of the evidence; and parent–child relationships, far from changing in the eighteenth century, are 'curiously resistant to change'.[32] The Puritans are frequently credited with introducing a more humane view of marriage in the sixteenth and seventeenth centuries; Kathleen M. Davies has shown that, far from being new, their ideas on marriage can easily be traced in pre-Reformation texts.[33] In a study of English society from 1688 to 1832, J.C.D. Clark has argued for its essential conservatism, the continuity of its social and political institutions and attitudes. One of his section headings is, 'The Survival of Patriarchalism; or, Did the Industrial Revolution Really Happen?'[34] This insistence by historians on the continuity of English society needs to be part of the dialogue between their work and that of literary criticism; and it offers further encouragement to take a long view of English comedy across the periods that have subdivided it.

None of this, however, puts us back into Heilman's 'way of timelessness'. Not every social change can be shown to be a myth (Clark's account of a stable society stops at the First Reform Bill) and writers are not simply each other's contemporaries. Not many years separate Wilde and Coward, but between the confident wit of the one and the nervous wit of the other lies the shell-shock of the twentieth century. Even writers who *are* each other's contemporaries (Shakespeare and Jonson being the obvious examples) can write about very different worlds. We need to find a way of studying comedy and society that acknowledges the play of difference and continuity but does not depend on long narrative curves and the unreliable generalizations that support them. The solution I propose is to send down a series of probes, looking for the way comedy in different periods treats a single issue, remaining alert to the way different treatments relate both to the writer's temper and to the temper of his age, but not allowing either factor a final power to shape the discussion. This does not mean an absolutely even-handed distribution of periods in each chapter; certain issues matter more to some periods (and writers) than to others. But I have concentrated on questions that never quite disappear, and provide common subjects across a wide historical range.[35]

## Spaces and bodies

Something should now be said of the theatricality of comedy, both for its own sake and by way of introducing the play of continuity and difference, and of drama and society, that will concern us throughout. A stage is a tightly defined space, and comedy concerns itself with the way people live in spaces, the open space of a park or a wood, the closed space of a room with practicable doors. Here, we can trace a social change that not only mattered to comedy but presented a sharp challenge to it. The free social interaction of Restoration comedy reflects the widespread availability of public space. People meet in the park and the mall, where men and women mingle in a relaxed and natural way, where assignations are made, and where clothes, manners and even feelings are on display.[36] In this period even stage sets that represent rooms in private houses sometimes feel like public spaces, where people come and go with remarkable freedom.[37] But through the eighteenth and nineteenth centuries public space declined, life became more domestic, and the quasi-theatrical art of self-presentation in a public arena suffered accordingly.[38] The turn towards the domestic is symbolized in the subtitle of George Colman the Younger's 1803 comedy *John Bull; or the Englishman's Fireside*. As the streets of nineteenth century London became (or were perceived to be) increasingly unsafe, the authorities urged women to stay home, effectively restricting their lives to the domestic sphere.[39] Colin McDowell notes that as the Victorian era was the great age of taxidermy, the Victorian lady was reduced to a specimen in a glass case, set up at home to be admired, beautiful but useless.[40] Houses were now designed for separate male and female activities. For men, the study, the billiard room, the smoking room, the library; for women, the boudoir and the drawing room. Even that happy couple Victoria and Albert were affected: most of the rooms at Osborne had the intertwined initials V and A over the doors; the smoking room had only A.[41]

The rituals of courtship in comedy are affected by this change. As we shall see in later chapters, in Restoration comedy, Etherege's *The Man of Mode* (1676) being a key example, men and women meet freely in public and talk frankly to each other, teasing, challenging, working through their relationships face to face. Sidney and Maud, the lovers in T.W. Robertson's *Society* (1865), meet in a semi-public space, a square; but they meet at night, when the square is locked, and their conversation is inhibited by shyness and social awkwardness: 'Are you not going to speak? . . . I don't know what to say' (I.ii.p.48). Later we see Sidney in the Owl's Roost, a public house that acts as a club where men smoke, drink, toast, talk politics and read newspapers. In that very masculine space, to the accompaniment of a raucous song about the deceitfulness of women, Sidney gets the news that Maud is engaged to another man. He turns '*deadly pale*', and '*his head falls on the table*' (II.i.p.58). The lovers of Restoration comedy are kept temporarily apart by their own personal wariness, their desire to keep their independence, their need not to lose face. Robertson's lovers are blocked by inhibition and misunderstanding embodied in tightly defined social spaces that make men and women seem like different species.

The detailed scenic realism in the Owl's Roost scene reflects another change in the nature of space – this time, theatrical space – to which comedy had to respond. In the theatres of the Renaissance and the Restoration, actors played close to the audience, in the same light; the auditorium was not darkened until the late nineteenth century. This allowed a free interplay between stage and audience, the equivalent of the free interplay between men and women in public spaces. The arrival of scenery in the Restoration did not really affect this, since the use of the forestage continued to encourage direct address, a convention that survived from the Renaissance into the early nineteenth century.[42] But as theatres grew in size this intimacy declined: in the late seventeenth century Drury Lane held around 800 people; by 1794 it held more than 3,600. The playing of comedy, which thrives on a close actor–audience relationship, must have been particularly affected.[43] (When comedy flourished in the nineteenth century, it was often in smaller theatres: the Prince of Wales's for the plays of T.W. Robertson, the Criterion for the plays of Henry Arthur Jones.) The darkening of the auditorium would have increased the separation. In the 1930s the actor-manager Seymour Hicks looked back to the old ways when he declared that 'for a comedy the house lights should be one-quarter up'.[44] In 1880 Squire Bancroft 'put a moulded and gilded picture-frame, two feet wide, around the proscenium of the Haymarket, flush with the front of the stage'. It was a defining moment: the actors no longer related directly to the audience; they had retreated behind the proscenium, into a fully pictorial set.[45] Modern experiments with theatre design notwithstanding, in many theatres, including theatres where modern and classic comedies are played, they are still there.

Direct address works naturally with comedy's self-conscious artifice, its willingness to admit we are in a theatre watching a play. In early English drama such admissions come easily. In Henry Medwall's *Fulgens and Lucrece* (c.1497), which has a claim to being the first extant English comedy, we are not even in a theatre; the play was written for performance in a banqueting hall during dinner. The clowns A and B are so far from being creatures of illusion that they have no character names, only the personalities of the actors who play them. They chat directly with the audience, twitting them with their silence: 'What mean ye, sirs, to stand so still?' (I.2). At one point B knocks on the door, A asks an audience member to let him in, and when nothing happens B enters on his own, complaining that the audience is useless. Much of the comedy depends on teasing the audience for behaving like an audience, just standing around and watching. In *Gammer Gurton's Needle* (c.1550), by 'Mr S.', there is some pretence that the stage represents the streets and houses of a village (the acting area of *Fulgens and Lucrece* represents nothing but itself). But the chief trickster, Diccon the Bedlam, still speaks to the audience directly, urging them to keep out of the actors' way and using their silence to enlist them as his fellow conspirators: 'Be still awhile, and say nothing. Make here a little roomth' (II.iv.2). Radical changes in stage space have modified this joke, but not killed it. In N.F. Simpson's *One Way Pendulum* (1959), Mrs Groomkirby, from behind the proscenium arch, takes with an ill grace the audience's observation of the set which is her living room: 'They'll have to take it as they find it. I haven't got time to go round scrubbing and polishing for them' (I.p.15). Towards the end of Orton's *Loot* (1965) the crooked policeman Truscott declares, 'What has just taken place is perfectly scandalous and had better go no farther than these three walls' (II.p.271). While Diccon enlists the audience in his misdemeanours, Orton's characters try to hide theirs. But the missing fourth wall makes the audience witnesses, and their silence makes them accomplices.

Through the radical changes in theatre space one thing, we might think, remains constant: the presence of the actor. But as space changes, the way in which the actor is present – directly demanding our attention, or simply observed – also changes. The most important change took place at the Restoration, and it involved the actors themselves. According to Michael Goldman, 'an actor's profession and desire are to interest people with his body'.[46] The actor's body is particularly important for comedy, which deals not just with the social level of life but with the physical level: food, sex, clothing. In the pre-Restoration theatre female roles were taken by boys, and the convention of the female character with the male body allowed playful experiments with theatrical illusion and questions of gender. In John Lyly's *Gallathea* (c.1585) two girls, disguised as boys, fall in love with each other. Uncertain about the right body language, they are uncomfortable as

11

boys (II.i.13–31). Lyly gives us boys disguised as girls disguised as boys, and not very good at it. In the end the goddess Venus promises that one of them will have a sex change. We never learn, and they do not care, which one it will be, and as they are still in disguise the final image is of two boys who are really girls (and two girls who are really boys) going off to get married. In Shakespeare's *As You Like It* (c.1600) Rosalind's disguise as a boy allows Orlando to play love scenes with a boy who looks like a boy and who is called Ganymede, the slang term for a boy prostitute. The nominally heterosexual basis of the action is further unsettled when Rosalind, in the epilogue, says she would kiss the men in the audience 'If I were a woman' (16–17), and we realize we have not just been watching Rosalind play Ganymede, we have been watching Ganymede play Rosalind.

In the Restoration theatre, when actresses took over, this playful ambiguity about gender was replaced by direct sex appeal.[47] The function of the breeches part, notoriously, was to let the actress show her legs; the more she pretended to be a man, the more she registered as a woman. The epilogue to Thomas Southerne's *Sir Anthony Love* (1690), which starred Susanna Mountford in a breeches part, tells the audience that what it came for was 'to see . . . the female Mountford bare above the knee' (14–16).[48] At the end of Jonson's *Epicoene* (1609), Dauphine whips off Epicoene's peruke and tells Morose flatly, 'You have married a boy' (V.iv.204–5), at once solving the play's problem and calling the bluff of a stage convention on which all plays of the time depended. Adapting this moment to Restoration conditions, Wycherley in *The Plain Dealer* (1676) has Vernish discover Fidelia's true sex: '*Pulls off her peruke, and feels her breasts*' (IV.p.487). He later refers to 'her pouting, swelling breasts' (V.p.503); our attention is not confined to the actress's legs. He tries to rape her, and she barely escapes. Fidelia was played by the popular and attractive Elizabeth Boutell, described in a contemporary satire as 'Chestnut-maned Boutell, whom all the town fucks'.[49] Here her body – exposed, pawed, threatened – is offered to the audience in a disquieting variation on the voyeuristic convention of the breeches part.

Comedy deals in social anxiety, and one of the sharpest of social anxieties is the fear of exposure. The revelation of Fidelia's true sex, not as part of a comic resolution, but to the wrong man at the wrong time, as part of the problem, invokes an unstable mix of sexual appeal and sexual shock; any laughter it provokes is likely to be unsteady. Elsewhere we find scenes of exposure that play on social anxiety by using stage space and the bodies of the actors, and show the play of continuity and change between different periods. At the end of Thomas Southerne's *The Wives' Excuse* (1692) Mrs Teazell invades Friendall's house to search for her niece; as she moves upstage the shutters at the back of the set part, indicating her opening the door to the next room: '*Scene draws, shows Friendall and Mrs Witzwould upon a couch*' (V.iii.283.1). The stage direction does not specify what they are doing, but they go into the room to have sex. In the 1994 Royal Shakespeare Company production, Friendall was seen mating with her from behind, bringing into the elegant setting the sight of copulating dogs. Friendall's response to being caught in the act before a large party of guests, including his own wife, is simple indignation: 'What a pox!

Disturb a gentleman's pleasures! And in his own house too!' When he learns the lady on the couch is not the one he was expecting, his apology is also an insult: 'Ha! Witwoud here! Nay then, would you had come sooner. Madam, I beg your pardon for some liberties I have taken with your ladyship. But, faith, I took you for Mrs Sightly' (V.iii.286–89). (I didn't want *you*.) Friendall's moral vacuousness is of a piece with the rest of the ending, where the embarrassing revelation produces no repentance, no resolution. Friendall and his wife coldly agree to part; Springame, who has been trying to get into bed with Witwoud from the start of the play, follows her offstage, assuming that if she'll do it with Friendall she'll do it with him. The cynical world the play has shown goes on its way, unredeemable.

Sheridan's *The School for Scandal* (1777) uses an equivalent revelation to totally different effect. *The Wives' Excuse*, like *The Plain Dealer*, will generate uncomfortable laughter at best. When at the first performance of Sheridan's play Charles Surface threw down the screen in his brother Joseph's apartment to reveal, not the little French milliner he and Sir Peter Teazle had been joking about, but Lady Teazle, the laugh was heard outside the theatre and down the street.[50] Once again a closed space has opened on an embarrassing revelation. But the audience's laugh can be an easy one: Lady Teazle is alone behind the screen, she has spent the first part of the scene resisting Joseph's attempts at seduction, and her one offence is the indiscretion of being there at all.[51] Satisfyingly, the masks have fallen: Joseph is exposed, Sir Peter enlightened, Charles vindicated, Lady Teazle repentant – though she has far less to feel guilty about than the unrepentant Friendall. Joseph makes a futile attempt to lie his way out of the situation, but Lady Teazle refuses to support him. With a whole act to go, her honesty lays the groundwork for a full reconciliation with her husband, and helps us measure the difference between *The Wives' Excuse*, a tough-minded Restoration comedy (too tough-minded even for its own time; it was not a success) and a good-natured, entertaining eighteenth-century one.

The revelation of the body when the space suddenly opens is much more innocuous in Sheridan: whatever Friendall and Witwoud are doing, Lady Teazle is just standing there. Such is the economy of Sheridan's management of the scene, that is all she needs to do. In Jonson's *Bartholomew Fair* (1614) the revelation of the body is more graphic and embarrassing. Justice Adam Overdo, who has been spying in disguise on the Fair, reveals his true identity and begins to pass judgment on all parties, when his own wife, who is onstage unknown to him and dressed as a prostitute, vomits: '*Mistress Overdo is sick, and her husband is silenced*' (V.v.67). The rebellion of her body summarizes one of the play's main themes: the flesh is uncontrollable. As Quarlous tells Overdo, 'Remember you are but Adam, flesh and blood! You have your frailty, forget your other name of Overdo, and invite us all to supper' (V.v.96–98). There is also the social embarrassment of seeing a Justice's wife on the game, confirming the complaint of a professional, earlier in the play, 'The poor common whores can have no traffic for the privy rich ones' (IV.v.69–70).

An equivalent social embarrassment, restrained by Victorian propriety but with distinct family resemblances, occurs in Arthur Wing Pinero's *The Magistrate* (1885).[52] The title character, Mr Posket, arrives at his court to do judgment rather the worse for wear. He has been nearly caught in a hotel after licensing hours, and bears the traces of his narrow escape, with rumpled clothing and a sticking-plaster on his nose. His one attempt to restore his dress has misfired, and he wears a vulgar, gaudy neckerchief. Clothes do for Pinero the work that the graphic comedy of the body does for Jonson. About to sentence a party of prisoners who were caught in the same hotel, and who were not so quick as he was when the police came, Posket stands on his precarious dignity, imagining he hears the voice of Mrs Posket: 'Strike for the sanctity of hearth and home, for the credit of the wives of England – no mercy!' (III.i.359–60). What he does not know is that Mrs Posket is one of the prisoners. The sight of her in the dock unhinges him: as if in a dream, he sentences her and her companions to seven days without the option of a fine, then wonders what he has done. Unlike the other scenes of exposure, the revelation and the sentencing take place just offstage: the main setting is the magistrate's room, and the inflexible scenic conventions of Pinero's time do not let us follow Posket into the court. Yet the concealment is comically appropriate to an age of propriety: something has just happened that is too shocking to watch. None of the play's indiscretions is literally sexual. But, strengthening the family ties with the other scenes, sexual hints hover over the language. Echoing Jonson's prostitute, a policeman describes the prisoners: 'Nice-looking women, too, though as I tell Mrs Lugg, nowadays there's no telling who's the lady and who isn't' (III.i.12–13). When Posket's own misconduct is revealed his fellow magistrate tells him, 'You have brought a stain upon a spotless Police Court!' (III.ii.319).

Through the changing proprieties, tastes and social conditions of different periods, the comedy of the disruptive body carries on, changing its language but not its essential statement. It is part of comedy's invitation to laugh at its characters' anxieties, on the principle that you never laugh at anything nice. The ending in which multiple couples come together in marriage is equally resilient. At the end of *As You Like It* (c.1600), four couples join hands on an open-air stage that represents an open-air setting, their harmony (with reservations about Touchstone and Audrey) symbolized in a dance. The celebration is public and communal; there is even 'mirth in heaven' (V.iv.107). At the end of Stoppard's *The Real Thing* (1982) two couples have come together. Henry has been reconciled to his wife Annie and they are about to make love, when he gets a phone call from Annie's first husband Max, who announces he has just become engaged. As Annie turns out the lights and retires to the bedroom Henry, '*impatiently patient*' with Max's display of happiness, declares 'she'll be delighted. I'm delighted, Max. Isn't love wonderful?' But he is '*trying to end it*' (II.xii.p.83). The couples do not form a new, larger social unit; one has intruded on the other's privacy. Absent-mindedly Henry turns on the radio, which is playing one of his favourite songs ('I'm a Believer' by the Monkees). As the setting is not an open space but a room, the music is not for a communal celebration but for Henry's private pleasure. The new couple has no onstage presence, and we never learn the woman's name; we cannot even hear what Max is saying. This is what has happened to the multiple-couple ending in the age of private space, of the telephone and the VCR. And yet there are two couples at the end, and the play concludes with Max still unheard but still talking, impossible to shake. The multiple-couple ending, if only just, has survived.

The persistence of comedy's conventions, and its use of those conventions to probe social anxiety, are the interconnected themes of the chapters that follow, beginning with an account of the strategies comedy uses to keep anxiety under control.

# 1

# GETTING CONTROL

## The baby in the handbag

In Sophocles's *Oedipus the King* the infant Oedipus, his ankles pierced, is abandoned on a pathless hillside to die. In Oscar Wilde's *The Importance of Being Earnest* (1895) the infant John Worthing is abandoned in a handbag in the cloakroom at Victoria Station (the Brighton Line). Each baby is rescued and grows up, his true identity unknown, among close relatives. Each discovers the truth about himself, and the discoveries have consequences. Oedipus learns that, fulfilling the prophecy of the Delphic Oracle, he has killed his father and married his mother; he is himself the unclean thing he has been searching for, the thing that has polluted Thebes. His mother Jocasta commits suicide, and Oedipus blinds himself and goes into exile. Jack (who has pretended his name is Ernest) learns his name really is Ernest; Algy, who has pretended to be Jack's brother, really is his brother. Oracles tell the truth, and so do lies. A problem is solved, a riddle answered. Jack, whose dubious identity left him with no social position, is now free to marry Gwendolen, who is his cousin; the relationship is close enough, but not *too* close.

Christopher Fry claimed that when he was writing a comedy the idea first presented itself to him as tragedy; Walter Kerr argues that comedy not only comes after tragedy, it comes *from* it.[1] It is as though comedy is created by taking the fear triggered by the tragic story, and controlling it by re-telling the story in a different mode. More is involved in this re-telling than twisting the ending a different way. The Oedipus story is one of relentless destiny; but in comedy, as Schlegel argued, 'The place of Destiny is supplied by Chance'. For Schlegel, this is because 'the latter is the empirical conception of the former'; for Allan Rodway, it is because life and fertility are matters of accident, while death is an absolute.[2] While Sophocles's characters act deliberately to circumvent the oracle, only to find their actions just as deliberately turned against them, Wilde's characters act through a curious absent-mindedness. Miss Prism, with a baby to deposit in a perambulator and a three-volume novel to deposit in a handbag, gets it the wrong way round in 'a moment of mental abstraction, for which I never can forgive myself' (III.359–60). In a similar fit of abstraction, the cloakroom attendant at Victoria Station gives the handbag to Mr Thomas Cardew, in mistake for his own. Jack, having lost both his parents, is accused by Lady Bracknell of 'carelessness' (I.540). While Oedipus gets his name from the piercing of his feet, Jack gets his from the fact that Mr Cardew 'happened to have a first-class ticket for Worthing in his pocket at the time'. There is no suggestion that Mr Cardew intended anything so purposeful as a trip to Worthing; he just happened to have the ticket.

Jack adds pedantically, 'Worthing is a place in Sussex. It is a seaside resort' (I.552–4). The practical detail is characteristic: Victoria Station, the Brighton line. Inspecting the handbag, Miss Prism not only notes the recognition tokens, the equivalent to Oedipus's wounded ankles, but recalls circumstances and locations: 'here is the injury it received through the upsetting of a Gower Street omnibus . . . . Here is the stain on the lining caused by the explosion of a temperance beverage, an incident that occurred at Leamington'. She has quite practical reasons for welcoming its return: 'It has been a great inconvenience being without it all these years' (III.391–400). The comedy puts us in a local, particular, highly material world. This fits with the fact that the anxieties driving the story are not murder, incest, and the malign will of the gods but social identity, social position, and the disapproval of Lady Bracknell, for whom the story of the handbag leaves Jack without 'an assured basis for a recognized position in good society' (I.579–80). Oedipus has a recognized position as ruler of Thebes, but the crisis triggered by the plague leads to a questioning of that position, with tragic results. Jack's crisis is triggered, as so often happens in comedy, by his desire to get married. He too has a recognized position – landed gentleman, Justice of the Peace – but his proposal to Gwendolen leads Lady Bracknell to ask searching questions about him. Is his town house on the fashionable or the unfashionable side, is his income from land or investments, does he smoke, who are his parents? On the last question, the truth comes out and he is, if not unclean, at least unacceptable. He cannot marry without producing 'at any rate one parent of either sex, before the season is quite over' (I.586–87). Considerations of marriage, family, position and identity are twined together in a knot of social anxiety the ending must untie.

## The right style: *Private Lives*

Of course no one listening to even the briefest snatch of dialogue from *The Importance of Being Earnest* would mistake it for a tragedy. We shall return to Wilde's play at the end of the chapter, considering how it exemplifies the general strategies of manner and presentation by which comedy keeps its anxieties under control. But our broader look at those strategies begins with Wilde's principle, stated by Gwendolen, that 'In matters of grave importance, style, not sincerity is the vital thing' (III.28–29). It is the vital thing because it determines, for both characters and audience, our distance from the problem, our choice of close emotional involvement or laughing detachment. It is a means of control. As creatures of the play's artifice Wilde's characters simply, effortlessly, *have* the style of comedy. In other comedies we see the effort: detachment is a conscious response to a problem, and implicitly recognizes its seriousness. We watch the process of which the apparently complete detachment of *Earnest* is the end product.

In Congreve's *The Way of the World* (1700) Fainall and Marwood have a passionate quarrel that threatens to become physically violent: he holds her, and she struggles: 'let me go. – Break my hands, do'. Fainall sees Mirabell and Mrs Fainall approach: 'Sdeath, they come; hide your face, your tears. – You have a mask; wear it a moment' (II.p.345). According to Jocelyn Powell, this means a full-face mask with a fixed smile; the wearer holds it in place by clenching her teeth on an amber bead.[3] The image is of real pain and anger, real tears, covered by the mask of comedy. This is a moment when the mask has in fact slipped, and it alerts us to the effort behind other moments that look effortless. As part of his plot against Lady Wishfort, Mirabell has married his servant Waitwell to her maid Foible. Greeting Waitwell on his wedding day, Mirabell rebukes him for looking as though he is enjoying it: 'why sure you think you were married for your own recreation, and not for my conveniency'. Imperturbable as Jeeves, Waitwell replies, 'Your pardon, sir. With submission, we have indeed been solacing in lawful delights; but still with an eye to business, sir' (II.p.523). Mirabell's use of Waitwell is strictly speaking outrageous. But both men deal with the issue by competing to see who can be cooler. Hazlitt calls wit 'the eloquence of indifference'.[4]

Constructing the right style is one of the key issues of Noël Coward's *Private Lives* (1930). The play begins where traditional comedies end, with two marriages. Elyot and Sibyl, Victor and Amanda, are beginning their wedding nights at a hotel in France. But as we listen to their voices the clashing styles tell us these couples are wrong for each other. Sibyl's gushing 'Just to think, here we are, you and I, married!' triggers Elyot's acid, 'Yes, things have come to a pretty pass' (I.p.185). Equally, Victor has the wrong style for Amanda. She appears, looking exquisite, and the best he can do is tell her she looks like 'a beautiful advertisment for something'. She retorts, 'Nothing peculiar, I hope' (I.p.191). Victor and Sibyl try, unsuccessfully, for the style of romance. Elyot and Amanda have the detached manner of comedy. They were once married to each other and when they meet their old love quickly rekindles. Elyot's 'You're looking very lovely you know, in this damned moonlight' (I.p.209) – romance controlled by an ironic protest against romance, irony controlled by an acknowledgement that the feeling is real – is the right style, the style to which Victor and Sibyl never attain.

Elyot and Amanda solve the immediate problem by running away together, but this means they are, as Amanda puts it, 'in the hell of a mess socially' (II.p.216). Their own relationship is not a steady happy-ever-after but a violently unstable compound of wit, romance, sex and screaming rows. Amid this insecurity, style is the one thing they can cling to, the one thing that gives them control. They consider what style to adopt when Victor and Sibyl finally hunt them down, and Amanda proposes they 'Behave exquisitely . . . I shall probably do a Court Curtsey' (II.p.226). In fact when the moment comes they are rolling on the floor together, screeching at each other and fighting like panthers. In the third act they disagree over the style in which to settle matters with Victor and Sibyl. Sibyl insists their violation of society's norms means, as in *Oedipus*, pollution:

SIBYL: (*with spirit*) It's all perfectly horrible. I feel smirched and unclean as though slimy things had been crawling all over me.
ELYOT: Maybe they have; that's a very old sofa.

(III. p.238)

Elyot takes Sibyl's metaphor, which insists on the seriousness of what has happened, and reduces it to material reality. His flippany outrages Victor, whose own style is 'bluster and invective'. Elyot tips his hand: 'Has it ever struck you that flippancy might cover a very real embarrassment?' It is also the best response to the social limbo he and Amanda have created by their defiance of convention: 'We have no prescribed etiquette to fall back on. I shall continue to be flippant' (III.p.238). Amanda, following her earlier proposal, tries social poise, which Elyot finds ludicrous. Presiding over breakfast, she is in the middle of a rattling, increasingly desperate tribute to the joys of travel (in which we can hear her silently pleading, 'Elyot, get me out of this') when he rescues her with a vulgar joke, capping her 'and then the most thrilling thing of all, arriving at strange places, and seeing strange people, and eating strange foods' with 'And making strange noises afterwards' (III.p.251). She chokes, they are silently reconciled, and they creep out of the apartment with their suitcases as Victor and Sibyl begin a violent row of their own.

In the long duologue that makes up the bulk of Act Two, Elyot and Amanda speculate anxiously about the non-comic realities of old age, the fading of passion, and death. Elyot insists that the answer to these things, and to 'the futile moralists who try to make life unbearable', is laughter. Even death is 'very laughable, such a cunning little mystery. All done with mirrors', and the traditional answer to it, *carpe diem*, is phrased as a joke: 'Come and kiss me darling, before your body rots, and worms pop in and out of your eye sockets' (II.p.226–27). The pain in their own relationship is harder to cover. Elyot has a moment of real hurt when he learns that Amanda has had affairs with other men. He tries to turn his protest into a matter of style – 'It doesn't suit women to be promiscuous' – to which she retorts, 'It doesn't suit men for women to be promiscuous' (I.p.218), and the result is the first serious quarrel in the act; the jokes have not relieved the pain but aggravated it. Their fights are not just verbal. The morning after, Amanda declares stiffly, 'I've been brought up to believe that it's beyond the pale for a man to strike a woman'. His reply, 'A very poor tradition. Certain women should be struck regularly, like gongs' (III.p.240), characteristically opposes flippancy to pomposity, and reduces the difficulties of their relationship to an epigram, a generalization in which women are simply material objects.[5] But the edge of cruelty in the joke shows its underlying anger. In conflict with Victor and Sibyl, Elyot and Amanda rise easily above the opposition by creating a comic detachment that endorses their violation of social convention; in conflict with each other, they let us sense the clenched teeth behind the comic mask.

## The wrong style: *A Chaste Maid in Cheapside*

In Elizabeth Inchbald's *Wives as They Were, and Maids as They Are* (1797) Bronzely, fancying himself in the role of vile seducer, tells the heroine, 'Lady Priory, you are in a lonely house of mine, where I am sole master, and all the servants slaves to my will'. She *'calmly takes out her knitting'* (V.i.p.64). In Alan Ayckbourn's *The Norman Conquests* (1973) Norman tries for a dramatic showdown with his wife Ruth, 'All right, you've had this coming', but as he *'pauses dramatically'* she announces a discovery of her own: it's her glasses, pressing on her sinus passages, that are making her sneeze (*Table Manners*, I.ii.p.50). The grand gestures, with their threats of adultery and marriage breakdown, collapse in the face of trivial material reality. In Etherege's *The Man of Mode* (1676) Dorimant's cast-off mistress Loveit keeps trying to act the tragedy queen, but she is in the wrong kind of play. When she begins, 'Faithless, inhuman, barbarous man', Dorimant instantly reduces her to a mechanism: 'Good. Now the alarm strikes' (II.ii.144–45). There is contemporary political resonance in the play's cool attitude to passion. Medley refers to Cromwell's porter, locked up as a lunatic: 'Were I so near marriage, I should cry out by fits as I ride in my coach, "Cuckold, cuckold!" with no less fury than the mad fanatic does "Glory!" in Bethlem' (I.i.312–14). The Puritan revolution, which not long ago turned England upside down, is reduced to a single crying voice calling helplessly from a madhouse; and that voice in turn is simply material for a Restoration-comedy joke about marriage and cuckoldry.[6] There are certain voices to which comedy refuses to give fair play: the fanatical, the passionate, the committed.

Such a voice is heard towards the end of Thomas Middleton's *A Chaste Maid in Cheapside* (1613). Sir Walter Whorehound, who has kept the Allwit family in comfort, sleeping with Mistress Allwit, getting the children and paying the bills – all with the husband's enthusiastic cooperation – is seriously wounded in a fight and, suddenly repentant, attacks the Allwits and the life he has lived with them:

> None knew the dear account my soul stood charg'd with
> So well as thou, yet, like hell's flattering angel,
> Wouldst never tell me on't . . . .
> Still my adulterous guilt hovers aloft,
> And with her black wings beats down all my prayers
> Ere they be half way up. What's he knows now
> How long I have to live? O, what comes then?
> My taste grows bitter; the round world all gall now;
> Her pleasing pleasures now hath poison'd me,
> Which I exchang'd my soul for . . . .
>
> (V.i.25–27, 74–81)

Sir Walter speaks with a passionate horror that suddenly extends the play's range beyond the cool material calculation that has been its keynote. But images of accounting and exchange cling to his language, and keep it from breaking free into the realm of the spirit; and he makes no headway with his listeners. The children are frightened of him, and Allwit claims he has gone mad. Then word is brought that Sir Walter is financially ruined, and the Allwits cannot get rid of him fast enough. (Mistress Allwit suggests they might put him in a small back room, but her husband points out they use it as a privy.) Allwit's final dismissal of the man who has supported his family for years, with himself in the role of willing cuckold, is the cool, ironic 'I thought you had been familiar with my wife once' (V.i.145).

As Sir Walter is banished with a joke, the comedy moves on to its end, with multiple marriages whose cynical, material spirit is captured when the father of one of the brides points out the saving involved: 'the best is, / One feast will serve them both' (V.iv.114–15). Sir Walter has tried to introduce the language of the spirit in a world that is resolutely material, where we have seen a christening feast become an orgy of eating and drinking, dominated by Puritan gossips who leave puddles under their stools. He sees sex as laden with religious guilt, in a play full of jokes like ''tis a husband solders up all cracks' (I.i.37). In a finale in which comedy's tendency to social accommodation is seen at its most cynical, Sir Walter may have, in theory, the right views; but he has the wrong style, and the world goes on without him.

## Material people

One of the stylistic tricks that creates comic detachment is the reduction of humanity to the material level (certain women should be struck regularly, like gongs). In the scene that most sharply defines *A Chaste Maid in Cheapside*, a country wench disposes of an unwanted baby by fooling a pair of promoters who are checking for violations of Lent into thinking it is a piece of meat. The scene is symbolic of the commodification of humanity; it is a traditional gag;[7] and it literalizes the process of metaphor, by which one thing is exchanged for another. The language of comedy is full of such exchanges, and they are usually reductive: 'She's just a bit of Knightsbridge candyfloss. A couple of licks and you've 'ad 'er' (Peter Shaffer, *Black Comedy* [1965], p.195); 'Marry her! O Lord, sir, after I have lain with her? Why, sir! how the Devil can you think a man can have any stomach to his dinner, after he has had three or four slices off the spit?' (Colley Cibber, *Love's Last Shift* [1696], V.iii.126–28). Sex is food, and having sex is consumption. In the opening scene of *The Man of Mode* an orange-seller brings Dorimant oranges, and news of the latest women, and the two seem interchangeable. After a bout with Dorimant, Bellinda, feeling faint, complains of a surfeit of nectarines. In Wycherley's *The Country Wife* (1675), after Lady Fidget has rifled Horner's china collection, Horner is forced to admit he has no china left. Only the cuckolded husband thinks they are talking about china. In *Gammer Gurton's Needle* (c.1550), by 'Mr S.', we are made to wonder if the missing object is really a needle when Hodge describes it as 'A little thing with an hole in the end, as bright as any silver; / Small, long, sharp at the point, and straight as any pillar' (II.i.43–44).

Bawdy double entendre is the small change of comedy, and like small change it is everywhere. It helps to create the detachment of comedy, by reducing the body and its desires to commodities, objects in an intellectual game. The recurring motif of baby-exchange symbolizes comedy's pervasive interchange of the human and the material. (Babies, being small and portable, lend themselves to this sort of thing.) In *Chaste Maid* a baby is exchanged for a piece of meat; in Christopher Fry's *The Lady's Not for Burning* (1948), for the church collection: Richard describes how as an infant he was found stuffed into the poor box, the money having been taken (I.p.5). Miss Prism's exchange of a baby for a three-volume novel is not just one more example: in a way it sums up all the others. It is in literary texts that the human can be dehumanized by the play of language, and painful feelings distanced by style. To put a text *in place of* a baby is the logical extension of this process.

It follows that sexual double entendre involves literature as readily as it involves food, and brings literary concepts down to a practical level. In Congreve's *The Double Dealer* (1693) there is double dealing in the language when Lady Froth, offering to let Brisk read her heroic poem *The Sillibub*, invites him to come into the next room 'and there I'll shew you all I have' (II.p.143); a later reference to their going into the garden together for a literary chat and 'making couplets' (V.p.203) helps illuminate the moments in *The Man of Mode* (V.ii.89–90) and *The Way of the World* (IV.p.378) in which lovers complete each other's couplets. More violently, in Wycherley's *The Plain Dealer* (1676) Major Oldfox, who has been trying all through the play to read his poetry to the Widow Blackacre, finally has her ambushed in a tavern and tied to a chair so that he can do the deed: 'You shall be acquainted with my parts, Lady, you shall'. To her protest, 'what, will you ravish me?' he replies, 'Yes, Lady, I will ravish you; but it shall be through the ear, Lady, the ear only, with my well-penn'd acrostics' (V.p.507). (Should we recall the tradition that the Holy Spirit impregnated the Virgin Mary through the ear?) In Joe Orton's *What the Butler Saw* (1969) Dr Prentice, about to seduce Geraldine, equates one kind of climax with another: 'Lie on the couch with your hands behind your head and think of the closing chapters of your favourite work of fiction. The rest may be left to me' (I.p.368). Elsewhere in the play sexual prowess is equated with typing speed (I.pp.365, 370).

The wit of such passages depends on claiming similarity where there is really difference. Prism's exchange is a revealing symbol, and a mistake that has to be put right. A baby is not a novel; and there are times when china is just china, and a cigar is just a cigar. The quiddity of the material world, its insistence on being itself, helps to ground comedy in material reality. Food is food, as the long-suffering servants of bankrupt gentlemen are constantly reminding their masters. In Congreve's *Love for Love* (1695) Valentine reads books as a substitute for having breakfast ('I'll walk a turn and digest what I have read') but his servant Jeremy, unimpressed by 'a very fine feast, where there is nothing to be eaten' insists he cannot live by metaphor alone (I.p.216). With some exceptions, the servants of English comedy are less given to intrigue than their Plautine ancestors: their role is more to keep an eye on the larder. Algy may use cucumber sandwiches to signify a whole way of life, but Lane buys the cucumbers. In *The Man of Mode*, after Dorimant and Bellinda have had sex, we glimpse Dorimant's servant Handy '*tying up linen*' (IV.ii.0.1). Having sex is not just eating nectarines, reading books or collecting china; it is also having sex, and it leaves stains on the sheets, which the servants have to deal with.

Comedy's insistence on material reality and its refusal of the high style come together in its quarrel with tragedy. One reason why Peter Quince and his actors make such a fine mess of the tragedy of *Pyramus and Thisbe* is they are 'Hardhanded men that work in Athens here' (*A Midsummer Night's Dream* [c.1595], V.i.72). They belong to practical trades: Flute the bellows mender, Snout the tinker, Snug the joiner, and so on. If this implies a snobbery about the inability of the working class to do tragedy (and it does) the snobbery is grounded in formal considerations. The actors are too concerned with practical matters – how to bring in the wall, how to make the chink, how to give a solid body to moonshine – and this means their performance is resolutely material. They also have a material sense of what it is worth: 'Sixpence a day in Pyramus, or nothing' (IV.ii.23–24). Tragedy suffers a similar fate in Francis Beaumont's *The Knight of the Burning Pestle* (c.1607), in which the Grocer's apprentice Rafe, put on the stage by his employers, cuts across the play's city comedy with an increasingly disconnected heroic romance of his own, ending with a death scene. Rafe enters with an arrow through his head, declaiming a parody of the opening lines of *The Spanish Tragedy*: 'When I was mortal, this my costive corpse / Did lap up figs and raisins in the Strand', and ending, 'fly, fly, my soul to Grocer's Hall' (V.277–78, 327). You can't do tragedy if your real business is selling groceries.

## A comedy for men: *The Case of Rebellious Susan*

Like the materialism of comedy, its tendency to social accommodation resists the grand gesture, the extraordinary commitment. But many comedies treat social accommodation itself with irony. In *A Chaste Maid in Cheapside* the material world in which Sir Walter's morality looks ludicrous deals in marriage, procreation and financial success; but to accommodate oneself to it is to accept a scheme of things that treats people as goods. In *Private Lives* Amanda and Elyot kick over the traces, and it is social accommodation, embodied in the conventional Victor and Sybil, that looks ridiculous. In *The Case of Rebellious Susan* (1894) Henry Arthur Jones plays a tricky double game, and here we confront – as we shall do in many other plays – the double-edged quality of comedy itself, its tendency to question its own premises. Susan Harabin, having discovered her husband's adultery, threatens to pay it back in kind by taking a lover. She has already flirted – at least – with Lucien Edensor. As Jones originally wrote the play, there was a strong suggestion that their affair had been consummated. The actor-manager Charles Wyndham, who was to produce it, was outraged that Jones should make a woman's adultery the subject of a *comedy*, and made him tone down the dialogue at the crucial point.[8] If Susan were to revenge her husband in kind she might be a good Restoration-comedy heroine, but by the standards of Jones' period she would be material for a fallen-woman tragedy along the lines of Pinero's *The Second Mrs Tanqueray*, produced with great success the previous year. Within the play, the attack is led by Sir Richard Kato (Wyndham's part), one of a troop of *raisonneurs* who patrol late Victorian and Edwardian drama. They speak, with wit and an air of experience, for worldly common sense and social accommodation, for not rocking the boat; as a sign of his authority, the *raisonneur* was generally played, as here, by the actor-manager.[9] Being a lawyer, Sir Richard has seen more than he cares to of the divorce courts, and he speaks for a society anxious about the prevalence of divorce and fearful of social breakdown.[10] His general view of the role of women in society is summed up in two words: 'Go home!' (III.p.154).[11] Telling Susan to stay with her husband, he insists, 'you are going to do just what is suitable for my niece, and for an English lady with her own reputation and the reputation of her family to consider' (II.pp.143–44). In backing the family, he is backing England.

He is also, in preserving marriage, doing the business of comedy, and he appeals not just to propriety but to material reality. He believes in the 'bread-and-cheese realities of life' (I.p.122), and when he finds Harabin depressed, offers to cure him with breakfast: 'What shall it be? A chop, steak, bacon and eggs –' (II.p.136). He urges Susan to accept the double standard in a line that is appropriately both a cliché and a food image: 'what is sauce for the goose will never be sauce for the gander. In fact, there is no gander sauce' (I.p.112). The double standard he speaks of was embodied in the law: a wife's adultery was sufficient grounds for divorce, but a husband's adultery had to be combined with desertion or cruelty.[12] Lady Darby, whose own husband is a philanderer, tells Susan that hers is 'no worse than a respectable average case'; she urges her to nag Harabin for a fortnight and then forget the whole thing (I.pp.110–11). She is cutting Susan down to size, as we have seen comedy do to characters who try to make too much of their personal griefs. The way of the world that Susan has to accept includes a comic tolerance of male infidelity. Admiral Darby, recalling his own adventures, is torn between maudlin lament – 'what an unfaithful rascal I've been' – and patriotic pride: 'Of course, in these matters . . . we must all make great allowances for men . . . especially for sailors. How do you account for it, Jim, (*suddenly brightening into great joviality and pride*) that the best Englishmen have always been such devils amongst the women? Always! I wouldn't give a damn for a soldier or a sailor that wasn't, eh?' (II.p.138). He fortifies himself through this searching self-examination with anchovy sandwiches and champagne. When Susan challenges her husband to give his word of honour that he will never stray again, he cannot bring himself to do it. Her lover Edensor also lets her down: he goes off into exile in New Zealand vowing eternal fidelity (to Sir Richard's sceptical amusement) and marries a girl he met on the ship. In the words of the long-suffering Lady Darby, 'men are men' (I.p.110).

Susan submits. Harabin does his best to restore their marriage by offering to take her shopping. Society is saved; but if we compare Jones' ending with Katharine's flamboyant speech of submission at the end of *The Taming of the Shrew* we see a world of difference:

LADY DARBY:   You see, dear, we poor women cannot retaliate.
LADY SUSAN:   I see.
LADY DARBY:   We must be patient.
INEZ:   And forgive the wretches till they learn constancy.
LADY SUSAN:   I see.
LADY DARBY:   And, dear, yours is a respectable average case after all.
LADY SUSAN:   Yes, a respectable average case after all.

(III.pp.160–61)

The comedy does not seem to be ending on a high note; Susan sounds brainwashed. The human cost, indeed the human damage, involved in bringing her under control creates misgivings about the ordered ending. The play's first audiences were not sure whether they had seen a defence of society or an attack on it.[13]

Jones allows these misgivings by raising the question: have we watched a comedy or a tragedy? The play's most experienced representative of the woman's point of view is the widow Inez Quesnel, who speaks of how much women, in their loyalty, have to conceal, and adds: 'You men will never see anything but a comedy in it. So we have to dress up our tragedy as a comedy just to save ourselves from being ridiculous and boring you. But we women feel it is a tragedy all the same' (II.p.126). In the male comedy, the tragic experience of women would look ludicrous, as the rejected Loveit does in *The Man of Mode*. In the male comedy, a philandering admiral is a figure of broad fun, a young lover whose eternal fidelity lasts for three weeks is quietly amusing, emotional problems can be solved by a good breakfast, and a happy ending is a repentant husband taking his wife shopping. But Inez sees these betrayals and sacrifices another way: 'Our own hearts aren't sacred to us. That's our real modern tragedy – we laugh at the tragedy of our own lives!' Sir Richard retorts, 'No, no, it's our real modern comedy and our truest wisdom' (II.p.126). At the end of the play these two are headed for marriage, and the last word belongs to Sir Richard. It is not a reconciliation but an invitation to shelve the question: 'Let us leave these problems (*Kisses her hand very tenderly*) and go in to dinner' (III.p.161). The Harabins and the Darbys are already in the dining room; three couples are consolidated, and the bread-and-cheese realities of comedy prevail.

Life is a tragedy for women and a comedy for men; the play seems to choose comedy, but at the end of his Epistle Dedicatory, ironically addressed to Mrs Grundy, Jones turns it the other way: 'P.S. My comedy isn't a comedy at all. It's a tragedy dressed up as a comedy' (p.107).[14] The comic world has controlled a recalcitrant woman, but unlike characters in other plays who overdo their potential tragedies Susan has never been laughable. We are all too aware that she has been browbeaten into submission, and what awaits her is not happiness but simply making the best of a bad job. Yet Jones, who writes Kato's speeches with confidence and panache, has not been able to get imaginatively inside the experience of the women: he describes Inez as '*fascinating*' and '*inscrutable*' (I.p.109), leaving the play's most strong-minded woman as a strange, exotic specimen. He scores more heavily at the formal level. Going to the theatre with Inez in the last act, Susan insists, 'we'll go to something merry and rakish, not to a tragedy. I hate tragedies' (III.p.148). She wants a comedy like *The Country Wife* or *Private Lives*, one that would find space for her desires. She hates tragedies because she is in one. The play itself, trying to make a comedy of it, has succeeded only in dressing it up.

## Laughing off death

Jones takes his comedy to, and possibly across, the border of tragedy not by threatening Susan with death but by seeing the social accommodation that preserves her as tragic renunciation, uncovering the dark side of the comic ending. It is more characteristic for comedy in its quarrel with tragedy to insist on the funny side of the tragic ending, to dismiss death as somehow unreal. Elyot in *Private Lives* calls it a laughable trick done with mirrors. (In Cocteau's film *Orphée* the messengers of death come through mirrors, but the explanation is chilling: look in the mirror, you will see death at work.) There are farcical mock-funerals, as in Nicholas Udall's *Roister Doister* (c.1552), with its mischievous parody of the Office for the Dead, and in Sir George's Etherege's *The Comical Revenge; or, Love in a Tub* (1664), where a funeral is interrupted by a comic Frenchman who comes running on stage dressed in a portable tub. Both funerals centre on a 'corpse' that is not really dead. Thinking of the plotting of romantic comedies like *Much Ado About Nothing*, Zvi Jagendorf claims that comedy can deal with death only by pretending it is an illusion.[15]

Some plays allow a real debate over whether death belongs in a comedy at all, making their control over it a matter of self-conscious effort. In Jonson's *Every Man out of his Humour* (1599) a miser tries to hang himself on stage, and two commentator characters debate whether such an incident is permissible in a comedy, settling the matter in Jonson's favour by citing classical precedent. Noël Coward's comedy of death, *Blithe Spirit* (1941), allows a debate over the tastefulness of death jokes. When Charles's second wife Ruth describes his late first wife Elvira as 'of the earth earthy', his reply, 'Well, she is now, anyhow,' is followed by an argument over whether such a remark is offensive or merely honest (I.i.p.17). Both plays were written at a time when death was an ever-present reality. Jonson's London was regularly visited by plague, and its sights included public executions and severed heads on London Bridge. Coward's London was enduring the Blitz. The programme for *Blithe Spirit* included the following notice: 'If an air raid warning be received during the performance the audience will be informed from the stage . . . those desiring to leave may do so but the performance will continue.'[16]

The performance will continue: the whole enterprise of comedy, with its insistence on love, marriage, immediate pleasure and day-to-day reality, is a defiance of death, an attempt to control one of the most basic human fears. Jonson and Coward in their different ways know that what comedy is resisting is real, and allow some discomfort on this point. More romantic plays go the route Jagendorf suggests: against the overwhelming power of love, death is an illusion, a game of let's pretend. Loving women return from apparent death to claim, and save, their erring men. In moral comedies on the Patient Griselda theme, like the anonymous *The London Prodigal* (c.1604) and *How a Man May Choose a Good Wife from a Bad* (c.1602) a wastrel husband, blamed for his wife's death, is saved by her return. In Shakespeare's *Much Ado About Nothing* (c.1599) Hero, apparently dead of grief at Claudio's slander of her, returns with the words, 'One Hero died defiled, but I do live, / And surely as I live, I am a maid' (V.iv.62–63). She makes it sound as though she really was unchaste, and really did die, but in dying saved them both from the old life in which all that happened, and left them ready to start a new one. A new life is literally beginning at the end of *All's Well That Ends Well* (c.1603) when Helena returns from apparent death not just alive but miraculously pregnant by the husband who claimed he would never sleep with her. On the night Bertram heard of her death he was actually in bed with her, thinking it was the Florentine girl Diana. It is Diana who gives Helena's entrance cue: 'Dead though she be, she feels her young one kick. / So here's my riddle: one that's dead is quick' (V.iii.303–4).

The defiance of death in the name of love (or at least sex) is broader and more flamboyant in *A Chaste Maid in Cheapside* (1613) and *The Knight of the Burning Pestle* (c.1607), where funeral ceremonies are farcically reversed as lovers spring alive out of coffins.[17] In Middleton's play there is a brisk wedding in doggerel verse and the groom's brother suggests the shrouds will do for wedding sheets. In Beaumont's, Old Merrythought, having greeted his son's apparent death with comic songs, greets his resurrection and that of his lover:

> With hey trixy terlery-whiskin,
> The world it runs on wheels,
> When the young man's ——
> Up goes the maiden's heels.
> (V.189–92)

We know what part of the young man goes up, and this tells us how to read the image of young people emerging upright from coffins. This bawdy vitality, like the stage action that accompanies it, translates the romantic defiance of death into material terms.

The conscious artifice of the reversed funerals in Middleton and Beaumont becomes flagrant theatricality in Tom Robertson's *Caste* (1867). As Esther mourns her husband George, killed in action, her sister Polly recalls a ballet they were both in, about the return of a soldier who was thought dead. As she plays the tune that accompanied the soldier's return, George enters. Polly's alleged purpose is to break the news gently; her real purpose, and the play's, is maximum stage effect. The play both asks us to believe in George's resurrection and admits it is a stage trick.

*Blithe Spirit* directly parodies the romantic return from death. Elvira and Ruth return not as living women but as ghosts; death is real. Even as ghosts they are material and unromantic: Elvira expresses a frustrated longing for cucumber sandwiches (II.ii.p.67) and Ruth is snappish at being called back from the great beyond: 'Once and for all, Charles, what the hell does this mean?' (III.i.p.96). Far from embracing his lost loves, Charles walks out on them in mocking defiance as, reduced to invisibility, they respond by wrecking the set. Edward Bond gives a further twist to the tradition in *The Sea* (1973), turning comedy's usual procedure directly against itself. Here, laughter is directed not at death but at the characters who try to deny it. Colin has drowned in a storm on the way to see his fiancée Rose. The villagers, led by the local dragon Mrs Rafi, respond to his death with a farcical mixture of blindness and self-importance. The day after the drowning we see them rehearsing a play about Orpheus and Eurydice, that great myth of the frustrated attempt of love and art to conquer death. They begin by drawing the curtains to shut out the sea (and therefore the memory of a real death) and the rehearsal proceeds in the *Pyramus and Thisbe* manner, with the Vicar (as Pluto) worrying about appearing before his parishioners in tights, Myfanwy Price (Cerberus) dog-paddling across the Styx and Mrs Rafi (Orpheus) punting across it to the Eton Boating Song. Later they make a shambles of the scattering of Colin's ashes, as Mrs Rafi and her companion Mrs Tilehouse turn the hymns into '*a rivalry for the most elaborate descant*' (vii.p.48), Mrs Tilehouse upstages Mrs Rafi's dramatic recitation with a quiet muttering search for her smelling salts, and the occasion degenerates into a brawl with ashes flung in all directions. Meanwhile Rose and Colin's friend Willy (who is first seen rising alive out of the sea, and on whom the play's hope for the future rests) have coped with his death more seriously, talking each other through it, agreeing not to shut out the horror of life but to face it honestly: 'Turn back and look into the fire' (vi.p.44). Willy draws Rose out of her despair at Colin's death, and in the aftermath of the mock-funeral scene he kisses her, then goes off to swim in the sea as she follows to hold his clothes. The suggestion is that he will swim naked, and they will make love. Though Bond has kept the relationship of Willy and Rose deliberately unromantic, we see in them a family resemblance to the lovers of earlier comedies who defy death by popping out of coffins. But there is no return for Colin.

*The Sea* directs its laughter at those who couch their response to death in self-important rituals that evade its reality instead of facing it realistically and then leaving the dead behind. When Willy kisses Rose she comments, 'In a dead man's shoes', and he replies, 'The dead don't matter' (vii.p.59). When Colin's body is washed up by the sea, and the mad linen-draper Hatch, thinking the corpse is part of an invasion from outer space, starts hacking it with a knife, Willy watches quite calmly: 'What does it matter? You can't hurt the dead' (vi.p.46). One way of denying death is to assume that a corpse has feelings; Willy sets himself against that. In the performances I have seen, however, audiences have some difficulty matching Willy's detachment: they watch Hatch's attack on the corpse with palpable discomfort edging into nervous laughter. Bond does not particularly call for laughter here, but he is just on the edge of what we might call the comedy of corpse abuse, where laughter becomes an uneasy mix of detachment (this is no longer a person) and discomfort (it used to be). Here comedy copes with death not by treating it as an illusion but by reducing it to physical knockabout. Attempting to refute Bergson's theory of laughter, Arthur Koestler claims, 'If "we laugh every time a person gives us the impression of being a thing" there would be nothing more funny than a corpse'.[18] There is actually something in that: a corpse is the ultimate expression of comedy's reduction of humanity to the material level.

In Tom Stoppard's *Jumpers* (1972) the death of Duncan McFee, philosophy professor and gymnast, makes him the centre of a series of sight gags. Literally the centre at first: as he is constructing a human pyramid with his fellow philosopher-gymnasts a shot rings out, he falls out of the pyramid, dying, and the pyramid slowly collapses around him. The retired singer Dotty, in whose apartment this happens, hides the body by hanging it on the back of a door, where it swings in and out of sight. At the end of Act One the body is disposed of by the play's master-trickster Archie, who enters with a team of gymnasts and a large plastic bag, which he unfolds like a conjurer doing a trick (a cunning little mystery, all done with mirrors); the gymnasts collect the body, pop it in the bag, and leave, all this in a dance-like movement timed to Dotty's singing 'Sentimental Journey'. Archie covers McFee's murder by constructing a suicide theory: deeply depressed, McFee 'crawled into a large plastic bag and shot himself' (II.p.55). Archie has a rogue's vitality in the face of death: his statement of his philosophy at the end of the play concludes, 'At the graveside the undertaker doffs his top hat and impregnates the prettiest mourner. Wham, bam, thank you Sam' (Coda, p.78). We see the affinity with the bawdy mock-funerals of earlier comedy; but we also note a certain heart-lessness. McFee, knocked out of the pyramid, is not just an object. As he dies, he crawls up Dotty's body, getting blood on her dress. We glimpse the reality that the play's comedy of death elsewhere controls and we sense, again, the clenched teeth behind the mask.[19]

Joe Orton is more ruthless in *Loot* (1965). Hal and Dennis, having pulled off a bank robbery, need somewhere to hide the money and, in a variation on the baby-exchange, they evict the corpse of Hal's mother from its coffin and put the money in its place. The interplay of sex and death turns necrophilic here. Mrs McLeavy's nurse Fay suggests McLeavy may want the coffin opened: 'Formaldehyde and three morticians have increased his wife's allure' (I.p.241). The sexual connections between Hal and his mother are more oblique. As Fay strips the body behind a screen and hands out the clothing to him, Hal chats away about the brothel he would like to run, imagining a variety of girls. As he gets his mother's corset, brassiere and knickers, he specifies 'a tall bird with big tits'; getting her teeth, he adds, 'and a bird that spoke fluent Spanish and performed the dances of her native country to perfection. (*He clicks the teeth like castanets,*)' (I.pp.226–27). In that last touch Mrs McLeavy seems more fun in death than she ever was in life.

The usual forms of exchange, literal and verbal, operate: the corpse is exchanged for money, Fay claims it is a dressmaker's dummy, and, with the natural leap of rhyme, Inspector Truscott thinks it is a mummy. He asks Hal whose it is and Hal replies, just as naturally, 'mine' (I.p.231). Watching the eyes and teeth restored to the corpse, Truscott tells Hal, 'Your sense of detachment is terrifying, lad. Most people would at least flinch upon seeing their mother's eyes and teeth handed around like nuts at Christmas' (II.p.272). Hal's detachment is an extreme version of the detachment of comedy, as the play as a whole presents an extreme version of the vitality of sex in the face of death, and of the reduction of humanity to the material.

## The Importance of Being Earnest

Orton's characters, like Coward's, achieve the cool style of comedy, and this brings us back to *The Importance of Being Earnest* (1895), where so many of the comic strategies we have examined in this chapter come together: the style, the concentration on material reality, the laughing dismissal of time and death. Here, we might think, the mask is firmly in place, the artifice complete. When Lady Bracknell, twenty-eight years after the fact, demands, 'Prism! Where is that baby?' (III.338–39), or Jack complains 'it is always nearly seven' (I.679) – always, that is, time for Algy to invite himself to dinner – time itself seems suspended as on Keats's Grecian urn. This suspension of time is part of what looks like the play's exclusion of reality, its creation of an innocent England of dotty vicars, eccentric governesses, tea in a sunlit garden. It looks like the ultimate triumph of comedy's control. Yet the play also offers an unusual opportunity to watch that control at work, to study the tensions that issue in laughter. To begin with, it is a listening post in which we can overhear some of the real concerns of late Victorian England. Lady Bracknell's view that investments are a better source of income than land, and Cecily's reference to Gwendolen's boredom with the country as 'agricultural depression' from which 'the aristocracy are suffering very much . . . just at present' (II.697–99), reflect one of the critical social changes of the time, the collapse of agricultural income and therefore of land values, resulting in a major shift in the basis of power.[20] Miss Prism's complaint about the excessive breeding of the lower classes (II.256–59), and Cecily's dislike of women who engage in philanthropic work – 'I think it is so forward of them' (II.562–63) – are not quaint paradoxes but attitudes many of Wilde's contemporaries held quite seriously.[21]

More strikingly, the play draws its comedy from strains and tensions in Wilde's own life. His passionate, destructive relationship with Lord Alfred Douglas was heading for the crisis of Wilde's court case against Douglas's father the Marquess of Queensberry, the upshot of which would be Wilde's own arrest on charges of gross indecency, and two years' imprisonment with hard labour. In *De Profundis*, the letter he wrote to Douglas from prison, Wilde was to complain of the way Douglas constantly sponged off him, inviting himself to extravagant luncheons, dinners and suppers: 'you had no motives in life. You had appetites merely.'[22] Algy's appetite, and his habit of inviting himself to meals, are jokes made out of Wilde's real irritation with Douglas's selfishness. Algy's constant attendance on the imaginary invalid Bunbury is an upside-down reflection of Douglas: Wilde nursed Douglas through a bout of influenza, but when he fell ill himself Douglas walked out on him, explaining his feelings in a letter: '*When you are not on your pedestal you are not interesting. The next time you are ill I will go away at once.*'[23] Douglas, like Lady Bracknell, did not approve of this modern sympathy for invalids. The play's jokes about divorce and bankruptcy – 'Divorces are made in heaven' (I.82–83); 'Half the chaps who get into the Bankruptcy Court are called Algernon' (II.27–28) – are very light shadows of coming trouble. After the crash Wilde went bankrupt and (though this threat was not carried out) his wife Constance was advised to sue him for divorce.

How far Wilde's homosexual activity, with its attendant dangers, is reflected in the play is a matter of debate. Alan Sinfield has cast cold water on suggestions that 'Ernest' and 'Bunbury' are homosexual code words.[24] To read jokes like 'All women become like their mothers. That is their tragedy. No man does. That's his' (I.625–26) as homosexual code is to make an over-easy equation of homosexuality with effeminacy. But the private jokes embodied in Wilde's choice of names include Jack's reference to his tenant Lady Bloxham: Jack Bloxham, whom Wilde called an 'undergraduate of strange beauty', started an Oxford magazine, *The Chameleon*, that promoted homosexuality.[25] The danger in which Wilde was putting himself is more broadly reflected in the themes of the double life (Ernest in town, Jack in the country) and the guilty secret: to Lady Bracknell, Jack's origins 'display a contempt for the ordinary decencies of family life' (I.571–72). Ultimately, Wilde's own technique was that of the chameleon, changing colour for protection, turning the danger of his life into jokes that could seem sufficient in themselves, with no need to be read as code.

The three-act *Earnest* that is commonly read and performed now stands between two other texts: it is preceded by a four-act *Earnest*, which exists in different versions; and it is followed by *De Profundis*. *De Profundis*, reversing the pattern we have seen elsewhere, is the tragedy that comes out of the comedy. It looks behind the jokes about Algy's selfishness to uncover pain and anger at Douglas's. It replays in a different key Gwendolen's reference to her father: 'Outside the family circle, papa, I am glad to say, is entirely unknown. I think that is as it should be' (II.583–84). Wilde, whose destruction stemmed from his being caught in the feud between Douglas and Queensberry, told Douglas, 'The fact that your father loathed you, and that you loathed your father, was not a matter of any interest to the English public.'[26] In prison, Wilde made an important discovery about class difference: 'The poor are wiser, more charitable, more kind, more sensitive than we are. In their eyes prison is a tragedy in a man's life, a misfortune, a casualty, something that calls for sympathy in others . . . . With people of our rank it is different. With us prison makes a man a pariah.'[27] When Algy asked,

'Really, if the lower orders don't set us a good example, what on earth is the use of them?' (I.33–35) it was a comic inversion of a conventional attitude.[28] Wilde has discovered that Algy spoke more truly than he knew.

In the four-act *Earnest* the tensions Wilde was transforming into comedy are more prominent. Algy's appetite is more extravagant: his depradations on the cucumber sandwiches are more conspicuous, and during his visit to Jack's country house he gets two lunches in quick succession, one of which includes twelve lobsters. There is a lengthy, dramatically inert passage in which Jack and Algy agree on the iniquities of fathers, a passage on which the shadow of Queensberry lies too heavily; reading it, we realize that the comic dynamic of the Jack–Algy relationship depends on their never agreeing on anything. Jack enlists the help of the other characters in his search through the Army Lists, mistakenly giving Lady Bracknell a copy of *The Green Carnation*, an actual novel in which Wilde and Douglas were lampooned. Money problems, and the threat of arrest, are embodied in the episode in which Mr Gribsby, of the firm of Parker and Gribsby, comes to arrest Ernest Worthing for a debt he owes to the Savoy Hotel. The debt was run up by Jack (Ernest in town), but the threat of arrest is to Algy (Ernest in the country), who protests, at the thought of going to Holloway Prison (where Wilde was later to be held pending his release on bail), 'I really am not going to be imprisoned in the suburbs for having dined in the West End.'[29] Jack pays the debt, and Gribsby leaves; but not before revealing that he is another Bunburyist: he is both Parker and Gribsby, Gribsby when he is about unpleasant business, Parker when he is about pleasant business. One of the boy prostitutes Wilde frequented was Charles Parker, who would later be a key witness for the Crown. Canon Chasuble remarks, as Gribsby leaves, 'There is thunder in the air.'[30]

Wilde, rereading the play after his release from prison, wrote to a friend, 'How I used to toy with that tiger Life!'[31] His biographer Richard Ellmann calls the play 'a wonderful parapet [constructed] over the abyss of the author's disquietude and apprehension' and 'a miracle of control'.[32] This control involves a reduction of the disturbing elements in the four-act version; it also involves gaining detachment from life by turning it into style: 'In matters of grave importance, style, not sincerity is the vital thing' (III.28–29). French and German are not so much languages as styles: to Lady Bracknell French sounds improper and German respectable (I.366–71). Style in turn imposes a filter on reality: Cecily complains, 'I know perfectly well that I look quite plain after my German lesson' (II.7–8). It creates detachment: Gwendolen's reaction to a major crisis in her life, Lady Bracknell's refusal of her engagement, is to pull back from the event into a series of generalizing epigrams: 'Ernest, we may never be married. From the expression on mamma's face I fear we never shall. Few parents nowadays pay any regard to what their children say to them. The old-fashioned respect for the young is fast dying out' (I.701–4). Along with the detachment goes a flattening of value. In her outrage at the news of Jack's unconventional origins, Lady Bracknell claims that his 'contempt for the ordinary decencies of family life . . . reminds one of the worst excesses of the French Revolution. And I presume you know what that

unfortunate movement led to?' (I.571–74). It is impossible to keep a normal sense
of proportion when the disgrace of being bred in a handbag is equated to one of
the cataclysmic events of European history, and that event in turn is dismissed as
'unfortunate'. The way is cleared for a series of jokes that invert conventional
expectations, as Wilde was in private practising inversion of another kind. Algy
complains of the scandal of married couples who flirt with each other, 'washing
one's clean linen in public' (I.251–52); Lady Bracknell has dark forebodings of
unrest among the upper classes and 'acts of violence in Grosvenor Square'
(I.501–2). As Jack was exchanged in infancy for a three-volume novel, the transformation of experience into style means that fictions can become realities. Cecily
and Algy both take the invented engagement with Ernest that she records in her
diary as a series of real events. The girls, learning that neither young man is Ernest,
still demand to know where Ernest is. Their insistence on taking fiction as reality is
vindicated at the end when Jack gets – significantly, out of a book, the Army Lists –
the information that he really is Ernest after all.

Wilde stated the play's philosophy as an inversion: 'we should treat all the trivial
things very seriously, and all the serious things of life with sincere and studied triviality'.[33] The serious things include muffins and cucumber sandwiches: 'And,
speaking of the science of Life, have you got the cucumber sandwiches cut for
Lady Bracknell?' (I.8–9). It is regularly suggested that the eating that goes on
through the play is a sublimation of sexual appetite, a Victorian substitute for the
pleasures of the Restoration rake. While Cecily claims that eating muffins looks
like repentance (III.4–5), to one critic it looks like fellatio.[34] But this may be taking
trivial things with the wrong kind of seriousness. Food, as food, is part of comedy's
reduction of life to the material level; Wilde may be taking a lead from W.S.
Gilbert's *Engaged* (1877), in which Miss Treherne, visiting her friend Minnie on the
latter's wedding morning, laments her own outcast state: 'Alas, I am out of place
here. What have I in common with tarts? Oh, I am ill-attuned to scenes of revelry!
(*Takes a tart and eats it.*)' (II.pp.151–52). Through the rest of the scene she continues
to eat tarts as Minnie, in real annoyance, tries unsuccessfully to stop her. The joke
depends not on the tarts' being symbols of anything else, but on their being tarts.
So in Wilde cucumber sandwiches are serious not because they are symbols but
because they are cucumber sandwiches.

The serious things are correspondingly trivialized. A christening is arranged as
casually as a haircut: Jack tells Canon Chasuble, 'I might trot round about five if
that would suit you' (II.282). He speaks with equal casualness of killing his brother,
and, having done so, turns up in full mourning only to find him, embodied in Algy,
enjoying rude health. The targets here include the Victorian cult of mourning,
which Wilde found over-elaborate and in serious need of reform,[35] and comedy's
own predilection for defying death with unlikely resurrections. The tragedy of the
fallen woman – from which Susan Harabin is rescued, and which Wilde himself
treated seriously in *Lady Windermere's Fan* and *A Woman of No Importance* – briefly
touches Miss Prism, in parody form, when Jack thinks she is his mother, and
grandly prepares to forgive her.

It is particularly painful that scandal should touch Miss Prism, however briefly; her dedication to Victorian propriety is such that she censors Cecily's economics textbook: 'The chapter on the Fall of the Rupee you may omit. It is somewhat too sensational' (II.94–95). One of the serious things Wilde trivializes, and needed to trivialize, is the constant threat of scandal. Many of the play's epigrams toy with this particular tiger. 'More than half of modern culture depends on what one shouldn't read' (I.131–32) could mean that the canon is created by exclusion, or that the books that matter are improper ones. There is a moment of shock when Miss Prism describes her manuscript as 'abandoned', followed by relief when she explains she means 'lost or mislaid' (II.58–59). When Algy claims that a married man needs to know Bunbury if he is not to have 'a very tedious time of it' Jack retorts that once married to Gwendolen he won't want to know Bunbury. Algy's reply, 'Then your wife will. You don't seem to realize, that in married life three is company and two is none' (I.264–71), not only endorses adultery but makes it a matter of equal opportunity, denying Jones's claim that there is no gander sauce.

Debauchery of a conventional kind is left vague: the imaginary Ernest gets into unnamed 'dreadful scrapes' (I.211–12). When we look for the rakish town life that makes Jack invent Ernest, we make a disconcerting discovery. Algy surveys all the things they could do after dinner – go to the theatre, the Club, the Empire – but what Jack wants to do is nothing. A passage from Wilde's *The Critic as Artist* provides a gloss: 'to do nothing at all is the most difficult thing in the world, the most difficult and the most intellectual. . . . It is to do nothing that the elect exist. Action is limited and relative. Unlimited and absolute is the vision of him who sits at ease and watches, who walks in loneliness and dreams'.[36] Jack's surface character is that of a respected and useful member of society, a landowner, a Justice of the Peace, a guardian. The other half of his double life, the half we never see because by its very nature it involves no action, is detachment, unlimited and absolute. The play has a similar double life. It can be taken as a charming entertainment, a relaxing escape from reality; in this light it belongs, like Jack, in respectable society. But in its inversions of value, its trivializing of the serious, its questioning of the whole notion of importance, in the sheer absoluteness of its detachment, there is a subversiveness all the more potent for being so painless.[37] The distancing devices of comedy – the detachment imposed by style, the reduction of life to the material level, the trivializing of tragedy and death – can in other plays reconcile us to the world, and to the accommodations society demands. *The Importance of Being Earnest* can be taken that way; Wilde may have used it that way himself, as a way of helping him live with the tensions of his life. But when detachment is absolute it is anti-social. Jack's origins make him, like Oedipus, an outcast.

Does comedy's detachment serve society or challenge it? *The Importance of Being Earnest* opened under police protection: Queensberry had threatened to make a disturbance in the theatre, and the actor-manager George Alexander, alerted by Wilde, cancelled Queensberry's ticket and called in the police.[38] Their presence has a curious double significance. Ostensibly, they were there to see that the fashionable audience of St. James's Theatre did not have its pleasure disturbed. But the police, all too soon, would come to Wilde on other business, playing not Parker but Gribsby, and in retrospect their presence at the theatre takes on an unintended meaning. The comedy of the baby in the handbag, denied a recognized position in good society, can be seen as an inversion of the tragedy of the outcast Oedipus. But the author of the comedy would shortly be an outcast himself.

# 2

# WATCHING SOCIETY

## On display: *The Man of Mode*

As comedy gets uncomfortable experiences under control by a detachment that can itself be disquieting, it organizes its presentation of social life through a stylization that reduces it to a system of clear signals. A gesture, an item of clothing, the choice of a word, will tell us how to place a character: a winner or a loser in the social game, in or out. The transactions of social life are likewise reduced to a few clear signals in the plots of comedy, as characters, at some cost to their full humanity, become counters in games played for money and property. In both cases the reductiveness has a paradoxical double effect: it aids the detachment of comedy, yet makes us uneasy at seeing humanity so reduced. Jean-Christophe Agnew has argued that in the early modern period theatre became a way of dealing with the anxiety of seeing identity and personal relations reduced to commodity transactions.[1] Comedy, with its interest in the material level of life and its willingness to stylize, is the natural medium for such anxiety. It allows us to watch people in the social arena, losing and establishing credit, trading in money, goods and each other. To have the right style is, we have seen, a way of establishing credit in formal terms within the special world created by comedy; it can also establish credit in the social world that comedy reflects. Watching comedy at work is watching society at work; and this dual process taps our anxiety, and our amusement, at watching social life reduced to the signs and systems in which comedy itself trades.

In the first scene of Sir George Etherege's *The Man of Mode* (1676) we see Dorimant preparing for the day, displaying a volatile mixture of pride, amusement and impatience at the necessity of being groomed for the arena:

DORIMANT: (*to* HANDY, *who is fiddling about him*) Leave your unnecessary fiddling. A wasp that's buzzing about a man's nose at dinner is not more troublesome than thou art.
HANDY: You love to have your clothes hang just, sir.
DORIMANT: I love to be well-dressed, sir, and think it no scandal to my understanding.

HANDY: Will you use the essence, or orange-flower water?

DORIMANT: I will smell as I do today, no offence to the ladies' noses.

HANDY: Your pleasure, sir. (*Exit* HANDY)

DORIMANT: That a man's excellency should lie in neatly tying of a ribbon or a cravat! How careful's nature in furnishing the world with necessary coxcombs!

YOUNG BELLAIR: That's a mighty pretty suit of yours, Dorimant.

DORIMANT: I'm glad 't has your approbation.

YOUNG BELLAIR: No man in town has a better fancy in his clothes than you have.

DORIMANT: You will make me have an opinion of my genius.

(I.i.323–39)

In the play as a whole Dorimant is preoccupied with his own power, his control of the interlocking games of social appearance and sexual intrigue; in the opening scene he naturally resents being in the hands of a servant, and resents having to present himself for the judgment of others. At the same time he takes pride in his appearance; like it or not, he is a creature of the market. His solution is to put himself on display on his own terms. He resents being reduced to a performance; but he ensures that the performance will be a good one, and his own.

He meets his match in Harriet, who in her first appearance is battling with her maid: 'Dear madam, let me set that curl in order . . . . Let me alone, I will shake 'em all out of order!' (III.i.1–2). Harriet's insistence on a natural wildness shows that like Dorimant she wants to control her own social performance. She contrasts herself with Lady Dapper, whose over-exactness in 'powdering, painting, and . . . patching never fail in public to draw the tongues and eyes of all the men upon her' (III.i.15–16). When Dorimant and Harriet meet they accuse each other of a similar over-eagerness to please, of playing too obviously to the audience, cheapening the goods (III.iii.88–98). Each is mocking the other, trying to keep the edge in a game in which the correct style is a carelessness that displays one's confidence. It is this confidence that Dorimant shows in his decision to use no perfume, and that Loveit, the play's chief loser, conspicuously lacks. When we first see her she is staring into a mirror, declaring, 'I hate myself, I look so ill today' (II.ii.3).

For those who lack the natural skill, there are books. Dorimant's friend Medley describes one: 'Then there is *The Art of Affectation*, written by a late beauty of quality, teaching you how to draw up your breasts, stretch up your neck, to thrust out your breech, to play with your head, to toss up your nose' (II.i.135–38) – and so on. 'A late beauty of quality' is damning; out of the game herself, the author is reduced to giving lessons. And the fact that there is a market for such books shows how many people are insecure about their performances.[2] Harriet and Young Bellair, pushed by their parents towards a marriage neither of them wants, construct between them an ironic imitation of textbook body language. Knowing their parents are watching, they put on a show, giving each other directions:

HARRIET: Your head a little more on one side. Ease yourself on your left leg and play with your right hand.

YOUNG BELLAIR: Thus, is it not?

HARRIET: Now set your right leg firm on the ground, adjust your belt, then look about you.

YOUNG BELLAIR: A little exercising will make me perfect.

HARRIET: Smile, and turn to me again very sparkish.

YOUNG BELLAIR: Will you take your turn and be instructed?

HARRIET: With all my heart.

YOUNG BELLAIR: At one motion play with your fan, roll your eyes, and then settle a kind look upon me.

HARRIET: So.

YOUNG BELLAIR: Now spread your fan, look down upon it, and tell the sticks with a finger.

HARRIET: Very modish.

(III.i.137–51)

*The Man of Mode* is among other things a nature documentary on *homo sapiens* in the mating season. Here the preening and display are ironized and turned into theatre by two people whose real interest is in staying apart, and who keep a comic detachment by mocking the tricks that are normally used to attract.

But the process can cut both ways; the performance they construct as comedy becomes real display, and betrays real interest. As they give each other detailed instructions they show a close concentration on each other's bodies. Harriet is concerned with the placing of Bellair's legs, and when he retorts in kind there is a small flash of electricity:

YOUNG BELLAIR: Clap your hand up to your bosom, hold down your gown. Shrug a little, draw up your breasts and let 'em fall again, gently, with a sigh or two, *etc*,

HARRIET: By the good instructions you give, I suspect you for one of those malicious observers who watch people's eyes, and from innocent looks make scandalous conclusions.

(III.i.152–57)

He is getting a little too interested, and for a moment she stops the game, implicitly warning him not to read too much in *her* eyes, and to keep his distance.

When Bellair (taking advantage of the contemporary fashion for low-cut dresses)[3] tells Harriet to display her breasts, he is also showing the interest in the actress' body that was one of the features of Restoration theatre. Dorimant and Harriet, in the deliberate naturalness of their self-display, show that they are bringing into the market not just their clothes but their bodies, the total physical presence that impresses and attracts. They are doing, in effect, what actors do when they walk on to the stage. As the opening stage direction implies, our view of

Dorimant's levee is a glimpse into an actor's dressing room: '*A table covered with a toilet; clothes laid ready*' (I.i.0.1). Restoration audiences could stroll backstage to watch the performers dress, showing special interest in the women.[4] Here that activity is transferred into the main playing area. The business of social display is easily reduced to a mechanical system, subject to mockery. But it is also a serious and fascinating part of the business of theatre, and of the business of society.

## Reading the signs

The custom of the levee allows us to see a leading character beginning the day, assembling the externals of his performance, entertaining visitors, establishing his place in the world. Dorimant's dressing-room is his command post. As we see him making his decisions about dress and perfume, we also see him planning his campaign against Loveit, and receiving from an orange-seller news of the latest new women in town. Part of the scene's impact is the fascination of watching a master at work. In Congreve's *Love for Love* (1695) Valentine (the same actor, Thomas Betterton, now pushing sixty) begins the day under seige from his creditors, reading a book for breakfast because there is nothing else left, with his servant complaining of starvation and his friend Scandal reporting that the town, into which he can no longer venture, regards him with a mixture of commiseration and contempt. A life of gentlemanly pleasure, a life like Dorimant's, has taken its toll, and the bills are in. The command post is now a place of retreat, and the levee is a sign not of social power but of social disgrace.[5]

Jonson's *Epicoene* (1609) begins with Clerimont in his lodgings '*making himself ready*' (I.i.3). His first visitor is Truewit, who rebukes the idle social round his friend indulges in: 'Why, here's the man that can melt away his time, and never feels it! What between his mistress abroad and his ingle at home, high fare, soft lodging, fine clothes and his fiddle; he thinks the hours ha' no wings, or the day no post-horse' (I.i.23–27). We are introduced not just to a character but to an idle society concerned with display and pastime, and to a comedy whose view of that society will have a critical edge. Sir Richard Steele in *The Conscious Lovers* (1722) uses the levee for a more simply moral effect. The play begins with Sir John Bevil asking his servant, 'Have you ordered that I should not be interrupted while I am dressing?' (I.i.1–2). As part of Steele's attempt to turn comedy away from frivolity and debauchery and on to serious matters of thought and feeling, this levee, if such it can be called, is strictly private. Yet Sir John is still on display: using his servant as a sounding-board, he expounds the philosophy that lies behind his serious, dignified relations with his son. Bevil Junior opens the next scene reading an improving essay from *The Spectator*, decking not his body but his mind: 'Such an author consulted in a morning sets the spirit for the vicissitudes of the day better than the glass does a man's person' (I.ii.2–5).

We might think that the social conditions of the twentieth century leave no room for the gentleman's levee. But, as the theatrical custom of holding court in the dressing room survives (Simon Callow confesses to having missed an entrance cue because his visitors were talking too loudly)[6] so does the levee. The second scene of Tom Stoppard's *The Real Thing* (1982) shows the playwright Henry on a Sunday morning, surrounded by records and newspapers, receiving visitors, serving drinks, arguing about his most recent play, and worrying about how he is going to present himself to the public on *Desert Island Disks*. We learn about his tastes, his philosophy, his anxieties. As in *The Man of Mode*, one's credit hinges on one's style, and Henry worries that the program will expose his love of cheap popular music: 'I'm supposed to be one of your intellectual playwrights. I'm going to look a total prick, aren't I, announcing that while I was telling Jean-Paul Sartre and the post-war French existentialists where they had got it wrong, I was spending the whole time listening to the Crystals singing "Da Doo Ron Ron"' (I.ii.p.17). Steele's gentlemen are serenely confident; Dorimant's confidence is edged with irritability; Henry betrays the anxiety that goes with being on display.

In all these scenes we get a fix on the central character, the world he inhabits, the kind of judgment the play will call for. In the main body of a play a single, quick signal can tell us, with or without guidance from the stage, how to place a character. In Shakespeare's *All's Well that Ends Well* (c.1603) Lafeu tells Parolles how he spotted him as a phoney: though his language was plausible, 'the scarves and the bannerets about thee did manifoldly dissuade me from believing thee a vessel of too great a burden' (II.iii.203–5). Throughout *The Real Thing* the merits and demerits of the working-class playwright and political vandal Brodie are argued back and forth; he appears for the first time in the last scene, wearing '*a cheap suit*' (II.xii.pp.79–80), and his fate is sealed. Voices function as clothing does. In Peter Shaffer's *Black Comedy* (1965) the 'unmistakable, terrifying deb quack' (p.139) of the hero's fiancée Carol, with her fondness for coinages like 'sweetipegs', 'daddipegs' and 'sexipegs', tells us this marriage had better not take place. In H.J. Byron's *Our Boys* (1875) the retired butterman Middlewick asks, 'Halloa – who's the gals?' and one of the ladies in question, his son Charles's fiancée, reacts in physical shock to his '*intensely vulgar voice*'. (Here the signals are mixed: Charles '*by his expression shows he resents her manner*' [I.p.130].)

There are right places and wrong places. In Noël Coward's *Private Lives* (1930) Elyot complains that in order to set up his divorce from Amanda 'I spent the whole weekend at Brighton with a lady called Vera Williams. She had the nastiest-looking hairbrush I have ever seen' (I.p.189). In Coward's *Blithe Spirit* (1941) Elvira complains to her husband Charles, 'Nobody but a monumental bore would have thought of having a honeymoon at Budleigh Salterton.' She elaborates: 'potted palms, seven hours of every day on a damp golf course, and a three-piece orchestra playing "Merrie England"' (III.i.p.91). Elvira is a ghost; some offences are worth pursuing beyond the grave. In Alan Ayckbourn's *The Norman Conquests* (1973) Ruth is reduced to hysterical laughter on learning that her husband Norman was planning to spend a dirty weekend with Annie at East Grinstead (*Table Manners*, I.ii.p.52). Quick signals like these, in matters of clothing, language and taste, tell us that a character, one way or another, will not do. The onstage characters who point this out (Lafeu, Elvira) gain an edge by doing so. Even one's taste in theatre counts. Olivia in Wycherley's *The Plain Dealer* (1676) caps a display of hypocrisy by attacking the obscenity of *The Country Wife* (II.ii.419–21). In Ben Jonson's *Every Man in his Humour* (1598; revised version published 1616) Bobadil instantly condemns himself by admiring *The Spanish Tragedy*, Jonson's shorthand for the old-fashioned drama he wanted to supplant (I.v.50–1). Nor can characters who simply have the wrong style help themselves by trying harder, since trying hard is itself an offence. In Jonson's *Every Man out of his Humour* (1599) the upstart Fungoso tries to follow the fashion by imitating the clothing of Fastidius Briske, always finding himself one suit behind. Lady Wishfort in Congreve's *The Way of the World* (1700) rehearses her body language: 'I'll give the first impression on a couch – I won't lie neither, but loll and lean upon one elbow, with one foot a little dangling off, jogging in a thoughtful way' (IV.pp.374–75). Waitwell, whom she is trying to impress (in his disguise as Sir Rowland), summarizes the results: 'Oh, she is the antidote to desire' (IV.p.389).

With the advent of realistic scenery, settings join clothes, voices and body language, helping us place the characters even before they appear. St John Hankin's *The Return of the Prodigal* (1905) opens: '*The Jacksons' drawing room, a handsome room, suggests opulence rather than taste. Not vulgar, but not distinguished. Too full of furniture, pictures, knick-knacks, chair covers, plants in pots. Too full of everything*' (I.p.81). Hankin counts on the audience to make the necessary judgments as soon as they see the set. Our ability to read such signals produces a bonding with the play, a sense of being in the know. We know, and congratulate ourselves for knowing, that one should not admire *The Spanish Tragedy*, use words like 'sexipegs', or be called Vera Williams. It is part of the comfort comedy offers: we feel we belong to a community of understanding. The effect operates with special power when there is no explicit guidance from the stage: when, for example, the curtain rises and one look at the set tells us the people who live here have no taste.

But satire can ricochet into the house. In a lighted auditorium, with more galleries facing each other than facing the stage, the audience will be particularly self-aware. Reading older comedies we come across frequent references to characters behaving badly in the playhouse, putting themselves on display in a way that competes with the performance. In *Every Man out* Carlo Buffone advises Sogliardo, 'look with a good starch't face, and ruffle your brow like a new boot; laugh at nothing but your own jests, or else as the noblemen laugh. . . . sit o' the stage, and flout; provided, you have a good suit' (I.ii.58–64). Sparkish in Wycherley's *The Country Wife* (1675) boasts that he and his friends 'find fault with their bawdy upon the stage, whilst we talk nothing else in the pit as loud' (III.p.297). We read such passages now as stage history, evidence (jokingly exaggerated, perhaps) of the playhouse behaviour of an earlier age. But in the original performances they would have been part of a real interplay of stage and auditorium, as audience members, scrutinizing the social behaviour of the characters, realized they were under scrutiny themselves, from the play and from their fellow spectators.

Lady Brute and her niece Bellinda, in Sir John Vanbrugh's *The Provoked Wife* (1697), know this and prepare accordingly, practising in a mirror the faces they will use in the playhouse (III.iii.72–77). As in *The Man of Mode*, the display is sexual. Lady Brute confesses, 'if I perceive the men whispering and looking upon me, you must know I cannot for my life forbear thinking they talk to my advantage' (III.iii.56–58). Comedies are particularly useful: 'I watch with impatience for the next jest in the play, that I may laugh and show my white teeth' (III.iii.61–62). However, bawdy comedies (like Vanbrugh's) pose a challenge: 'when they come blurt out with a nasty thing in a play . . . all the men presently look upon the women.' Behind the obvious, unspoken question (did they get it?) lies the question Horner asks in *The Country Wife*: who will, who will not? To laugh is to betray oneself, not to laugh is dull; Bellinda's solution is to blow her nose (III.iii.78–80). The theatre as a place of sexual display survives into the Victorian period, where in Dion Boucicault's *Old Heads and Young Hearts* (1844) it is given an earnest and sentimental turn as Littleton complains of Lady Alice's behaviour at the Opera: 'I don't think there was a fool in the house whom she did not flirt with through her opera-glass' (IV.p.86). The emphasis is not on the lady's skill at putting herself on display, but on the lover's pain at watching her. The basic situation is the same.

In *The Country Wife*, in Vanbrugh's *The Relapse* (1696) and in Susanna Centlivre's *The Beau's Duel* (1702), sexual intrigues begin with sightings in the playhouse, suggesting the importance of display for initiating comic action. In *The Relapse* Loveless sees on stage a play that predicts his own story, that of a reformed rake who falls again, and sees in the audience Berinthia, who will help him fall. It is easy for the audience to laugh at characters who preen and posture, putting themselves on display; but the play regularly asks the audience if it is any better. The audience comes to be seen; as for the actors, being seen is their essential business; and the plotting of comedy regularly takes display as its starting point. It is laughable and reductive, and there is no doing without it.

## Class as reality

Among the classifications in which comedy deals (right and wrong style, in and out), few operate so powerfully as class. Some historians tell us that the idea of class is a nineteenth-century invention, and that class divisions with a corresponding 'vertical antagonism' came into being with the Industrial Revolution.[7] It is true that in the Victorian period class-consciousness seems more acute and class divisions more elaborate. But in some comedies of the sixteenth and seventeenth centuries class distinctions, simpler than the nineteenth-century ones but still palpable, define the characters and drive the plot. In Thomas Dekker's *The Shoemakers' Holiday* (1599) the division is between citizens who earn and aristocrats who spend. In the first scene the Lord Mayor tells the Earl of Lincoln he does not want his daughter Rose marrying Lincoln's cousin Lacy, 'Who will in silks and gay apparel spend / More in one year than I am worth by far' (I.i.13–14). They debate an episode in Lacy's past, in which, out of money on a trip to Germany, he became a shoemaker. Lincoln is disgusted: 'A goodly science for a gentleman / Of such descent' (I.i.30–31). The Lord Mayor returns this contempt in kind: 'And yet your cousin Rowland might do well / Now he hath learn'd an occupation' (I.i.42–43). The class abrasiveness of this scene shows the barrier the lovers have to cross. Dekker's interim solution is to have Lacy return to his old role of shoemaker. This does not mean class fluidity: Lacy as shoemaker is in disguise, playing a part, and he adopts a heavy Dutch accent to emphasize the point. The final solution is romantic, reinforced by the power of the King, who declares as he joins the lovers, 'Dost thou not know that love respects no blood, / Cares not for difference of birth or state?' (V.v.103–4).

Elsewhere the play puts its main weight on the life of work. When Lacy joins the shoemakers' establishment, one of the workers asks him, 'Have you all your tools? A good rubbing pin, a good stopper, a good dresser, your four sorts of awls, and your two balls of wax, your paring knife, your hand and thumb-leathers, and good Saint Hugh's bones to smooth up your work?' (I.iv.70–74). This is a class that defines itself not by style or gesture but by the hard facts of work; its principal signs are tools. Lacy can never really break into this class; his stay in the shop is a romantic interlude. On the other hand, the class division that drives Philip Massinger's *A New Way to Pay Old Debts* (c.1625) is a matter of blood and breeding, and while Dekker privileges the workers Massinger privileges the gentry. Sir Giles Overreach, who made his money as a city usurer and is now devouring country estates and ruining gentry who are down on their luck, wants to marry his daughter Margaret to Lord Lovell. Lovell's objection rests not, as in *The Shoemakers' Holiday*, on a contrast of different ways of life, but on a fundamental difference in nature defined in physical terms:

> I would not so adulterate my blood
> By marrying Margaret, and so leave my issue
> Made up of several pieces, one part scarlet
> And the other London blue.
> (IV.i.222–25)

The play is built not on a contrast of working or not working but on a difference between good blood and bad. The final test of whether one has the right blood is military action. Lovell has a fine reputation as a soldier, and Wellborn, restored to the estate he squandered, determines at the end of the play to restore his lost honour by going to war. Overreach bullies other characters by threatening to use his sword simply as a sign of his own power. In the final mad scene that follows his defeat he tries to draw his sword, and fails.

His daughter marries a gentleman she loves, Tom Allworth; as in *The Shoemakers' Holiday*, comic structure suggests the possibility of truce in the class war. But it does so through a romantic story convention, placed at the end of the play, so that the awkward question of whether such a marriage can work out in a class-ridden world does not have to be raised. T.W. Robertson, on the other hand, places just this question at the centre of *Caste* (1867). The Hon. George D'Alroy has married the dancer Esther Eccles. His friend Hawtree deplores the match, declaring that

George has violated 'the inexorable law of caste . . . that commands like to mate with like, and forbids a giraffe to fall in love with a squirrel' (I.p.349). He sees a mingling not just of different bloods but of different species. Speaking from the other side of the barrier, the plumber Sam Gerridge agrees: 'People should stick to their own class. Life's a railway journey, and Mankind's a passenger – first class, second class, third class. Any person found riding in a superior class to that for which he has taken his ticket will be removed at the first station stopped at, according to the bye-laws of the company' (I.p.359). His image draws on the daily reality of class divisions in Victorian society. He is also, like Hawtree, expounding a law, and his style slips into that of an official notice.

Much of the play's comedy stems from the collisions of one class with another. Sam's paper cap, in which he takes a workman's pride, is to Hawtree an unfamiliar object, and he handles it as a monkey might handle something dropped in its cage: '*examines it as a curiosity, drops it on the floor and pushes it away with his stick*' (I.p.358).[8] There is also pathos in Esther's exclusion from George's class. His mother, a tyrant who regards Esther's very name as deplorable – 'Eccles! Eccles! There never was an Eccles. He don't exist' (II.p.373) – shows her pride in George's military ancestry by quoting great chunks of Froissart. The Marchioness is comic; but it is not so comic when Esther, challenged by the Marchioness to buckle on George's sword-belt as he goes to war, is so overcome by grief that she faints instead.

The marriage of George and Esther is treated sympathetically, and Hawtree's objections to it are rendered ironic when his own fiancée jilts him to marry the son of a Marquis (caste within caste) and we learn that his father was in trade. But to Robertson caste is essential: it is a source of comedy, a source of pathos, and finally an inescapable reality. At the end of the play George delivers the message: 'Oh, Caste's all right. Caste is a good thing if it's not carried too far. It shuts the door on the pretentious and the vulgar; but it should open the door very wide for exceptional merit' (III.p.405). It is the willingness to allow exceptions (like his own marriage) that keeps class tolerable. The casualness of 'Oh, Caste's all right' suggests that no strenuous thought is needed to defend the system; we take it for granted, like the weather.

## Class as performance: *Pygmalion*

The signs of class are to some degree external: voices, behaviour, dress, the stock in trade of comedy. But they are generally presented as signs of innate nature, not performance tricks that can be adopted or discarded at will. Romantic love and good feeling can reach across the barriers (in *Caste*, Sam and Hawtree shake hands when they find they have both been aiding Esther in her difficulties) but the barriers themselves hold. Characters who try to switch class can only give temporary performances, not change their essential natures: examples include Lacy as a shoemaker, and the young gentlemen of Richard Brome's *A Jovial Crew* (1641), whose attempt to pass themselves off as beggars comically founders when they ask for huge sums of money and, when insulted, challenge the offender to a duel. The test case is Bernard Shaw's *Pygmalion* (1914), where Henry Higgins passes the flower girl Eliza Doolittle off as a duchess by changing her voice and giving her a decent wardrobe. Shaw does not sentimentalize the flower girl: when we first see her Eliza is ignorant, dirty, and *'needs the services of a dentist'* (I.p.15). A tough life has made her fearful; she is deeply suspicious when she finds that Higgins has been copying her words into a book. On her first visit to him she betrays a pathetic snobbery, thinking he will be impressed to learn she has come in a taxi. There is more to get rid of here than ingrained dirt and vulgar vowels. The difficulty of the transition shows when we catch it half-way, on Eliza's visit to Mrs Higgins's drawing-room, her first outing in society. She speaks in two voices simultaneously: the flower girl presents a comic version of the squalid, desperate life of the poor, with grammar to match; the lady shapes it all in perfect vowels and consonants: 'Lord love you! Why should she die of influenza? She come through diptheria right enough the year before. I saw her with my own eyes. Fairly blue with it, she was. They all thought she was dead; but my father he kept ladling gin down her throat till she came to so sudden that she bit the bowl off the spoon' (III.pp.78–79). Here, class barriers hold firm: a lady cannot be created by a change of accent, and all Higgins has managed is a comic scrambling of the signals.

The Eliza of the last two acts is another matter. Not only are her voice and appearance fully transformed; she is now a strong-minded, intelligent woman who debates with Higgins on equal terms. It is as though Shaw, in order to get her out of her class, has to make her into a new character. (And because she no longer stands out as different she is no longer funny.) Yet even this is not enough to win her a new place in the class system. On the day she passes her test, appearing at a number of demanding social functions, Higgins confesses to a worry that she does it too well, revealing herself as a professional imitation, too good to be the real thing. In the last scene, startled by the sight of her father in his wedding finery, she reverts to one of her gutter noises: 'A-a-a-a-a-ah-ow-ooh!' (V.p.128). Socially, she is in limbo. Through the last two acts her urgent questions, 'What am I fit for? What have you left me fit for? Where am I to go? What am I to do? Whats to become of me?' (IV.p.106), go essentially unanswered. The news that she will marry Freddy Eynsford Hill and run a flower shop belongs not to the play but to the postscript Shaw added for the 1916 printing. Eliza's own verdict on what Higgins has achieved is 'I wish youd left me where you found me' (IV.p.107).

Strictly speaking, Eliza's new strength and intelligence ought to make her class irrelevant. She herself, praising Colonel Pickering's courtesy towards her, sees class not as an immutable reality but as a perception: 'the difference between a lady and a flower girl is not how she behaves, but how she's treated' (V.p.127). Higgins (who is equally rude to everyone, as Pickering is equally polite) goes further, arguing the 'great secret' is 'having the same manner for all human souls: in short, behaving as if you were in Heaven, where there are no third-class carriages, and one soul is as good as another' (V.p.132). But the England of *Pygmalion*, like the England of *Caste*, is not Heaven, and there are third-class carriages. *Pygmalion* experiments with using performance not to confirm class identity but to break it; but its comedy depends on the existence of the barriers it challenges, on the interplay of class voices and class manners; and Eliza's success in leaving her original class leaves her socially dislocated. She demonstrates her mastery of her new role in a public performance Shaw brought on stage when he revised the play in 1941; in the original play we never see it. Instead we are taken backstage once the show is over to watch the frustrating, uncertain aftermath.

## In disgrace: *The School for Scandal*

As a woman, Eliza Doolittle feels particularly dislocated and vulnerable in the social arena. The arena allows not just display but disgrace and exposure, and for a woman, there can be more at stake than taste or class; in communities that expect modesty and circumspection from them, any kind of publicity can be damaging. Christian Custance, in Nicholas Udall's *Roister Doister* (c.1552), finds that just to be the subject of the title character's ludicrous attentions leads her fiancé to suspect her honesty; she has committed the offence of being talked about.

In *The Way of the World* (1700) the offence and the threat are more specific. Marwood terrifies Lady Wishfort by threatening to expose her daughter's adultery in court. She begins with a grim sexual pun and goes on from there: '[to] have your case opened by an old fumbling lecher in a quoif like a man-midwife to bring your daughter's infamy to light. . . . while the good judge, tickled with the proceeding, simpers under a grey beard, and fidges off and on his cushion as if he had swallowed cantharides, or sat upon cow-itch' (V.pp.397–98). She then adds a further terror: 'it must after this be consigned by the shorthand writers to the public press; and from thence be transferred to the hands, nay into the throats and lungs of hawkers, with voices more licentious than the loud flounder-man's or the woman that cries "grey peas"' (V.p.398). So long as you are operating immediately in front of an audience, you have a chance to control the performance. Gossip is unfixed and volatile. But the printed word is fixed and widely distributed; your story will be told to hundreds, even thousands of people, who have never seen you and whose view you cannot correct. In that respect a press report is the antithesis of a performance. And, as Marwood points out, you will become a commodity, hawked about in the streets for money.

The power of the press is comically shown in Dion Boucicault's *Old Heads and Young Hearts* (1844), when *The Morning Post* reports a double elopement but gets the names wrong, and the women assume they are now bound to marry the men to whom the newspaper has attached them (IV.p.95). It is less comic in Arthur Wing Pinero's *The Benefit of the Doubt* (1895), whose heroine Theophilia is disgraced not so much because the judge in a case involving a marriage breakup has rebuked her for indiscretion, as because the papers are sure to pick it up (I.pp.59–60). She compares her shame to a violation of the clothing code: 'I felt like a woman caught with bare shoulders in daylight' (I.p.67). She is rescued by a friend who arranges for her to be seen regularly in public with the Bishop of St Olpherts. It is not the

Bishop who will save her (he is so senile he can barely put a sentence together) but the society reporters.

The scandalmongers of Sheridan's *The School for Scandal* (1777) use the press for all it is worth. The play's opening line is Lady Sneerwell's, 'The paragraphs, you say, Mr Snake, were all inserted?' (I.i.1). Mrs Candour, old-fashioned enough to prefer the spoken word, fears being scooped: 'We shall have the whole affair in the newspapers with the names of the parties before I have dropped the story at a dozen houses' (V.ii.7–9). The old medium is more personal, but the new medium is faster. When Lady Teazle is present the scandalmongers stick to relatively tame jokes about bad makeup and missing teeth; Sheridan protects his heroine from association with gossip at its worst. But when she is absent the scandalmongers cut much deeper, hitting each sex where its credit is most vulnerable. They turn on a number of women with tales of elopement, adultery and illicit pregnancy. They turn on Charles Surface with reports of his financial ruin. Their slanders actually destroy: Snake credits Mrs Clackitt with 'six marriages being broken off and three sons disinherited, . . . four forced elopements, and as many close confinements, nine separate maintenances, and two divorces' (I.i.13–16). As Pinero's Theophilia feels her body exposed, Sheridan's gossips, when Sir Peter Teazle catches his wife with Joseph Surface, turn his social wounds into literal ones: 'a thrust in segoon quite through his left side . . . a bullet lodged in the thorax' (V.ii.70–71). When he walks on to the stage, uninjured, Sir Oliver remarks, 'we had just given you over' (V.ii.136).[9] The notional wounding of Sir Peter is broadly comic as well as symbolic; the gossips' treatment of Lady Teazle is quietly chilling:

LADY SNEERWELL: Well, there is no trusting appearances, though indeed she was always too lively for me.

MRS CANDOUR: To be sure, her manners were a little too free; but then she was so young!

LADY SNEERWELL: And had, indeed, some good qualities.

(V.ii.31–35)

They talk about her as though she were dead. Socially, she is; they have killed her.

Sir Peter sees scandal as a public matter. It circulates like banknotes, and all parties involved are responsible: 'in all cases of slander currency, whenever the drawer of the lie was not to be found, the injured parties should have a right to come on any of the endorsers' (II.ii.176–78). Sheridan's rough notes on the last page of the manuscript include: 'A sort of brokers in scandal – who transfer lies without fees – reputation like the stocks.'[10] For Snake, as for a newspaper owner, it is a commercial matter. He apologizes to Lady Sneerwell: 'You paid me extremely liberally for the lie in question; but I unfortunately have been offered double to speak the truth' (V.last.184–86). At the same time he has to be concerned with his own public credit, and asks not to have his one good deed exposed: 'I live by the badness of my character. I have nothing but my infamy to depend on' (V.last.221–22). When Lady Teazle declares jokingly, 'Sir Peter is such an enemy to scandal he would have it put down by Parliament', Sir Peter takes her more than half seriously: "Fore Heaven, madam, if they were to consider the sporting with reputation of as much importance as poaching on manors and pass an Act for the Preservation of Fame, I believe there are many who would thank them for the Bill' (II.ii.162–67). One's name is one's property, and in England property is sacred. Against the solidity of property we may set the money market, volatile and potentially destructive, where fortunes may be lost on a rumour. Slander circulates, and destroys, like money.

## In the marketplace

Society is an arena where people are on display; it is also a market where they are bought and sold. The systems of exchange, literal and metaphoric, in which comedy deals – a baby for a novel, china for sex – become embedded in the plots of comedy. Marriage, the end to which comedy normally strives, becomes corrupted when men and women are put on the market. In Steele's *The Tender Husband* (1705) Sir Harry Gubbin announces, 'my business in town is to dispose of an hundred head of cattle and my son' (I.259–61). He objects to the price the lady's guardian is setting: 'you rate her too high; the war has fetched down the price of women' (I.269–70). The man becomes livestock by verbal association; the woman seems to be livestock quite literally.

In the seventeenth and eighteenth centuries the London social season became a marriage market,[11] and in comedy complaints about this continued well into the nineteenth century.[12] In Shakespeare's *The Taming of the Shrew* (c.1594) Baptista auctions his daughter Bianca off to the highest bidder, with the competitors offering houses, plate, gold, cattle and argosies. Shaw parodies the convention in *Arms and the Man* (1894) when Bluntschli establishes his claim to Raina by challenging Sergius to a contest of possessions. Sergius has twenty horses and three carriages; Bluntschli has two hundred horses and seventy carriages, not to mention four thousand tablecloths, nine thousand pairs of sheets and blankets, two thousand four hundred eiderdown quilts, ten thousand knives, forks and dessert spoons. He has just inherited a string of hotels from his father.

In most periods the exchange of people for property in marriage is a normal social practice, sharpened and stylized in comedy for satiric effect. Even good marriages, like that of Millamant and Mirabell in *The Way of the World*, come with financial transactions attached. The materializing of human relations invades the black market when it touches adultery. In Thomas Middleton's *A Chaste Maid in Cheapside* (1613) the marriage market operates in the usual way, with the usual metaphors. Sir Walter Whorehound, bringing his mistress to London to find her a rich husband, promises, 'I bring thee up to turn thee into gold, wench' (I.i.100), while Yellowhammer, keeping his daughter from wasting herself on the wrong kind of suitor, plans to 'lock up this baggage / As carefully as my gold' (III.i.40–41). More startling is Allwit's arrangement with Sir Walter, who sleeps with Mistress Allwit and in return looks after the family, paying rent and church duties and supplying all the household necessities: Allwit notes smugly that the coalhouse is full, the yard is stacked with firewood, and having checked on the supplies 'I say nothing, / But smile and pin the door' (I.ii.28–29). Mistress Allwit's body has been turned not into gold but into coal and wood.[13] The suburbanites of Giles Cooper's *Everything in the Garden* (1962) live off a similar arrangement, but it is a sign of the progress made by the middle class that their needs are more elaborate. The wives bring in substantial incomes as call girls (at one point there are banknotes all over the stage, posing a storage problem) and when there is a threat that the business may close down, the husbands worry about school fees, a new greenhouse and a daughter's pony (III.p.202). As Allwit congratulates himself on freedom from church duties, one of Cooper's husbands, shocked at first when he learns what his wife is up to, comes round when he realizes the money is tax-free.

As the necessity of display in the arena can reduce people to performances, so the materialism of social life reduces them to commodities. Their value is not the credit they win by having the right style or belonging to the right class, but cash value. In Henry Fielding's *The Modern Husband* (1732) Lord Richly, paying Mr Modern for having an affair with Modern's wife, complains to the lady that he has made a bad bargain: 'I am £1500 out of pocket, which, in my way of counting, is fourteen more than any woman's virtue is worth' (II.vii.p.276). Maggie, the simple Scottish girl in W.S. Gilbert's *Engaged* (1877), puts an even more modest value on herself. When her lover indignantly refuses to sell her to an English gentleman for two pounds she urges him not to be hasty: 'twa pound is twa pound' (I.p.146).

## *Money*

This reduction of humanity, one of those jokes that as Bergson would put it has a bitter aftertaste, is not the whole story. Money is also power, and in the plotting of more good-natured comedies it is power to do good, to rescue the indigent and deserving, to let unfortunate lovers marry. It is, by the same token, a way of testing the moral nature of characters. The generosity test runs through comedy, especially in the eighteenth and nineteenth centuries. This is the test (in the form, what will you do for an indigent relative?) that in *The School for Scandal* Charles Surface passes and Joseph Surface fails. In Richard Cumberland's *The West Indian* (1771) the worthy but penniless Captain Dudley needs money to outfit him for an expedition to Africa. Though the mean-minded Lady Rusport refuses, the play is so full of good characters that he is bombarded with offers.

Cumberland's title character is a rich, naïve, good-natured young man who has just come to England from Jamaica, and scatters his wealth benevolently around London. Sheridan's source of benevolent wealth is Sir Oliver Surface, who made his money in India. Though Sheridan was later to take part in the impeachment of Warren Hastings, neither play asks how the English got so rich in these exotic lands. The money is magic gold from a fabulous foreign source, and solves all problems. In *The Nabob* (1772) Samuel Foote exposes what the other playwrights suppress. Sir Matthew Mite (there was an actual East India Company official called Sir Matthew White) has become rich in India by cruelty and extortion, and now tries to use his money to spread corruption in England. When he declares, 'riches possess, at least, one magical power, that, being rightly dispensed, they closely conceal the source from which they proceeded' (III.ii.p.111) he might be stating the principle of *The West Indian* and *The School for Scandal*: don't ask where the money comes from; watch what it does.

The mainspring of the plot of Edward Bullwer-Lytton's *Money* (1840) is the will of the late Mr Mordaunt, who grew wealthy in India and from beyond the grave passes a series of judgments through the medium of money. To the parasites who have fawned on him, sending him unwanted presents in the hope of a rich legacy (the central device of Jonson's *Volpone*) he gives insulting bequests: a cousin who sent him the parliamentary debates gets their cash value in return, 'deducting the carriage thereof, which he always forgot to pay': £14.2s.4d. A relative who sent him 'every year the Cheltenham waters which nearly gave me my death' gets the empty bottles (I.i.pp.60–61). The bulk of his estate goes to a distant, impoverished relation, Alfred Evelyn: 'being, I am told, an oddity, like myself – the only one of my relations who never fawned on me, and who, having known privation, may the better apply wealth' (I.i.pp.61–62).

Evelyn quickly finds himself surrounded by parasites. In a variation on the convention of the levee, we see tradesmen buzzing around him like wasps, all wanting him to spend his money on the material things they supply.[14] Evelyn, who has always been a sardonic moralist, despises his wealth and the people who feed on him; but he values it as a chance to do good to the unfortunate: 'Fools – knaves – hypocrites! By the way, Sharp, send £100 to the poor bricklayer whose house was burnt down yesterday' (II.ii. p.66). He prefers to do good by stealth, believing in 'a charity that shuns the day' (II.ii. p.77) as though the passing of money is a lower bodily function that should not be done in public. But it is the business of theatre to demonstrate its ideas, and Evelyn obliges, contriving a satiric action that shows the absurd power of wealth to establish credit in society. He pretends to lose his fortune by gambling and investing in an unsafe bank; predictably, the world turns against him. At the end of Act One, newly wealthy and surrounded by flatterers, he asks, 'Lend me £10 for my old nurse' and '*Chorus put their hands into their pockets*' as the curtain falls (I.i.p.62). At the end of Act Four he makes the same request and '*Exeunt* OMNES, *indignantly*' (IV.ii. p.106). The comic stylization embodies the reductive power of money, which makes people act like robots.

Evelyn's relations with the women in his life are also bound up with money. His first attempts to raise money for his old nurse come early in the play, when he is still poor. The generosity test operates in the usual way. Clara Douglas, though she can barely afford it, responds; Georgina Vesey promises to help, but only if she inherits Mordaunt's fortune: she has her eye on a pair of earrings. She manages, however, to take the credit for Clara's gift as though it were her own. Money also poisons the relations between Evelyn and Clara. She has rejected him in his poverty, and (misunderstanding her motives) he allows himself to accumulate the trappings of wealth in a bitter attempt to show her what she has lost: 'the luxuries, the gaud, the splendour I thought you prized' (III.i.p.83). He professes mean motives even in giving her a secret gift of £20,000: it was to give him hidden ownership of her future life. If she found domestic happiness with another man, he could reflect, 'that smile was mine – due to me' (V.iii.p.114). He is, in effect, buying her, in what he himself calls an act of revenge. However, if money drives the lovers apart for a while, it draws them together in the end. A banker's letter (not, in this play, an incongruous love-token) shows that Clara has deposited £10,000 to Evelyn's account to save him from apparent ruin. He had thought the sum came from Georgina, and felt obliged to marry her; the news frees him to marry Clara. But for a while it looked as though the wrong woman had bought him.

Money has a double effect in the play's love relationships: it puts men and women in the market, dehumanizing them; but it also allows them to confirm their worth, and their affection, by acts of generosity. Evelyn's gift to Clara was meant to degrade; her gift to him is meant to save; what is essentially the same action carries two different kinds of moral weight. The play's final lesson is that money is as necessary as display and as inescapable as caste. Clara rejected Evelyn in his poverty because of bitter memories of her own parents, who married without enough to live on: 'the humiliation – the proud man's agony – the bitter life – the early death! – and heard above his breathless clay my mother's groan of self-reproach!' (V.iii.p.114). The grim lesson is transformed into an upbeat finale as Evelyn proclaims a double happiness – 'you are mine! We are rich – rich!' (V.iii.p.118) – and in the last moments different characters, displaying their own comic obsessions, list the qualities necessary to get on in life ('Enlightened opinions, Constitutional principles') with Evelyn getting the last word: 'And – plenty of Money' (V.iii.p.120).

## Money and the body: *The Merchant of Venice* and *Volpone*

There is a more searching treatment of money as the medium through which characters express their natures and their relationships in Shakespeare's *The Merchant of Venice* (c.1598). As a usurer, Shylock illustrates one of the classic arguments against usury by making money breed like ewes and rams (I.iii.92–94). In other plays, the system of exchange equates money with people, dehumanizing the latter; here, Shylock equates money with animal breeding, bringing it up a little in the scale of existence to give it a grotesque pseudo-life. But he also makes the standard equation: when his daughter Jessica elopes, Shylock's double lament, 'my ducats, and my daughter!' (II.viii.17), puts them on the same level of importance. In his bond with Antonio Shylock equates three thousand ducats with a pound of his enemy's flesh. Shylock presents it as a joke; and in theory it operates as other exchanges in comedy do, a baby for a novel (or a piece of meat), a bride for a string of hotels. It is a joke, however, whose inner hostility is so overtly exposed that it no longer functions as a joke, any more than a watch with its face and hands removed can function as a watch.

When Shylock claims his due – 'The pound of flesh which I demand of him / Is dearly bought, is mine, and I will have it' (IV.i.98–99) – the grotesque equation of money and human flesh is reinforced by a crabbed possessiveness. In the give-and-take exchanges of life, it is Shylock's business to take. Portia, the rich heiress of Belmont, is a giver. While Shylock deals in precise sums, carefully weighed out, she offers, hearing of Antonio's plight, 'Pay him six thousand, and deface the bond; / Double six thousand, and then treble that' (III.ii.299–300). A similar free-flowing generosity is conveyed in the last scene when Lorenzo tells her 'you drop manna in the way / Of starvèd people' (V.i.294–95). But this time the manna is Shylock's money, wrested from him in court. And Shylock's money has been the mainspring not just of the bond story but of the romantic action as well. He lends money to Antonio, who gives it to Bassanio, who uses it to journey to Belmont and win Portia. From the beginning Bassanio makes it clear that whatever romantic value Portia has for him, she has financial value as well: he needs her money to pay his debts. Shylock is not the only one to put cash value on another human being. Portia anticipates Shylock's claim that Antonio's flesh is dearly bought, and puns on romantic and cash value, when she tells Bassanio, 'Since you are dear bought, I will love you dear' (III.ii.313). Keys lock Shylock's house and coffers; keys, with sexual significance, unlock the caskets of Belmont. Shylock's cry of 'mine!' echoes through the play. His claim on Antonio's body is not far off the claims husbands and wives make on each other's bodies in marriage, symbolized in the ring Portia gives Bassanio, 'A thing stuck on with oaths upon your finger, / And so riveted with faith unto your flesh' (V.i.168–69). Her echo of the key word in Shylock's bond is no accident.

While it may seem inhuman for Shylock to equate his ducats with his daughter, Jessica is not far from his thinking when she increases her market value by stealing Shylock's money as she elopes: 'I'll gild myself / With some more ducats' (II.vi.50–51). As in *Money* there is no doing without money, so in *The Merchant of Venice* there is no doing without Shylock: his money drives the action, and his concern with possession and property, with the material reality of life, informs the apparently more humane exchanges of the other characters. The couples claim each other's bodies as he has claimed Antonio's; the bawdy joke with which Gratiano ends the play, 'while I live I'll fear no other thing / So sore as keeping safe Nerissa's ring' (V.i.306–7) is a gloss on Shylock's own proverb, 'Fast bind, fast find' (II.v.55).[15]

*The Merchant of Venice* shows a long chain reaction of deals involving money and people. Ben Jonson's *Volpone* (1606), with the tightness of Shylock's 'Fast bind, fast find', shows a closed system. Volpone's dupes bring the apparently dying magnifico presents in the hope of inheriting his estate. But Volpone does not give; he only takes. In his impersonation of an invalid, the only moving part of his body is a single grasping hand. Unlike Shakespeare's characters he stands apart from the exchanges of commerce – 'I use no trade, no venture' (I.i.33) – and from the relations of personal life: 'I have no wife, no parent, child, ally, / To give my substance to' (I.i.73–74). Lacking a family himself, he fractures other families, making Corbaccio disinherit his son and Corvino prostitute his wife. Goods and people, their other relationships broken, are caught up in a one-way flow towards the magnetic centre of Volpone's bedroom.

Goods and people are also equated, in the manner of *A Chaste Maid in Cheapside* and other plays, when Corvino, an insanely jealous husband, is led to offer his wife Celia to Volpone, allegedly as a medical cure to win his favour. This makes Celia the equivalent of the mountebank's oil Volpone hawks under her window. She is also, like the women of *Chaste Maid*, turned into gold by the language. Mosca sparks Volpone's interest in her:

> a beauty ripe as harvest,
> Whose skin is whiter than the swan, all over,
> Than silver, snow, or lillies! a soft lip,
> Would tempt you to eternity of kissing,
> And flesh that melteth in the touch to blood!
> Bright as your gold, and lovely as your gold!
> (I.v.109–14)

The soft, sensual body suddenly hardens into metal. Corvino justifies prostituting her by turning her into material goods: 'What, is my gold / The worse for touching? clothes, for being looked on?' (III.vii.40–41). When Volpone, tempting her with his wealth, offers her pearls to dissolve and drink, jewels to wear and lose, the fantasy of waste echoes Mosca's sense of Celia's body as melting flesh. If she is evanescent, so is wealth. (Antonio's wealth has a similar quality: it vanishes mysteriously, and just as mysteriously returns.)

Celia's body is to be touched, used, handled, consumed. It is also to be put on obscene display, scarred and tortured. Corvino, in a jealous rage at finding her watching a mountebank from her balcony, accuses her of flaunting her body in public 'To give your hot spectators satisfaction' (II.v.9), and imagines her copulating in the position that will give the fullest view:

> Would you not mount?
> Why, if you'll mount, you may; yes, truly, you may:
> And so you may be seen, down to th' foot.
> (II.v.18–20)

When she refuses to give herself to Volpone, Corvino threatens to bind her alive to a dead slave and hang the bodies out of the window, with the name of 'some monstrous crime' (III.vii.103) burned into her flesh. As Shylock wants Antonio carved up in the open court, Corvino wants Celia displayed, in various forms of copulation; he also threatens to dissect her and read an anatomy lecture over her 'to the city, and in public' (II.v.72).

Volpone's body actually undergoes what Celia's is threatened with: it becomes goods to trade in, an object of eager attention, an anatomy, and finally an object of punishment. The dupes who gather around his bed waiting for him to die are all named for birds of prey; they come sniffing carrion. Mosca encourages them with a series of anatomy lectures: 'His mouth / Is ever gaping, and his eyelids hang' (I.iv.41–42). As Volpone offers presents to Celia in exchange for her body, his dupes give presents as admission money for viewing his. His body is the site of his final punishment, as he is locked forever in the role he played: 'Thou art to lie in prison, crampt with irons, / Till thou be'st sick, and lame indeed' (V.xii.123–24).

But while Volpone and the other malefactors are to be tucked out of sight, banished or incarcerated, Corvino, who planned to make an obscene public display of Celia, is made a public spectacle himself, rowed through the Grand Canal in a cap with ass's ears, 'and so to mount (a paper / Pinn'd on thy breast) to the *berlino*' (V.xii.138–39), where he will be pelted with fish, fruit and rotten eggs. The body is a commodity to trade in, in commercial scams and prostitution; it is finally, as in Kafka's *In the Penal Colony*, the medium on which the state writes the offender's crimes. The ultimate nightmare in a world whose characters are constantly on display is public humiliation of the body. This was a specialty in the justice of Jonson's time; but a milder comic punishment in Arthur Wing Pinero's *The Magistrate* (1885) shows that comedy, and the law, can still find ways of getting at the body in a more genteel age. After a night in prison Colonel Lukyn complains indignantly, 'I have been washed by the authorities' (III.ii.309).

## The authorities

The characterization of comedy is bound up with systems of social display that give the audience, and the other characters, signals to read, entailing a reductive-ness that leaves characters vulnerable to laughter. The action of comedy turns its characters into commodities traded in the marketplace. In both cases the body, that essential medium of the theatre, is on display, at once fascinating and vulnerable. In all these transactions there is risk, insecurity, instability. In the background, beyond plotting and beyond performance, are the permanent institutions of society: law and government. We might expect comedy to treat these sardonically, and often enough this expectation is fulfilled. The censorship that operated through most of the period in question meant that comedy's treatment of government had to be circumspect; but comedy is full of mad laws and crooked lawyers. The court in *Volpone* is as venal and corrupt as the malefactors it sentences. Shakespeare's comedies often begin with inhuman laws that provide a starting point for the action, a problem to solve. Legal documents are ominous. In *New Men and Old Acres* (1869), by Tom Taylor and Augustus William Duborg, the house-keeper of Cleve Abbey says of the lawyer Secker, 'Drat them papers of his! There's mischief in 'em – I know there is!' (I.p.246). She is right; they spell the family's ruin. In *A New Way to Pay Old Debts* (c.1625) Overreach's power is broken when the deed conveying Wellborn's estate to him turns out to have been written with disap-pearing ink. It is a basic wish-fulfilment fantasy; if only all awkward legal documents were written so.

Yet it is the law that saves Antonio in *The Merchant of Venice*, when Portia points out the literal meaning of Shylock's bond. It is a legal document, the conveyance of her estate to Mirabell, that rescues Mrs Fainall from her husband at the end of *The Way of the World* (1700). Though Dion Boucicault's *London Assurance* (1841) includes a stock crooked lawyer, Meddle, who tries to stir up trouble to get fees for himself, it also includes a gesture of respect for the law itself. Max Harkaway explains to his niece Grace that the law of entail prevents him from leaving his estate to her, much as he would like to, and adds, 'nor can I say I'm sorry for it, for it is a good law' (V.243–44). It is a good law because it protects the long-term integrity of property (and therefore the status of the family) from the whims of a single generation; it is part of what holds England together.[16] There are foolish judges and jargon-spouting lawyers, concerned only with their fees. But there are also (especially in the early period, where hands-on local justice is the norm) wise and good-humoured magistrates, like Master Bailey in *Gammer Gurton's Needle* (c.1550) who sees through the chaos the trickster Diccon has created, rebukes those who have been taking themselves too seriously, and goes easy on Diccon for the fun he has provided; and Justice Clement in *Every Man in his Humour* (1598, revised version published 1616), who ensures among other things that some really bad poetry is publicly burned.

Faith in the law is bound up with faith in that distinctly English institution, Parliament. Sir Peter Teazle's solution for scandal is that Parliament should pass a law against it. The villain hero of Charles Macklin's *The Man of the World* (1764, revised 1781), Sir Pertinax Macsycophant, crawls and connives his way through society, but the House of Commons exposes him; unable to speak, he becomes the butt of laughter. In T.W. Robertson's *Society* (1865) a parliamentary election does the work Robertson attributes to caste in his later play: it shuts out the pretentious and the vulgar. The hero Sidney Daryl, whose family has long associations with the borough of Springmead (the name evokes warm feelings about the English countryside) defeats the unspeakable Chodd, who thinks he can get anything he wants with his chequebook. Old family beats new money, and there is a rousing patriotic finale with a band playing 'Conquering Hero' and church bells ringing.

In the flashes of patriotism scattered through English comedy, the liberty of the subject, protected by the law, is a recurring theme. In *The Man of the World* Lord Lumbercourt complains that a tradesman he has beaten for the impertinence of asking to be paid has successfully gone to law against him; Lumbercourt wishes he were in a decent foreign country where 'a nobleman might extinguish the reptile in an instant' (II.p.38). There is a cluster of tributes to English liberty around the Glorious Revolution of 1688, notably in Thomas Shadwell's *Bury Fair* (1689), where Wildish debates with a comic Frenchman over the constitutions of their respective countries. Wildish declares, 'Your king is a king of dogs . . . ours . . . is a king of men, and free men! Ours governs the willing, he the unwilling.' The Frenchman is revolted by this slackness: 'your King can do nothing; dere is de law, de Parliament, I don know vat, begar: my king can send for my head when he please' (II.ii.407–12).[17] (His king is Molière's, the all-seeing power who alone can defeat the villain-hero of *Tartuffe*.) In the same play Gertrude invokes the principles of 1688 to defend her freedom of choice in marriage: 'I am a free heiress of England, where arbitrary power is at an end, and I am resolved to choose for myself' (III.iii.295–97). Less than a decade later, but in a more ironic spirit, Lady Brute in *The Provoked Wife* (1697) justifies breaking her vows to her husband by invoking the contract theory used against James II (I.i.63–68).

Given comedy's tendency to show restrictive social structures, these invocations of liberty provide a breath of air. Yet whether the English constitution truly guaranteed liberty for women or for anyone else is, to put it mildly, a matter of debate.[18] The Glorious Revolution did not in fact relax the laws of marriage, and Lady Brute knows it. Most of the passages we have glanced at are decorative. As they evoke underlying institutions that exist beyond the traffic of the world, they stand apart from the play's action, bonding with the audience through a shared patriotism. National pride provides flourishes to end the performance, as the National Anthem used to begin it. Thus the final celebrations of *The Shoemakers' Holiday* (1599) are capped with the King's words, 'When all our sports and banquetings are done, / Wars must right wrongs which Frenchmen have begun' (V.v.190–91); and Arthur Murphy's *The Citizen* (1761) ends with two ringing declarations, 'May Britain's thunder on her foes be hurled . . . And London prove the market of the world' (Epilogue, p.141) to which we may add the last words of Steele's *The Tender Husband* (1705): 'And English be the language of mankind' (Epilogue, 30). Many of these flourishes invoke the sovereign. *Roister Doister* (c.1552) ends with a prayer for the Queen in which the individual characters, each taking two lines, submerge their identities in the general statement of loyalty. A great offstage shout greets the restoration of Charles II at the end of Sir Charles Sedley's *The Mulberry Garden* (1668), linking the final harmony of the characters with 'this all-healing day' (V.v.176). Hannah Cowley not only dedicates *The Belle's Stratagem* (1780) to George III's consort Queen Charlotte, but has one of the play's moral spokesmen advise a husband whose wife has had a near miss with adultery to take her to the court and 'Bid her keep her eye on the bright example who presides there' (V.iv.p.480).

Behind the follies of display and the inhumanity of material exchange lie the eternal verities that guarantee the fundamental health of society: the law, Parliament, the empire, the crown. But of course it is impossible in the late twentieth century to write those words without irony. In *Cloud 9* (1979) Caryl Churchill takes the old style patriotic ending and moves it to the beginning of the play, where it is immediately vulnerable. In an African outpost of the empire in the nineteenth century, Clive and his family gather round to celebrate the flag, the Queen, the whole imperial order of which Clive is the domestic centre. All join in an old patriotic song: 'The forge of war shall weld the chains of brotherhood secure; / So to all time in ev'ry clime our Empire shall endure' (I.i.p.5). Through the first act the order the opening celebrates is revealed as oppressive and hypocritical; through the second act, the characters liberate themselves from it not by invoking the British constitution but by coming to terms with their own identities, desires and sexual natures. Yet the patriotic flourish is still a way of bonding with the audience through a shared belief: irony about the Empire is as conventional in the twentieth century as celebration of it was in the eighteenth.

Joe Orton saves the patriotic note for the end in *What the Butler Saw* (1969), invoking a figure who for many of his contemporaries was as sacred as any monarch. Sergeant Match produces the missing piece of a statue of Sir Winston Churchill, and there are '*Deep intakes of breath from everyone.*' Dr Rance calls up heroic memories of the war: 'How much more inspiring if, in those dark days, we'd seen what we see now. Instead we had to be content with a cigar – the symbol falling far short, as we all realize, of the object itself.' Finally, '*The dying sunlight from the garden and the blaze from above gild* SERGEANT MATCH *as he holds high the nation's heritage*' (II.pp.447–48). Accused of libelling Churchill Orton replied, 'That isn't libel, surely. . . . I wouldn't sue anybody for saying I had a big prick. No man would. In fact I might pay them to do that.'[19] He might have added that the Earl of Rochester paid a similar tribute to Charles II: 'His sceptre and his prick are of a length.'[20]

But as Orton's partner Kenneth Halliwell pointed out, the detachment of the prick from the statue meant that the father figure, the symbol of authority, had been castrated.[21] There may also be a link with Orton's reaction to his prison term for defacing library books: 'The old whore society really lifted up her skirts and the stench was pretty foul.'[22] Churchill, admittedly in statue form, has been caught flashing the audience, obscenely displaying a part of his body that decorum requires should be hidden. The final celebration of authority, like earlier patriotic flourishes, creates a sense of England: this time as a place where social authority, embodied in Doctors Rance and Prentice, abuses its power. The ironic celebration of the phallic power of the father figure ends a play that began with Prentice trying to seduce Geraldine, who turns out to be his daughter. It also evokes the metaphoric exchanges, the bawdy double entendres, of comedy. *That* cigar was not just a cigar. Through the principle of synechdoce, the part standing for the whole, the great man is held up for display, like Dorimant; he undergoes the obscene exposure and dismemberment threatened to Celia; and like Corvino he is pilloried.

# 3

# LONERS

## Comedy and the loner

Characters who are reduced to figures on display or goods to trade in are denied their full humanity. Yet it is through such reductions that comedy makes characters usable in its stylized presentation of social life; in order to show society's reductiveness, comedy must exploit its own. And comedy itself is inescapably social, as its theorists keep insisting. As Robert Bechtold Heilman puts it, 'comedy and solitude are incompatible: the essence of comedy is in relations with others . . . . The comic mode is social.' For Henri Bergson, 'Any individual is comic who automatically goes his own way without troubling himself about getting into touch with the rest of his fellow-beings.' We laugh, he maintains, not at immorality but at unsociability.[1] These are standard views. The structures of society may dehumanize; but absolute solitude is also inhuman. For Peter L. Berger and Thomas Luckmann the Promethean loner is an impossibility: 'self-production is always, and of necessity, a social enterprise'.[2]

When Hebble Tyson in Christopher Fry's *The Lady's Not for Burning* (1948) retires to his study with the words, 'You can knock, but I shall give you no reply. / I wish to be alone with my own convictions' (III.p.74), he exemplifies comedy's mockery of the loner. Tyson is obsessed with his own authority. The fantasizers of Jonsonian comedy have a similar desire to be alone with their fantasies. Sir Politic Would-be in *Volpone* (1606) boasts that he lives apart, an observer of life: 'Free from the active torrent, yet I'd mark / The currents and the passages of things' (II.i.102–3). Far from observing reality, he uses his solitude to spin crazy fantasies of projects to serve the state; he is last seen literally retired into his shell, disguised as a tortoise to avoid arrest. Bobadill in *Every Man in his Humour* (1598, revised version published 1616), puts a good face on his cheap lodgings by calling them 'a cleanly and quiet privacy, above all the tumult and roar of fortune' (I.v.45–46). His project of disposing of an enemy army forty thousand strong by having his picked group of twenty fighters kill twenty a day shows a detachment from reality that matches Sir Pol's. Both characters, in the end, are publicly humiliated.

Both are also harmless fools. The villains of Philip Massinger's comedies *A New Way to Pay Old Debts* (c.1625) and *The City Madam* (1632) exemplify the loner

58

as destructively anti-social. Sir Giles Overreach in the first play devours his neighbours' lands, showing complete indifference to the suffering he causes. In his final mad scene he sums himself up: 'Why, is not the whole world / Included in myself?' (V.i.355–56). Luke Frugal in the later play likewise spreads ruin in the service of his own greed. He celebrates his birthday in the last scene by feasting alone; his victims are paraded before him, and he takes them as a show put on for his amusement. Jonson's fools allow an easy laughter; but if there is anxiety behind that laughter, Massinger's villains, dramatizing the dark potential of solitude, show us why.

Jonson's fools and Massinger's villains are self-satisfied in their isolation. Malvolio in Shakespeare's *Twelfth Night* (c.1600), prickly in company, is happy and expansive when alone, constructing imaginary relationships, fantasizing about his marriage to Olivia and 'practising behaviour to his own shadow' (II.v.17). For other characters, however, solitude is a source of anxiety and discomfort. In Elizabeth Inchbald's *Everyone has his Fault* (1793) Mr Solus, a discontented bachelor, and Sir Robert Ramble, who has recently divorced his wife, meet in a tavern, both at loose ends, both registering unease at having to dine at such places, having no company at home (II.i.1–14). But as it is a mistake to try too hard for the right style, it is a mistake to try too hard to be companionable; comedy's fools include compulsively gregarious characters, driven by a fear of solitude, who construct only the emptiest relationships. Friendall in Thomas Southerne's *The Wives' Excuse* (1692) invites the whole town to his house, tells a dozen different women they inspire his poetry (I.ii.229–34), and drops famous names, claiming acquaintance with 'Jack Dryden and Will Wycherley' (III.ii.188–89). He is really the friend of no one. He refuses to walk with his wife in St James's Park, seeking out more select company; but everyone he hails snubs him. The universal benevolence of Honeywood in Oliver Goldsmith's *The Good-Natured Man* (1786) is really anxiety to please. His uncle Sir William rejects his professions of affection – 'how can I be proud of a place in a heart where every sharper and coxcomb find an easy entrance?' (I.p.5) – and his servant Jarvis tells him bluntly, 'You have no friends' (I.p.6).

To be desperately social is not to be social at all. Boyet in Shakespeare's *Love's Labour's Lost* (c.1594) and Sir Jolly Jumble in Thomas Otway's *The Soldiers' Fortune* (1684) are both chatty, gregarious characters whose compulsive sexual joking betrays their essential solitude. Boyet, an elderly courtier who attends the Princess of France and her ladies, banters and flirts with them, but when he demands a kiss he is put off (II.i.221–24) and when his joking with Rosaline becomes bawdy she puts him in his place: 'Thou canst not hit it, hit it, hit it, / Thou canst not hit it, my good man' (IV.i.125–26). Sir Jolly is an enthusiastic elderly pimp who is past it himself but loves bringing couples together and fantasizing about the results: 'Ah, my little son of thunder, if thou hadst her in thy arms now between a pair of sheets, and I under the bed to see fair play' (II.i.24–26). The most he can imagine for himself is 'Od, I could find it in my heart to put my little finger in your bubbies' (III.i.216–17). Though he brings others together, he himself is restricted to peering and pawing.

Yet in the joking detachment of Boyet and Sir Jolly there is something of comedy's own perspective: standing back, observing, keeping an amused distance. More specifically, Boyet is a loner in a comedy in which no one gets married; Sir Jolly disapproves of marriage, which he calls 'a destroyer of civil correspondence' (IV.i.173); his view is borne out in the play by the marriage of Sir Davy and Lady Dunce, and in the sequel, *The Atheist* (1681), in which the marriage of Sylvia and Courtine, contracted at the end of *The Soldiers' Fortune*, turns into a snakepit of mutual hatred. There is a sense in which each loner's position is ultimately justified by the comedy's own scepticism about relationships.

One of Jonson's most extraordinary loners is the scurrilous jester Carlo Buffone in *Every Man out of his Humour* (1599) who in the last act turns comic festivity into a private fantasy, holding behind closed doors a drinking party all by himself, taking the parts of different characters, drinking toasts in different cups, and finally staging a quarrel in which he '*overturns wine, pot, cups and all*' (V.iv.90). From the beginning the play presents Buffone in a critical light, and in the end he is punished and humiliated by the other characters. Yet the play also uses his perspective, letting him guide the responses of the audience, as when he comments on the pretentious rogue Shift showing off in St Paul's (III.v.36–40) or directs a spying party to watch through the keyhole as Shift gives a private lesson in tobacco-taking to the country gull Sogliardo (IV.iii.91–96). Like Sir Jolly, Buffone is a voyeur, but the audience themselves are also voyeurs, and as he directs them to watch the other fools, he is doing the play's work. Jonson's Volpone, examined in the last chapter, is a destructive loner taking pride, as Massinger's villains do, in his lack of relationships. But as his scam drives the plot, so his sardonic amusement at his dupes is the audience's view as well. It is not enough to see comedy as defending sociability and mocking the loner, since in the loner's perspective there is something of comedy's own detachment.

## Tricksters

The trickster is a recurring character type whose essential solitude lets him direct the play's laughter. Tricksters usually appear gregarious and sociable, but creating that impression is one of their tricks. Dazzle in Dion Boucicault's *London Assurance* (1841) claims kinship with everyone he meets, sponges off other people by falling in with their interests, and when asked to preside over a duel promises to be 'the intimate and bosom friend of both parties' (V.159–60). (He also turns the threatened violence of the duel into comedy by proposing that it take place in the billiard room over madeira and cigars.) But as Friendall has no friends, Dazzle has no kin and no real social identity. He introduces himself as 'Richard Dazzle, late of the Unattached Volunteers' (I.377–78) and when at the end of the play Sir Harcourt Courtly asks the pregnant question, 'who is Mr Dazzle?' he cheerfully replies, 'I have not the remotest idea' (V.481–84). In a play concerned with family and property, Dazzle, rootless and constantly improvising his identity, is a disruptive force.

The play's last speech, Sir Harcourt's lecture on the true nature of a gentleman, is designed to squash him; but it is Dazzle's impudence that gives the play its title.

The trickster's power is bound up with his freedom from settled relationships. Mosca in *Volpone* has only one relationship that matters – 'I shall begin to grow in love / With my dear self' – and boasts his freedom to 'be here, / And there, and here, and yonder, all at once' and 'change a visor, swifter than a thought' (III.i.1–2, 26–27). Merrygreek in Nicholas Udall's *Roister Doister* (c.1552), has a long list of houses where he is an occasional guest (I.i.13–26) and Diccon the Bedlam in *Gammer Gurton's Needle*, by 'Mr S.' (c.1550) declares, 'South, East, North or West, I am never out of my way' (II.i.10). Having no home, the trickster has no loyalties, and uses this freedom as a licence to create mischief. Diccon sets neighbours against each other by telling lies: he tells Gammer Gurton that Dame Chat has her needle, and Dame Chat that Gammer Gurton has accused her of stealing her cock, producing for the audience's amusement a screaming row between the women. In stirring up trouble he is doing the business of the play, and this may be reflected in the easy judgement he gets from Master Bailey at the end. His opposite number is Harmony in Inchbald's *Everyone has his Fault*. While Diccon tells lies to stir up trouble, Harmony tells lies to bring about reconciliation. His favourite trick, which works with the speed of Puck's flower, is to tell people who are at enmity that when their backs are turned they speak well of each other. He himself is a gregarious loner. He wishes he could greet every stranger he meets, shaking hands with the men and kissing the women; there is a touch of Friendall here (I.ii.10–15). Entering the coffee room at a tavern he demands to see *all* the newspapers. But while his curiosity and benevolence are universal, when offered marriage for himself he is guarded and evasive, and he manages to get through to the end of the play as a bachelor.

The first joke of the central trickster in Thomas Southerne's *Sir Anthony Love; or, the Rambling Lady* (1690) is on the audience: the title and subtitle, one would think, must be describing two different characters: in fact they are the same. Lucy has robbed her keeper Golding of £500 and escaped to the continent in male disguise to pursue her former lover Valentine. If Merrygreek and Diccon are of no fixed address, Lucy-Sir Anthony is of no fixed sex. She has to fight off unwelcome attentions from men who know her true sex, and from a lecherous French priest who doesn't, and who describes her as 'every thing with every body, a man among the women, and a woman among the men' (II.i.81–82). In this case the loner's rootlessness includes a sexual ambiguity like that of the sex-changing tricksters of traditional native cultures. Lucy lives by her wits; besides developing a lucrative sideline as jewel thief and blackmailer, as a man she wins Valentine's friendship and as a woman she tricks him into bed with her. She also disrupts plot expectations by remaining unattached at the end of the play. The breeches heroine usually gets her man;[3] but Lucy, having bedded Valentine, lets him marry Floriante on the grounds that he will soon get tired of a wife; she has a more secure future with him as a mistress.[4] Instead she marries Golding, whom she has described as 'that nauseous fool' (I.i.46), in order to get a separate maintenance and thus keep her freedom. She gets what she wants from each man, sex from Valentine and money from Golding, with no commitment to either.

Tricksters characteristically have a strong relationship with the audience; the conventions of earlier drama allow figures like Diccon to address them directly. But Jonson exploits the essential solitude of the trickster to break even that convention in *Epicoene* (1609). Dauphine confides neither in his friends nor in the audience;[5] we do not even know he is the central trickster until the end of the play when he removes Epicoene's peruke and reveals for the first time his underlying mastery of the plot. This play's fun is more competitive than communal, and it is no coincidence that when Truewit acknowledges Dauphine as the winner of the competition – 'you have lurch'd your friends of the better half of the garland, by concealing this part of the plot' (V.iv.224–26) – he is quoting a phrase from *Coriolanus*, Shakespeare's tragedy about a loner.[6]

## The Country Wife

Horner, the central trickster of Wycherley's *The Country Wife* (1675), has apparently made himself a social outcast through the false report of his impotence. Pitied or despised by the men, he is regarded with disgust by the women. But he predicts that his reputation for harmlessness will give him a trickster's freedom of movement, able to enter at will houses that would otherwise be barred to him, becoming 'the *passe-partout* of the town' (I.p.263). As he has freedom of access to the women, which he uses to demonstrate that he is not impotent at all, he seems gregarious with his male friends, with whom he has long, relaxed conversations. But behind his apparently free relations with both sexes there is something ultimately guarded and withdrawn. In what he intends to sound like a display of sour grapes, he declares to his friends, 'Well, a pox on love and wenching, women serve but to keep a man from better company; though I can't enjoy them, I shall you the more: good fellowship and friendship are lasting, rational and manly pleasures' (I.p.264). He also maintains that a balanced relation between the pleasures of different sexes is impossible: 'I tell you, 'tis as hard to be a good fellow, a good friend, and a lover of women, as 'tis to be a good fellow, a good friend, and a lover of money: you cannot follow both, then choose your side' (I.p.264). But which side has Horner chosen? As he plans his encounter with Lady Fidget, his friends complain of desertion: 'Engag'd to women, and not sup with us?' (III.p.294). He never lets them in on his secret, and they never know that his relations with women are not what he claims in their apparently frank man-to-man conversations.

He is detached from the women as well. The demands of courtship make him impatient: he wants to get straight to the sex. Comparing sex with eating and fighting, he declares, 'falling on briskly is all that should be done on these occasions' (V.p.351). In the china scene he couples with Lady Fidget just offstage, and the onstage dialogue that covers the encounter can be played in under two minutes. When it's over, it's over: he has no china left. Nor has he any interest in building a relationship around the encounter. In the game of sex, 'next to the pleasure of making a new mistress is that of being rid of an old one' (I.p.262); as for marriage, 'nothing makes a man hate a woman more than her constant conversation' (III.p.294). Though her frankness and simplicity make him like Margery Pinchwife better than his other women, he clearly does not share her view that once they have had sex they will be together forever.

Horner's trick has been compared to a Royal Society experiment determining the nature of women;[7] or as he puts it, 'she that shows an aversion to me loves the sport' (I.p.263). Lady Fidget, who talks compulsively of her honour, is his key example: when she challenges him, 'How, you saucy fellow, would you wrong my honour?' there is a barbed ambiguity in his reply, 'If I could' (I.p.261). (What the others hear is, I can't wrong your honour; what we hear is, you have no honour to wrong.) Just before they go offstage to do the deed, Horner has a revealing moment of performance anxiety, in which the lie almost becomes truth: 'If you talk a word more of your honour, you'll make me incapable to wrong it' (IV.p.324). He cannot have sex with a woman who challenges his theory about women. Horner's sexual encounters can be seen not just as a way of gratifying his physical desire but as a way of confirming his ideas, and the play's. The prudery of women like Lady Fidget is mere hypocrisy; they are as lecherous as he is. His conversation is full of satiric set-pieces attacking women: a woman, like a spaniel, 'barks at your friends, when they come to see you; makes your bed hard, gives you fleas, and the mange sometimes; and all the difference is, the spaniel's the more faithful animal, and fawns but upon one master' (II.p.286–87). Yet speeches like this pose a problem of interpretation. Do they represent a real misogyny which he then translates into action, proving the worthlessness of women by the ease with which he takes them? Or is their contempt a pretence, simply part of the trick, to put husbands (like Sir Jaspar Fidget, to whom the 'spaniel' speech is addressed) off the scent? Horner is clearly willing to risk a hard bed, fleas and the mange, over and over. There is something in his attitude to women that resists decisive interpretation.[8] Like Dauphine he hides from the audience; unlike Dauphine he keeps his secret to the end.

Like other tricksters, he is doing the play's work, controlling the intrigue and offering satiric commentary. But he leaves the nature of that work enigmatic. Like other tricksters he is seemingly gregarious, finally alone and hidden. We glimpse this at the beginning of Act Five, when the Quack calls on him and declares in surprise, 'What, all alone, not so much as one of your cuckolds here, nor one of their wives!' (V.p.342). Shortly after this the action starts up again, as Horner's lodgings are invaded by Pinchwife, Margery, and the women's drinking-party. But for a moment we have glimpsed a solitude that may be more than just a contrast to Horner's bustling, comic panache: it may be the key to it. The freedom that lets him operate so effectively in society depends on his being ultimately alone.[9]

## The fop and his mirror: *The Man of Mode* and *The Relapse*

Horner is on display: everyone gossips about him; he shows himself in the play-house to face down the disgrace of his reputation for impotence (I.p.263). The recurring figure of the fop is likewise on display, likewise gregarious; and like the trickster he is ultimately alone. As Malvolio practises behaviour to his own shadow, the fop's true relationship is with his mirror. Sir William Mode in Susanna Centlivre's *The Beau's Duel* (1702) is a Jonsonian fantasizer: alone in his chamber, he prepares for the day by studying himself in a looking-glass and acting out a conversation with an imaginary lord who pays him pretty compliments. At the end, losing the woman he had designs on, he renounces the whole sex and retires to his lodgings. The title character of John Crowne's *Sir Courtly Nice* (1685) is gregarious, but his relationships are trivial: 'he's the general guitar o' the town, inlaid with everything women fancy . . . the ladies love to have him in their chambers, and play themselves asleep with him' (II.112–17). Courteous, gentle and inoffensive, he 'writes a challenge in the style of a billet-doux' (II.125–26).[10] His chief mania is a fastidiousness that makes him squeamish about any kind of physical contact. This naturally limits his relations with women, who in any case are not his first priority, for all his professions of gallantry. Paying court to Leonora, he becomes transfixed by his image in a looking-glass, and she comments, 'he's making an assignation with his own foolish face' (V.362–63).

If there is such a thing as an archetypal fop, it is Sir Fopling Flutter in Sir George Etherege's *The Man of Mode* (1676). In a play whose sexual intrigues are frequently crafty and malicious, and whose main characters are given to tense dialogue full of undercurrents, it is possible to have quite a simple conversation with Sir Fopling:

LADY TOWNLEY:  The suit?
SIR FOPLING:  Barroy.
EMILIA:  The garniture?
SIR FOPLING:  Le Gras.
MEDLEY:  The shoes?
SIR FOPLING:  Piccar.
DORIMANT:  The periwig?
SIR FOPLING:  Chedreux.
LADY TOWNLEY, EMILIA:  The gloves?
SIR FOPLING:  Orangerie.
(III.ii.206–15)

Around this time the makers of fashion were emerging from anonymity and demanding attention for themselves as artists;[11] Sir Fopling is an assemblage of brand names. Naturally, the names are French; the ingredients of foppery are almost universally seen as French imports. When the conversation turns to French *authors*, Sir Fopling is quickly out of his depth (IV.i.226–30).

His amiability shows in his first scene. He is as eager to compliment as to be complimented, praising Dorimant for his French air, Emilia for her lace, Medley for his understanding of an 'equipage' (retinue). When Medley demurs, 'By my own you would not guess it', Sir Fopling has a neat reply, 'There are critics who do not write, sir' (III.ii.176–77). Criticized on a point of detail, he instantly agrees rather than start an argument (III.ii.198–200). In the previous chapter we saw display as a means of getting an edge in a competitive world; for Sir Fopling it is an end in itself. Critics have called him 'a creature of pure play' and 'pure mask, pure performance'.[12] Visting Dorimant's lodging, he dances by himself and complains of the lack of mirrors. When Young Bellair points out, 'Here is company to entertain you', he replies, 'In a glass a man may entertain himself' (IV.ii.85–87). Self-sufficiency of another kind is evoked when in a scene that corresponds in time to Dorimant's sexual encounter with Bellinda he leads the other men in a drinking song whose innuendo suggests a schoolboys' masturbation contest:

> Let every man stand
> With his glass in his hand
> And briskly discharge at the word of command.
> (IV.i.398–400)

Frustrated in his one attempt at a love intrigue, he reacts like an athlete who will not have sex before a big game:

> An intrigue now would be but a temptation to me to throw away that
> vigour on one which I mean shall shortly make my court to the whole sex
> in a ballet . . . . No one woman is worth the loss of a cut in a caper.
> (V.ii.339–43)

If Horner's solitude is what ultimately allows his control over the plot and his role as satiric commentator, Sir Fopling's solitude leaves him free for what he sees as his public responsibility. In a comedy in which display is used as a weapon in the sex war, he lets us see pure display, for its own sake, divorced from relationships.

The potential coldness in that divorce does not touch Sir Fopling; but it touches Sir Novelty Fashion in Colley Cibber's *Love's Last Shift* (1696) and his successor Lord Foppington in Sir John Vanbrugh's *The Relapse* (1696). In Sir Novelty, Sir Fopling's good-natured self-deprecation becomes a false modesty obviously designed to elicit praise (I.i.250–51).[13] Sir Fopling's delight in displaying the right brand names becomes Sir Novelty's arrogant claim to have invented all the details of the prevailing fashion himself (II.i.260–71). In the playhouse he sits with his back to the stage. His notion of playing a love scene is to praise himself, and when the lady objects, 'but still you ha'n't told me why you love me', he replies, 'I think 'tis sufficient, if I tell a lady, why she should love me' (II.i.307–11).

Vanbrugh in his sequel not only raises the character to the peerage but expands him into a magnificent comic monster. While other fops are content with one mirror, Lord Foppington prefers to be surrounded by mirrors: 'let my people dispose the glasses so, that I may see myself before and behind, for I love to see myself all raund' (I.iii.30–2). The advantage of a chocolate-house is 'you have looking-glasses all round you' (II.i.221–22). It seems he wants not just to contemplate himself but to shut out the world, replacing humanity with multiple images of the only person who matters. When he insists that his periwig is too small, since it leaves his cheeks visible – 'a periwig to a man should be like a mask to a woman, nothing should be seen but his eyes' (I.iii.141–43) – we wonder if he is displaying himself to the world or hiding from it. He has a private gallery 'furnished with nothing but books and looking-glasses' but he looks only at the outsides of the books, 'Far to mind the inside of a book is to entertain oneself with the forced product of another man's brain. Naw I think a man of quality and breeding may be much better diverted with the natural sprauts of his own' (II.i.195–96, 202–5). While Sir Fopling loves the give-and-take of compliment, Lord Foppington is testy in conversation, and irritable with the tradespeople who dress him.

Like other fops he is a collection of parts, and his essential emptiness is conveyed when Lory, servant to his brother Young Fashion, advises his master, 'Say nothing to him, apply yourself to his favourites, speak to his periwig, his cravat, his feather, his snuff-box' (I.ii.82–83). Foppington himself contemplates the emptiness of his life with total complacency, describing the social round – walking in the park, going to Locket's, going to a play – as a Beckett-like exercise in killing time: 'So there's twelve of the four-and-twenty pretty well over' (II.i.231–232). Summarizing his life as 'an eternal raund O of delights' (II.i.235), he does not seem to mind that he has just described a hollow figure. As his life is an empty circle, his heart is a rotating mechanism: 'Why, my heart in my amours – is like my heart aut of my amours – *à la glace*. My bady, Tam, is a watch, and my heart is the pendulum to it; whilst the finger runs round to every hour in the circle, that still beats the same time' (III.i.45–48). That summarizes his relations with women; his family feeling is indicated when he assumes that his younger brother must have been delighted to hear he was run through the body; he remembers his own joy at learning his father was shot through the head (III.i.20–25).

The amiable fop is amiable because his isolation from humanity leaves him above (or beneath) the fray. Lord Foppington is not amiable, his detachment is a comic cold-bloodedness, and his wit is aggressive. He is unusual among fops in having a trickster's ability to direct laughter; surprisingly, he has (like Horner) one of the sharpest minds in the play. When he claims that he reads, but never thinks of what he reads, Amanda seems to speak for good common sense when she objects, 'can your lordship read without thinking?' But he has a satirist's response: 'O Lard! Can your ladyship pray without devotion, madam?' (II.i.189–91). Amanda suddenly looks conventional against his sardonic awareness of the way of the world. He will not let his brother get away with a softened and tactful appeal for money: when Young Fashion says, 'I do not ask it as a due, brother; I am willing to receive it as a favour', Foppington cuts to the heart of the matter: 'Thau art willing to receive it anyhaw, strike me speechless' (III.i.86–89). When his brother in turn denounces his meanness, 'Now, by all that's great and powerful, thou art the prince of coxcombs', he replies, unperturbed, 'Sir – I am praud of being at the head of so prevailing a party' (III.i.116–19). He fails the generosity test, but he wins the scene. Heartless and mechanical, Lord Foppington is isolated from normal decent humanity; but normal decent humanity is something this play has little time for. The characters who exemplify it, Amanda and (briefly, till he learns better) Young Fashion, are out of step. Vanbrugh shows a world driven by sexual appetite and the need for money. Foppington plays both games only to lose, but his brazen cynicism about himself and his world leaves him fully in tune with the play's style. The descendant of the fop is the dandy, and in his classic work on that subject Jules Barbey d'Aurevilly declares 'There is in Dandyism, something cold, sober and mocking.'[14] He might be describing Lord Foppington.

## The fop reformed: *London Assurance*

As times change, the fop changes. Sir Harcourt Courtly, in Boucicault's *London Assurance* (1841), shows a traditional indifference to relationships, declaring satisfaction that when his wife ran off with another man he got a handsome financial settlement (I.186–92). Living in an age of less elaborate male dress, he strikes attitudes where an earlier fop would have shown off his wardrobe (I.i.159–63); the impulse to display is the same. But we are now in an age of drama that puts a premium on good feeling. Earlier fops are performances, and performances only; Sir Harcourt lets us see the man beneath the role. His response to a visit from the plainspoken Max Harkaway is revealing: '(*Throwing off his studied manner*) Max, Max. Give me your hand, old boy. (*Aside*) Ah, *he* is glad to see me! There is no fawning pretence about that squeeze' (I.145–47). The aside suggests that his formality springs from a distrust of other people and a need to keep his distance to avoid being hurt. In the scene that follows Sir Harcourt defends his foppery, and Max attacks it in the name of honesty and good feeling; but once Sir Harcourt is offstage Max takes a different view of him: 'That's a good soul. He has his faults, and who has not?' (I.267). He attacks the performance, but he likes the man.

Earlier fops are defined against a generalized nature which their artifice violates. Lord Trinket, in George Colman the Elder's *The Jealous Wife* (1761), boasts, 'Nature never made such a thing as me' (II.ii.p.73). Sir Harcourt is played off against a more fully detailed and narrowly defined nature, the English countryside, in which he is comically out of place. When he visits Max at his country estate, Max rebukes him for using perfume when there are flowers all around him (II.354–60). The play is full of lyrical celebrations of country life – flowers, birdsong, foxhunting – and audience members who find it all a bit much will cheer when Sir Harcourt responds to Max's challenge to rise with the lark, 'Haven't the remotest conception of when that period is' (III.151). Sir Harcourt is also set against the physical reality of his own body. His rouge and black wig are not just showing off but attempts to conceal his age; again, there is a man beneath the performance. The precedent here is Lord Ogleby in *The Clandestine Marriage*

(1766), by David Garrick and George Colman the Elder. Though Ogleby has a fop's preoccupation with style, his valet's principal job is getting his old body wound up and moving for the day, a process the valet compares to reviving a corpse (II.p.125). His keynote is the elderly vanity of assuming he still has a chance with the ladies, an illusion Sir Harcourt shares.

As beneath Lord Ogleby's carefully managed appearance there is a creaking old body, beneath his vanity there is a good heart, revealed at the end when he throws his support behind the play's lovers. This is what happens when the fop character, instead of being a pure performance, comes in layers. While Lord Foppington is triumphantly unashamed of his selfishness, Sir Harcourt, realizing the other characters have been duping and laughing at him, turns with nineteenth-century earnestness to his inner humanity, and achieves self-knowledge and repentance: 'I have been a fool, a dupe of my own vanity. I shall be pointed at as a ridiculous old coxcomb, and so I am . . . . Have I deceived myself? Have I turned all my senses inwards, looking always towards self, always self? And has the world been ever laughing at me? Well, if they have, I will revert the joke. They may say I am an old ass, but I will prove that I am neither too old to repent my folly, nor such an ass as to flinch from confessing it' (V.188–96). He looks with critical detachment at his own performance, realizes he is the butt of laughter, and comes out of the mirrored room, the enclosure of the self, that is the fop's natural habitat. This gives him the authority to deliver the lecture on the true nature of an English gentleman that ends the play.[15] He speaks for the play, not as a loner but as a member of the community, who has re-joined it after a spell away.

## Misanthropes

The trickster directs the play's laughter; the fop (with some exceptions) acts as the butt of it; the misanthrope does both. While his anti-social nature makes him vulnerable to mockery, his outsider's perspective gives him the authority to mock the world in turn. But as the fop and the trickster are more alone than they may originally appear, the misanthrope is more social. For someone who persistently claims he wants to be alone, Jaques in Shakespeare's *As You Like It* (c.1600) spends a remarkable amount of time seeking out other people to share his melancholy with. His greeting to Rosalind-Ganymede is typical: 'I prithee, pretty youth, let me be better acquainted with thee' (IV.i.1–2). His satiric attacks on the world (his meditation on the wounded deer, his party piece on the seven ages of man) give him the status of public entertainer. His ostentatious refusal to join in the final dance is as much his contribution to the occasion as the good wishes he addresses to the four couples about to get married. His last words as he leaves, 'What you would have / I'll stay to know at your abandoned cave' (V.iv.194–95), show that he expects Duke Senior to join him. He seems, if anything, afraid of solitude; his misanthropy is a role he plays to keep himself supplied with company.

Thomas Mendip in Fry's *The Lady's Not for Burning* (1948) claims he has given up on the world and ostentatiously demands to be hanged. Hebble Tyson sees something anti-social in his wit, accusing him of 'A sense of humour / Incompatible with good citizenship' (I.p.17). But to the satirist's detachment Thomas adds the gregariousness of the entertainer, leading two other young men in a series of collective yawns as 'a toast of ennui' (III.p.67), and generally making a public display of his despair. Others find him attractive for the things that set him apart. Humphrey complains, 'You're mad and you're violent, / And I strongly resent finding you slightly pleasant' (III.p.64). Jennet warns him that by solitude and mystery 'You are making yourself / A breeding-ground for love and must take the consequences' (II.p.57). In the end he and Jennet run off together.

Morose in Jonson's *Epicoene* (1609) is forced to play the role of public entertainer that Shakespeare's Jaques and Fry's Thomas Mendip adopt willingly. He has a pathological hatred not just of noise, but of any sound made by someone other than himself: even common greetings like 'God save you' he finds irksome (V.iii.26–31). Paradoxically, his acute sensitivity gives him a closer than normal relation with the world, since he is pained by sounds an ordinary person would hardly notice. His solution is to retreat into 'a room with double walls, and treble ceilings; the windores close shut, and caulk'd; and there he lives by candlelight' (I.i.184–86). There of course society seeks him out, to provoke him and make him display his humour: 'he would grow resty else in his ease. His virtue would rust without action' (I.i.171–72). The raucous wedding celebration contrived by his tormentors is like a skimmington ride, a public shaming of one who has offended society.[16] His bursts of pain and anger are for public amusement, and even Truewit's claim at the end of the play that the audience's applause will cure him may be simply enlisting the audience in providing one more torment.[17] But while Morose's tormentors make him the butt of laughter, the play's depiction of society as an arena of competitive noise actually endorses his loner's perspective on it. Jabbering lawyers, fools and women who won't stop talking – it is a world anyone would want to retreat from.

As Morose is bound to his world by a hypersensitivity that is at once laughable and valid, Macilente, the satiric commentator who guides the audience through Jonson's *Every Man out of his Humour* (1599), is bound to it by envy. His hatred of the world stems from his resentment of other people's good fortune; standing apart from his fellows, snarling at them, he cannot take his eyes off them. Despising Deliro's domineering wife Fallace, he still envies Deliro for having 'a wife of this exceeding form' (II.iv.136). Like Morose he shrinks from the simplest human contact, resenting the fact that as he accepts Deliro's hospitality he has to speak 'this word "I thank you" to a fool' (II.iv.8). Yet he has his own kind of gregariousness: his way of showing indifference to a pair of fools is not to leave the stage when they enter but to lie down on it, keeping himself in the way (I.i.38). In the original version of the play he was cured miraculously by the sight of Queen Elizabeth; in the final version he is cured when the other characters, one by one, are broken and humiliated, leaving him nothing to envy: 'Now is my soul at peace' (V.xi.54). There is no dance, no wedding, no reconciliation, no stage full of people; the other characters simply crawl off defeated as the play's world seems to wither and die at the will of its most malicious character. Though the other commentators Jonson plants on stage in the framing action may encourage us to keep our distance from Macilente, and though his claim of isolation is vitiated by his obsession with other people's superior fortune, the play ends on his terms.

## *The Plain Dealer*

As Wycherley's Horner is one of the most ambiguous tricksters in English comedy, his Manly, the title character of *The Plain Dealer* (1676), is one of its most controversial misanthropes. Even within the play he provokes disagreement. His misanthropy is so extreme that it puts him, like Jaques and Morose, constantly on display, as other characters debate whether it is admirable honesty or mere foolishness. He himself sets the terms of the debate when he declares in the Prologue that he acts 'a fool's part . . . / An honest man' (p.386). In the first scene two sailors recall that in the recent war he sank his own ship. The first sailor, calling him 'our bully Tar', sees this as a grand gesture to keep it out of the hands of the Dutch, and of the courtiers who might have made it a prize; the second complains, 'A pox of his sinking, Tom, we have made a base, broken, short voyage of it' (I.p.392).

Manly has a satirist's contempt for relationships. An embrace is the act of a pickpocket; as for himself, 'I'll have no leading-strings, I can walk alone; I hate a harness, and will not tug on in a faction, kissing my leader behind, that another slave may do the like to me' (I.p.389). The play's depiction of a conniving, hypocritical society appears to endorse this view, but Manly also rejects genuine kindness; one of the sailors recalls that when he and his fellows saved Manly's life and welcomed him ashore, 'he gave me a box on the ear, and call'd me fawning water-dog' (I.p.393). Is he mad, as by one interpretation the Gulliver of Book Four is when he recoils from the captain who rescues him, convinced the man is a Yahoo? Or is this a performance, as his later gesture of giving his last £20 to his boat's crew would suggest? In any case, he is, like Morose and Macilente, obsessively bound to the world he claims to reject. When he tells the sailors to let no one into his lodging, not even a woman, or a man bringing him money, the second sailor retorts that the one visitor he would accept is a man with a challenge, 'for though you refuse money, I'm sure you love fighting too well to refuse that' (I.p.395). Manly explodes and kicks the sailors out; the barb has hit home.

His own darkest, most obsessive relationship is with Olivia, with whom he trusted his fortune while he was at sea. From the beginning his idealized view of her is subject to strain and inconsistency. Claiming to trust her absolutely, he gives her his fortune as a sign of that trust; his interlocutor Freeman accuses him of buying her constancy with money (I.p.407). His frequent tributes to her purity and virtue keep veering into tributes to her sex appeal: 'her form would make a starved hermit a ravisher' (I.p.406). Taking Freeman to see her, he warns, 'thou, who art so much my friend, wilt have a mind to lie with her' (I.p.408). There is something in him that needs to imagine Olivia having sex, and when he learns she has betrayed him, purloining his fortune and marrying another man (Vernish, Manly's equally idealized and equally false friend) it is this side of Manly's nature that is activated as he plans his revenge. In a grim parody of *Twelfth Night*, Olivia has become infatuated with Manly's page Fidelia (a woman in disguise, following him for love) and Manly arranges that Fidelia will keep an appointment to consummate the affair; but while Fidelia will do the wooing Manly, in the dark, will get the sex: 'so much she hates me, that it would be a revenge sufficient, to make her accessary to my pleasure, and then let her know it' (IV.p.484). As Horner, by one reading, uses sex to act out his satiric contempt for women, Manly uses it to act out his hate for Olivia, a hate he continues to refer to as love (III.p.440). The china scene is covered by two minutes of dialogue, letting the audience laugh at the deceived husband who does not know what is going on in the next room. Manly's bout with Olivia is covered by a twelve-line speech of lament from Fidelia, who knows too well what is going on; it is the woman offstage who does not know. The brutal speed and simplicity of the encounter are underlined when Manly, emerging from the room, reports, 'I have said not a word to her' (IV.p.485).[18] This quick, anonymous sex expresses the dark side of Manly's obsession with Olivia, and, like the china scene, provides a reductive mockery of sexual relations. The mockery in *The Country Wife* was broad and farcical; this is grim.

As Manly couples in the dark with Olivia, he seems cut off from normal humanity. In fact he is never so much a loner locked in his private fantasy as he is in his relations with Olivia and Vernish. His dream of the ideal friend and the ideal mistress, and his insistence that there can be only one of each, substitute a mythic simplicity for the compromises of reality, the give-and-take of real love and friendship. The play never explains how he came to pick Vernish; but it is quite clear about Olivia. One of her other dupes explains her technique: 'she stands in the drawing-room, like the glass, ready for all comers to set their gallantry by her: and like the glass too, lets no man go from her, unsatisfied with himself' (IV.i.479). She caught Manly by mirroring his misanthropy: 'I knew he lov'd his own singular moroseness so well, as to dote upon any copy of it, wherefore I feign'd an hatred of the world too, that he might love me in earnest' (IV.p.482). With a fop's devotion to his looking-glass, Manly fell in love with an image of himself.

All this suggests that the play maintains a critical distance from Manly, showing him as a foolish idealist cut off from reality, whose relationships are simply narcissistic fantasies. Yet there are ways in which the play's perspective is disconcertingly like Manly's own. Olivia's worthlessness is as complete as Manly in his anger would want to imagine it. In her opening scene her hypocrisy is so flagrant as to be unreal: everything she declares to be her 'aversion' is immediately revealed as nothing of the kind. She shows intelligence in her view of how she snared Manly, and in the occasional wit of her attacks on him; otherwise she is a compound of dishonesty, cynicism and sexual voraciousness. Vernish is equally unrelieved in his villainy: discovering Fidelia is a woman, for example, he immediately tries to rape her. Manly's initial idealism about the characters is not challenged but inverted: they are as perfect in their villainy as he imagined them in their virtue. In the end they suffer crushing, humiliating defeat. Confirming Manly's own final view of them, the play enacts one of the lowest and most compelling of human fantasies: those who have wronged us are complete villains, with no redeeming features, and will get just what they deserve.

The play confirms Manly's fantasy of the ideal, faithful mistress through Fidelia, who follows him in disguise, puts up with abuse and insult, protests against his coupling with Olivia but waits by the door while he does it, and finally reveals her sex, her income (substantial) and her complete devotion. It is a certain kind of male fantasy of the perfect woman: loyalty, patience, unshakable love, great legs (it was a breeches part for Elizabeth Boutell) and two thousand pounds a year. There are occasional glimpses of a less obliging woman, just enough to encourage our scepticism about this fantasy. When Manly accuses her of cowardice, her response is tart: 'Can he be said to be afraid, that ventures to sea with you?' (I.p.399). When she reports that Olivia has levelled the same insult, cowardice, at Manly, she seems to get in an extra kick on her own behalf:

FIDELIA: . . . she had the baseness, the injustice, to call you coward, sir, coward, coward, sir.
MANLY: Not yet? –
FIDELIA: I've done. Coward, sir.

(IV.p.465)

There are also hints that she is a figure from a dream. At her first entrance, after Manly has told the sailors to let no one in, she somehow appears, without explanation. The literal answer is easy enough: she was in his lodging all the time. But there is just a hint that she can walk through walls. In the last scene she tells Manly the truth about herself after pulling him aside from the company, and promises to finish her story when there are 'fewer auditors' (V.p.514), as though she is offering a private fantasy for his ears alone.

While the play identifies with Manly's point of view, there is a hint of irony about that identification. In the end he gets back his fortune, and his old dream of one good mistress and one good friend is restored through Fidelia and Freeman. His satiric perspective has to a great extent been endorsed. But Freeman agrees to Manly's own suggestion that it appears he is reconciled to the world only because at last he has done well out of it, retrospectively turning his satire into sour grapes. By signing the Epistle Dedicatory 'The Plain Dealer', Wycherley identified himself with his creation, and from then on the label 'Manly Wycherley' stuck to him. But Wycherley (or is it Manly?) addresses the Epistle to Mother Bennet, a famous procuress. He tells her they are in the same line of work: 'the vices of the age are our best business' (p.381). As Mother Bennet gratifies the desires of her clients, Wycherley gratifies the fantasies of his, through Manly's vision of himself as an honest man betrayed by a world that confirms his satiric view of it, but finally rewarded with love, friendship, wealth, and the ruin of his enemies. The signature at the end of the epistle may encourage our identification with the play's vision, but the direction at the beginning awakens our sense of irony.

Manly's solitude gives him a satiric and idealizing purity of vision, which his relationships so complicate that we are left wondering how much that vision is compromised. The true plain dealer may be Olivia's cousin Eliza, who appears as part of a double act with her, countering her pretenses with straight common sense. Eliza is always cool, clear and right. No emotional entanglement, no hidden agenda, no hint of sour grapes taints her commentary. But we also note that apart from her essentially theatrical role as Olivia's interlocutor she has no relationships: no love affairs, no friendships, no relations other than her cousin, no part in the story and no existence outside the scenes in which she appears. In contrast to Manly's pained involvement in the world, Eliza truly stands alone.[19] The purity of her commentary and the purity of her isolation go together, and in both she is unreal. As through Manly, Wycherley may be telling us that involvement in the world always compromises us, through Eliza's incredibility he may be saying in a backhanded way that complete detachment is impossible.

## The mirror and the other

*Twelfth Night* (c. 1600) is full of images of solitude: Malvolio in his fantasy world and then in his dark prison, Viola describing her sister's pining, unrequited love (II.iv.110–15). As Malvolio's only relationship is with his own image, practising behaviour to his shadow, Viola in describing her sister's loneliness is really describing her own. At the end the frustrations of the romantic plot are resolved when Viola's twin brother Sebastian, whose mirror image she has become through her male disguise, appears on stage together with his sister for the first time. Sebastian seems at first to be looking not at his sister but at his own reflection:

> Do I stand there? I never had a brother;
> Nor can there be that deity in my nature
> Of here and everywhere. I had a sister . . . .
> (V.i.226–28)

From this point the recognition tokens of a traditional discovery scene ('my father had a mole upon his brow') clarify and separate their identities, and Sebastian speaks Viola's name, the first time it is heard in the play. The mirror has become the other, and relationships are restored. Viola can now turn to Orsino and Sebastian to Olivia. The lovers are freed from the solipsistic world of mirrors in which so many of the loners of comedy – characters as different as Manly and Lord Foppington – are trapped.

One modern comedy that appears for a while to endorse solitude is Caryl Churchill's *Cloud 9* (1979). The conventional family and sexual relationships of Act One are oppressive; Act Two frees the characters to seek other forms of satisfaction. Gerry, a gay man who prefers living alone (II.iii.p.99), finds pleasure in a quick bit of oral sex with a perfect stranger in a railway carriage, in the time it takes to go from Victoria to Clapham. The one thing that spoils it for him is his partner's attempt to get personal: 'I felt wonderful. Then he started talking. It's better if nothing is said. Once you find he's a librarian in Walthamstow with a special interest in science fiction and lives with his aunt, then forget it' (II.ii.p.77). In *The Country Wife* and *The Plain Dealer* quick, impersonal sex seemed a parody of relationship; here it is accepted as a valid way to find pleasure, and the satire is directed against the man who tries to spoil it by talking. (Manly, we recall, said not a word to Olivia.)

Betty, who has left her husband, is at first so terrified by solitude that even a walk in the park frightens her (II.ii.p.83). But she eventually finds satisfaction alone, through her own body; and not just satisfaction but the reality of her identity. In her marriage, 'I thought if Clive wasn't looking at me there wasn't a person there.' Now, 'I touched my face, it was there, my arm, my breast, and my hand went down where I thought it shouldn't, and I thought well there is somebody there' (II.iv.p.105). This, like the ending of *Twelfth Night*, is a recognition scene. The discovery of herself – 'do I stand there?' – frees Betty for new relationships; she goes on to strike up a friendship with Gerry.[20] At the end of *Cloud 9*, the Betty of Act One, played by a man, re-enters, and '*Betty and Betty embrace*' (II.iv.p.111). When Viola and Sebastian confronted each other Shakespeare's audience saw two male actors, identically dressed, creating an image of mirroring and same-sex bonding that gradually dissolved into an image of otherness, relationship, and heterosexual love. In *Cloud 9* a man and a woman, dressed in different periods (Betty I comes from the nineteenth century) meet and embrace, using a traditional theatrical image of heterosexual union, the ending of conventional comedy (boy gets girl) to suggest same-sex bonding (both are dressed as women) and a reconciliation with the self. This image expresses in performance terms what Betty achieved through the discovery of her own body. Even a play that celebrates the discovery, and the sexuality, of the solitary individual, does so through the language of relationship.[21] But *Twelfth Night* and *Cloud 9* both suggest that relationship begins with a look in the mirror, an awareness of the self. The condition is that when one looks in the mirror there has to be somebody there.

# 4

# OTHER PLACES

### Into the woods

One possible answer to the reductiveness of society is the loner's attempt to stand apart from it. But comedy's depiction of this character, we have seen, is full of contradictions: loners find themselves on display to the world they thought they had left, and more involved with it than they intended. Society continues to make its claims. Another possible answer is to escape to another place, a place of liberty. In Northrop Frye's still-influential analysis of Shakespearean comedy, this is the 'green world', a place of freedom where the 'comic resolution is achieved', after which the characters can move back to normal society.[1] But the other places of comedy are not always green, and what is achieved in them is not always resolution. Comedy's treatment of the other place is as complex and contradictory as its treatment of the loner.

At its simplest level the other place is a site of freedom, where the restrictions of normal society are suspended and desires can be acted out. In Aphra Behn's *The Rover* (1677) and *The Feigned Courtesans* (1679) Italy allows a sexual licence unavailable in England. In *The Rover* the spirit of Naples in Carnival time is, for a party of English gentlemen exiled from the land of Cromwell, 'a kind of legal authorized fornication, where the men are not chid for't, nor the women despised, as amongst our dull English' (I.ii.119–21). In *The Feigned Courtesans* the sexual freedom of Rome is attributed to the climate (I.i.p.9). France has a similar function for Wilde in *The Importance of Being Earnest* (1895): French songs sound improper to Lady Bracknell, and Canon Chasuble fears that Ernest's desire to be buried in Paris 'hardly points to any very serious state of mind at the last' (II.239–40). (Wilde himself left for France on his release from prison, and he too is buried in Paris.) The English who cannot cross the channel can always make do with woods, fields and parks. Elizabethan comedy in particular cheerfully confirms Puritan diatribes against the improprieties that took place when traditional folk-festivals allowed young couples to go into the woods.[2] The lovers of John Lyly's *Gallathea* (c.1585), two girls disguised as boys who fall in love despite a growing suspicion that they are the same sex, exchange vows in the woods (III.ii.49–51), and while they are not sure what they can do with each other, they know where they should go to do it:

'Come, let us into the grove and make much of one another, that cannot tell what to think of one another' (III.ii.55–56).

There is more boisterous comedy in the outdoor night sequence in Henry Porter's *The Two Angry Women of Abingdon* (c.1588). The outspoken heroine Mall Barnes sets the tone as she waits by a coney-borrow to elope with her lover, and ponders the bawdy appropriateness of the setting: when men hunt rabbits, 'they put ferrets in the holes – fie, fie! – / And they go up and down where conies lie' (IV.i.p.162). The lovers miss each other in the dark, other characters get caught up in the confusion, and the inhibitions of the daylight world are suspended. Masters are taken for servants and vice versa. Mistress Goursey's servant Coomes demands a kiss from her, and suggests more: ''twere a good deed to come over you for this night's work' (IV.iii.p.172). But he is actually talking to his fellow servant Hodge, who is impersonating his mistress and who leads Coomes into a pond. The local squire Sir Ralph Smith is out hunting, and the rumour spreads that his real quarry is Nan the dairymaid. Sir Ralph encounters Mall and, unaware of each other's identities, they engage in a bit of bawdy flirtation. But when they learn each other's names normal social distance is restored, and the tone changes: Mall asks quite seriously for Sir Ralph's help in winning her lover against her parents' opposition, and he just as seriously offers it. In the impenetrable darkness of the countryside at night – created by the actors' words on an Elizabethan stage illuminated by normal daylight – social identities have been suspended in what Mall's brother Philip calls a Christmas game of hoodman-blind (IV.iii.p.182). But the game produces confusion, not (as in Frye's pattern) resolution; the restoration of order and the fulfilment of the characters' desires depend on the coming of daylight and the return of normal social identity.

In later comedies, city parks take the place of woods, and retain something of their character.[3] Lord Bonville, in James Shirley's *Hyde Park* (1632), plans to use the park in his seduction of Julietta, and echoes the hunting imagery of *Two Angry Women*: 'There have been stories, that some have / Struck many deer within the Park' (IV.i.20–21). Darkness makes the parks of London convenient places for sexual licence: in Wycherley's *Love in a Wood, or St. James' Park* (1671) the widow Flippant complains, 'What unmannerly rascals are those that bring light into the Park? 'Twill not be taken well from 'em by the women certainly' (II.p.34). In Colley Cibber's *Love's Last Shift* (1696) Young Worthy says of the same location, 'Look how lovingly the trees are join'd . . . as if Nature had design'd this walk for the private shelter of forbidden love' (III.ii.2–4).

Darkness can shelter less amiable crimes, and in her study of the park in comedy Anne Barton has commented that in modern drama as in modern life city parks have become violent, dangerous places.[4] There is a partial exception, however, in Caryl Churchill's *Cloud 9* (1979). In Act One, set in an African outpost of the British Empire in the colonial period, the social and family structure dominated by Clive is oppressive, denying the honest expression of the characters' natures and desires. Betty is limited to the role of Clive's wife; his son Edward is forced into being a manly boy when he would rather play with his sister's doll; a gay man and a lesbian woman

are coerced into marriage. The women in particular are so repressed they have literally nothing to say to each other; in a recurring effect, two or three women are left on
stage by themselves and '*There is a silence*' (I.i.p.13, I.ii.p.29). Act Two is set in a park in
modern London, and its first scene is dominated by a conversation between two
women, Clive's daughter Victoria and her friend Lin. At the end of the scene Lin
asks Victoria to have sex with her, and Victoria, thinking in traditional categories
and wondering what her husband would say, asks, 'Does it count as adultery with a
woman?' Lin replies simply, 'You'd enjoy it' (II.i.p.75). The park is a free space where
relationships shift, dissolve and re-form. Edward and his lover Gerry break up;
Betty, divorced from Clive, starts a friendship with Gerry. Sexual identities shift:
Edward, stroking his sister's breasts, decides he's a lesbian (II.ii.p.92). He moves in
with Lin and Victoria.

So far *Cloud 9* echoes Restoration comedy's use of the park as a place for free
love, extending it beyond ordinary coupling, straight or gay, to free-wheeling
experiment. Churchill moves to a deeper level when in the park at night Lin,
Victoria and Edward, all drunk, try to call up the goddess of the old matriarchal
world. They imagine her as the embodiment of sexual liberty: 'the women were
priests in the temples and fucked all the time' (II.iii.p.94). She is also the answer to
the father-dominated order of Act One: 'Goddess of breasts . . . Goddess of
cunts . . . Goddess of fat bellies and babies. And blood blood blood' (II.iii. p.95).
Lin pretends, as a joke, that she can see something in the dark, and the ceremony
collapses in laughter. But something has happened. A stranger appears, and Lin
calls, 'Come and have sex with us'; then she sees it is her brother Bill, who has just
been killed in Belfast and who brings on to the stage not the sexual energy of the
goddess but the sexual desperation of the soldier: 'Spent the day reading fucking
porn and the fucking night wanking. Man's fucking life in the fucking army? No
fun when the fucking kids hate you. I got so I fucking wanted to kill someone and I
got fucking killed myself and I want a fuck' (II.iii.pp.97–98). The once-censored
word whose casual use through the rest of the play is a sign of freedom[5] is obscene
again, reflecting an obscene life.

It looks as though the invocation of the goddess has backfired, producing a
nightmare return of the oppressive order of Act One. But from Bill's appearance
onwards time breaks down, as characters from Act One mingle with characters
from Act Two, and the effect is mostly liberating.[6] In an echo of the assignations of
Restoration comedy two of the play's gay men, Harry from Act One and Gerry
from Act Two, pick each other up. Betty confronts and dismisses her long-dead
mother, and finally Betty from Act One embraces Betty from Act Two. As we shall
see elsewhere, time often seems different in the other world; here, it is as though the
invocation of the goddess has actually torn a hole in time. Bill is first through the
gap, and brings with him a sense of nightmare. The play then relaxes back into
comedy, and the suspension of normal life becomes liberating; but not before we
have touched on the fear this suspension can trigger, a fear of something dark and
other that the comedy acknowledges, and then controls. It is a fear we shall meet
again.[7]

The young men of *The Importance of Being Earnest* use the freedom of the second world to adopt new identities: Jack, whose base is the country, is Ernest in town; Algy, whose base is the town, is Ernest in the country. Jack in particular may be trying to use the uncertainty about identity embodied in his curious origins. Algy, who is more active than Jack in creating confusion, calls this Bunburying, and in going to the country to do it he is the more typical of the two. Young Fashion in Vanbrugh's *The Relapse* (1696) goes to Sir Tunbelly Clumsy's country house in the role of his older brother Lord Foppington, and gets the marriage with Sir Tunbelly's daughter Hoyden that was designed for his brother. Archer and Aimwell, the fortune-hunting heroes of Farquhar's *The Beaux' Stratagem* (1707), journey through the country under assumed names, alternating the roles of master and servant. In a more complicated case, Young Courtly in Boucicault's *London Assurance* (1841) visits Max Harkaway's country estate both as Augustus Hamilton and as a caricatured version of himself, pretending to be a shy, pedantic young man. The country setting allows the trickster-hero, living by his wits, to get away from places where he is known (and where he generally owes money), into a new identity that lets him win the woman of his choice, who can pay his debts.

Alan Ayckbourn creates a female Bunburyist in *Relatively Speaking* (1967). That is not his only variation on the tradition: Ginny sows confusion not about her own identity but about the identity of other characters and their relationships with her. She goes off to the country, telling her lover Greg she is visiting her parents. She is actually visiting Philip, an older man she has been having an affair with, to persuade him to leave her alone. Greg, reading the country address off a cigarette packet in an echo of the Act One curtain of *Earnest*,[8] not only follows her to the country but gets there first. The result is a tangle of identity confusion and cross-purpose dialogue: Greg, for example, asks Philip's permission to marry Ginny, but since he uses only pronouns Philip thinks Greg is his wife Sheila's lover, proposing to marry *her*; and so on. Understandably, the characters start to accuse each other of being 'unhinged' and 'completely mad' (II.ii.pp.75, 78). We touch, lightly, on the fear that lies beyond the confusions of the other place. Nor is there a full restoration of clarity and order: Philip and Sheila eventually catch on, but Greg never does; and a pair of slippers Greg finds in Ginny's apartment at the beginning of the play, which the audience thinks at first is a clue to her affair with Philip, turns out not to be his; Ginny has a third, unknown lover, a secret kept from the audience to the last minute. Greg returns with her to London, not knowing how much he does not know.

## As You Like It

Rosalind in Shakespeare's *As You Like It* (c.1600) is one of the most accomplished Bunburyists in English comedy. In the freedom provided by the Forest of Arden – anticipated by her own words, 'Now go we in content / To liberty, and not to banishment' (I.iii.135–36) – she not only changes identity, she changes gender. Like the tongue-tied women of *Cloud 9* she and her lover Orlando when they first meet in the court are virtually speechless. All she can do is drop broad hints, to which he responds with baffled silence, complaining when he is alone, 'What passion hangs these weights upon my tongue?' (I.ii.248). In Arden he not only finds his voice as a lover but does considerable ecological damage carving love poetry on the trees. Confronted with Rosalind herself (pretending to be Ganymede pretending to be Rosalind) he woos her with the language he was unable to find at court, not knowing she is the real thing. She in turn uses the freedom of her disguise not only to provoke Orlando's wooing but to go through a mock-marriage ceremony and to warn him what an uncontrollable wife she will be. The licence of the disguise, and the freedom of Arden, allow her simultaneously to act out her desires and to tease her unknowing lover, in a state of suspended identity that holds off final commitment either to romance or to mockery.

Celia at first sees Arden simply as a place of holiday: 'I like this place / And willingly could waste my time in it' (II.iv.90–91). Orlando's casual attitude to appointments suggests that for him time is suspended: 'There's no clock in the forest' (III.ii.297). This in turn leads to Rosalind's set-piece on the relativity of time, which moves at different speeds for different people (III.ii.303–27). In *Cloud 9* the invocation of the goddess calls up an ancient power, and figures from the past return. In Arden, an ancient power actually appears when the wedding-god Hymen presides over the finale, and Arden itself is a place where the past comes to life. Charles the Wrestler imagines the banished Duke and his followers reviving lost worlds: 'there they live like the old Robin Hood of England . . . and fleet the time carelessly as they did in the golden world' (I.i.111–14). In Arden Rosalind recovers her lost father, and Orlando finds his late father's memory held in honour. Robert Pogue Harrison observes that forests 'have the psychological effect of evoking memories of the past . . . . They are enveloped, as it were, in the aura of lost origins.'[9] He takes his examples mostly from the Romantic period, but he might be writing of *As You Like It*.

In Arden the destructive work of time, when it is not reversed, is viewed with comic detachment, as in Jaques's speech on the seven ages of man or Touchstone's meditation on his watch: 'And so from hour to hour we ripe and ripe, / And then from hour to hour we rot and rot' (II.vii.26–27). But there is also winter and rough weather in the golden world; Rosalind, Celia and Touchstone arrive in Arden tired, hungry, and complaining. Orlando, going into exile with his servant Adam, protested that he could not beg for food or hold travellers up at swordpoint (II.iii.31–3); but for Adam's sake he does both, invading the Duke's banquet with his drawn sword, threatening and finally begging. In the freedom of Arden his romantic inhibitions are broken down; in the deprivation of Arden so are his social ones. Duke Senior sees Arden as a place where he is finally told the truth: as the icy wind blows on him he tells himself, 'This is no flattery; these are counsellors / That feelingly persuade me what I am' (II.i.10–11). In his determination to find 'tongues in trees, books in the running brooks, / Sermons in stones, and good in everything' (II.i.16–17) he seems to be the opposite of Orlando who, far from reading what the book of nature has to tell him, inscribes his own romantic obsessions on the countryside: 'O Rosalind! These trees shall be my books, / And in their bark my thoughts I'll character' (III.ii.5–6).

Yet the contrast may be more apparent than real: for both men Arden is a blank space on which to write their own thoughts. Orlando's are of Rosalind, the Duke's of the court flattery that preceded his downfall. As the loners we examined in the last chapter find their truest relationships in mirrors, the characters who come to Arden find in it reflections of themselves. Rosalind and Touchstone, on their first encounters with the denizens of Arden, find themselves facing mirrors. Rosalind says of Silvius's display of love, 'Jove, Jove! This shepherd's passion / Is much upon my fashion' (II.iv.57–58). When Touchstone hails Corin as 'you, clown!' Rosalind tells him, 'Peace, Fool! He's not thy kinsman' (II.iv.62–63); the pun allows us to see one clown confronting another. Coming across the Duke's banquet, Orlando appeals to lost values ('If ever you have looked on better days, / If ever been where bells have knolled to church . . . ') only to find the Duke echoing his language: 'True is it that we have seen better days, / And have with holy bell been knolled to church . . . ' (II.vii.112–22). Jaques, on the other hand, sees Duke Senior's hunting as a re-enactment of Duke Frederick's usurpation (II.i.27–28, 60–63); for him Arden mirrors not the best values of the outside world, but its injustices.

Each world is touched with thoughts and images of the other. There are trees, real or imagined, on stage from the beginning of the play: the opening scene takes place in an orchard, and in that scene we first hear of Arden from Charles the wrestler. The family name of Orlando and his brothers, de Bois, suggests an origin in the woods. As foreshadowings of Arden touch the court, Touchstone's satiric routines bring memories of the court to haunt Arden: the most elaborate of these, his set-piece on the degrees of the lie, comes in the last scene as though to anticipate the impending return of the Duke and his party to the world he is mocking. There is in fact a curious suspension in the ending. Duke Frederick approaches Arden but never quite gets there; at its outskirts, in a liminal space, he meets an old religious man and is converted (V.iv.153–61). Like Caesar in Dryden's *All for Love* or the boy in Beckett's *Endgame* he comes from outside at the end of the play to invade the special, isolated world the play has created, but he never makes it on to the stage. Dryden's Caesar is 'just entering' as the play ends. By the same token, the Duke and his followers are *about* to leave Arden as their play ends; like Beckett's Clov, packed and ready for the road, they are just leaving, but we never see them go. As Arden and the court have been places from which to view each other, the play begins and ends suspended between the two locations.

There is also something consciously theatrical about Arden. It is at the Duke's banquet that we are told, by the Duke as well as by Jaques, that all the world's a stage (II.vii.135–65). The normally down-to-earth Corin calls Silvius's wooing of Phebe 'a pageant truly played', and Rosalind promises to 'prove a busy actor in their play' (III.iv.50,57). It is in Arden that Rosalind not only plays a role, Ganymede, but by her appearance reminds us of what 'she' really is, a boy actor; when Ganymede plays Rosalind it is like watching the company's leading boy at a non-dress rehearsal, playing a woman in doublet and hose. Arden's function as a blank space on which the characters inscribe their thoughts, and the ease with which it dissolves from English sheep-farming country to a classical forest with lions and olive trees, make it a reflection of the free, unlocalized Elizabethan stage. In *As You Like It* the second world is a place where identity and normal social reality are (for the visitors) suspended, allowing freedom to make holiday and play roles; but the characters who come to Arden find in it reflections of themselves and of the world they left behind. Arden is like the theatre itself, a place of escape, a second world that holds up a mirror to those who enter it.

## Palaces of truth

A journey to the country is not just an occasion to Bunbury. Characters who take that journey may find themselves not escaping the truth but confronting it. In Shakespeare's *The Taming of the Shrew* (c.1594) Katharine arrives at Petruchio's country house cold and wet, to find herself deprived of food and sleep. As Petruchio nags and bullies his servants, she is provoked into defending them: 'Patience, I pray you, 'twas a fault unwilling' (IV.i.144). One of the servants offers a reading of Petruchio's method: 'He kills her in her own humour' (IV.i.168). In other words, he is breaking her of her anger by forcing her to confront a mirror image of it. The main impression is of a comic nightmare with an edge of real cruelty. As J. Dennis Huston puts it, Petruchio's house is like a dream 'where the self is strangely powerless to repel violence; the object world of food and clothes keeps slipping into insubstantiality; . . . and time passes illogically and indeterminately.'[10] In this dream-world Katharine, by the servant's reading, confronts images of her own violence.

The Paris apartment that forms the setting for Act Two of Noël Coward's *Private Lives* (1930) looks like a perfect place of escape for lovers to be alone. The apartments above and below are empty, the one phone call is a wrong number, and as the act opens Elyot and Amanda have finished dinner, sent the maid home, and are lounging about, Amanda in pyjamas and Elyot in a dressing-gown. They have not been out for several days. Amanda's line, 'Darling, you do look awfully sweet in your little dressing gown' (II.p.216) suggests a cosy regression to childhood. They play language games and spin fantasies: 'Is that the Grand Duchess Olga lying under the piano?' (II.p.219). But they also rake up old grievances, reveal past infidelities, and have screaming rows. The escapist fantasy keeps breaking down as they act out the full range of their love–hate relationship, replaying the past at high speed. They do so with a compression and intensity that reflect the special conditions of the second world, and of the theatre. A consciousness of performance touches this world as it touches the Forest of Arden. Coward saw the play as a vehicle for himself and Getrude Lawrence, and the second act in particular, with its rapid changes of mood, as a test of the performers' skill, demanding 'the maximum of resource and comedy experience'.[11] Elyot's dressing gown was part of the Coward image, and when Elyot plays the piano and he and Amanda sing together, the use of music to cement the characters' relationship is also a chance for

Coward and Lawrence, as themselves, to perform a small cabaret for the audience. As Katharine confronts an image of herself in a world of grim physical reality that has also the fluidity of a dream, Elyot and Amanda confront their demons in a secluded apartment (just down the road, I imagine, from where Ernest Worthing is buried) that is also a stage set on which two gifted artists entertain the audience.

It is W.S. Gilbert's *The Palace of Truth* (1870) that presents the most literal form of the other world as a place of seclusion where characters confront the truth – in this case, not about themselves but about each other. All who enter the palace (twenty miles from the normal location of the court) are compelled by magic to speak the truth, without knowing they are doing so; the effect on their relationships can be imagined. The beauty of the palace leads one unsuspecting character to ask, 'Where will you find / A fitter nursery for love than this?' (II.p.45). Arden may encourage love, but the palace encourages embarrassing revelations. King Phanor admits his philandering; Prince Philamir declares he needs the love of Princess Zeolide, who is nothing special to him, only to feed his vanity; the apparently modest lady Azema flirts outrageously and goes so far as to allow a glimpse of ankle (II.p.50). The play draws laughter from a basic fear, the fear (especially sharp in love relationships) of having one's inner thoughts known.

The other plot trick is a magic box that allows its possessor to defeat the spell of the palace and go on lying as usual. Paradoxically, the box, flawless crystal of 'exquisite transparency! / The perfect emblem of a spotless life!' (I.p.41), looks like an image of truth. When at the end of the play it is broken the spell of the palace is broken with it. Behind the Gilbertian plot gimmick is the suggestion that lies and truth are mutually dependent, that the palace of truth and the court that gets by on lies are (like the court and the forest in *As You Like It*) closer to each other than one might suppose. Lies are the truth of social life, in that without them social life would be impossible; and a world in which everyone told the truth all the time would look flagrantly artificial, as it does here. The special form Gilbert gives to the theatricality of the second world is a consciousness of the actors: because the characters do not know they are speaking the truth, everything they say becomes an acting exercise in which the words say one thing and the actor's manner says another.[12] The flattering courtier Chrysal responds to a song from Princess Zeolide by '*applauding as if in ecstasies*' while declaring, 'No voice – no execution – out of tune – / Pretentious too – oh, very, very poor!' (II.p.43). The curmudgeon Aristaeus admits that his misanthropy is simply a ploy to entertain the court and declares '(*very savagely*) . . . . No child's more easily amused than I' (II.p.44). As social life depends on lies, declarations of truth look grotesquely strained and artificial. When the spell of truth-telling is finally broken, King Phanor declares, 'We shall get on much better' (III.p.71).

The logical culmination of the theatricality of the second world[13] is found in Noël Coward's *Hay Fever* (1925), which reverses Gilbert's myth by creating a Palace of Untruth. At the Blisses' country house everything is theatricalized, thoughtless flirtations are blown up into grand passions, and the unsuspecting weekend guests who are the visitors to this strange world find themselves caught up in a series of plays within the play. This theatricality centres on the family's actress mother Judith; when her guest Richard innocuously kisses her hand he gets a melodramatic response: 'David must be told – everything! . . . There come moments in life when it is necessary to be honest – absolutely honest . . . the truth must be faced fair and square' (II.p.152). As in Gilbert's play, 'facing the truth' is really playing a scene. The stunning revelation that provides the Act Two curtain – 'Don't strike! He is your father!' (II.p.166) – is lifted straight from one of Judith's old vehicles, *Love's Whirlwind*. At breakfast the following morning one of the guests, Jackie, breaks down: the house gets on her nerves, the dragon wallpaper in her room gives her nightmares, her hosts are 'all mad, you know', and her own identity has been called in question when David Bliss, having invited her for the weekend, asks 'Who the hell are you?' (III.pp.167–68). The country-house weekend in real life, like the journey to the second world in comedy, provided chances for erotic adventure; in *Forty Years On* Alan Bennett includes among the sounds of an English country house at night Edward VII returning to his own room.[14] But the Blisses' house takes its guests – comically and theatrically – from light flirtation to madness, nightmare, and the breakdown of identity.

## *Heartbreak House*

Bernard Shaw's *Heartbreak House* (1920) presents a country-house weekend that is also a visit to a second world – a place of erotic adventure and truth-telling, a place of nightmare, and an image of the world outside. Ellie Dunn arrives at Captain Shotover's country house, as Katharine arrives at Petruchio's country house and the refugees arrive in Arden, exhausted, dying for a cup of tea as they are fainting for lack of food. She is greeted by a lack of social nicety that will be matched by the Bliss family; though she has been invited by the daughter of the house, Hesione Hushabye, no one seems to expect her. Though tea and introductions are eventually produced, the house remains a place of ordeal both for its visitors and for those who live there. One of its ordeals is the exposure of truth: Hector Hushabye warns Randall Utterword, 'In this house we know all the poses: our game is to find out the man under the pose' (II.p.133). Characters' true names are revealed, with humiliating effect: Marcus Darnley is really Hector Hushabye, Randall Utterword is Randall the Rotter, Boss Mangan is Alfred, immediately shortened by Hesione Hushabye to 'Little Alf' (II.pp.112–13). The reduction to childishness is typical. Lady Utterword deals with Randall's petulance by treating him like a spoiled child, ragging him till he cries and drops off to sleep. Lady Utterword herself, back home after years abroad, tries to stand on her dignity as the wife of a man who has been governor of all the crown colonies in succession, but Nurse Guinness insists on using childhood pet names for her ('Addy' and 'Doty') and when Shotover refuses to recognize her as his daughter, she pleads, 'I'm little Paddy Patkins' (I.pp.56–57).

It is Boss Mangan – like the Chaplain in *St. Joan*, one of those unfortunate characters Shaw uses as a punching bag – who suffers particularly from the house's function as a palace of truth. He is goaded into revealing that his generosity to Ellie's father was a sham, and his image as a millionaire captain of industry is hollow. Ellie, who was engaged to him at the beginning of the play, reveals she never intended to marry him; she was just testing her strength. For Mangan 'this is a crazy house. Or else I'm going clean off my chump' (II.p.97) and in desperation he tries to tear his clothes off: 'Weve stripped ourselves morally naked: well, let us strip ourselves physically naked as well, and see how we like it' (III.pp.146–47). Captain Shotover himself is not immune to exposure. Ellie points out the trickery behind his performance as mad, inspired prophet: 'You pretend to be busy, and think of fine things to say, and run in and out to surprise people by saying them, and get away before they can answer you' (II.p.127). Shaw is exposing his own theatrical trickery here; looking back from this moment, we can see how much he has depended on the device of giving Shotover striking exit lines. Part of the Captain's mystique is that he is trying to reach the seventh degree of concentration; but the seventh degree of concentration turns out to be, by his own admission, rum (III.p.146).

As a place of erotic adventure, Heartbreak House is disconcertingly sterile.[15] It seems like a sexual free house: when Randall apologizes for kissing Hesione, Shotover retorts, 'Stuff! Everyone kisses my daughter. Kiss her as much as you like' (I.p.77). Hesione admits to inviting pretty women to the house to give Hector another chance at the grand passion he once had with her; but 'it has never come off' (I.p.84). The Shotover women have a strange power over men, but Hesione uses her power to break and humiliate Mangan, and Ariadne reduces Randall to tears. Hector, having kissed Ariadne more violently than either of them expected, recoils from what he has done, striking himself on the chest and exclaiming, 'Fool! Goat!' (I.p.84). The last two acts take place in a moonlit night that Hesione compares to 'the night in Tristan and Isolde' (II.p.123), but the only love charm that operates in Heartbreak House is the power of predatory women over enervated men.

The house's theatricality lies not only in Shotover's contrived performance as the mad mystic but in the house's own contrived resemblance to a ship, which leads Hector to turn it into an image of England, the special world functioning as a critical reflection of the normal one. He asks, 'And this ship we are all in? This soul's prison we call England?' to which Shotover replies, 'She will strike and sink and split' (III.p.156). In the air raid that ends the play the house that is also a ship that is also England passes through a storm in which it is nearly wrecked. The raid, like the invocation of the goddess in *Cloud 9*, seems to be a supernatural intervention. Literally it reflects the war Shaw and his audience had just passed through; but the enemy is never named, and Hector identifies the 'splendid drumming in the sky' not as planes or Zeppelins but as 'Heaven's threatening growl of disgust at us useless futile creatures' (III.p.140). In Shaw's terms, this is the Life Force in action. It is also an artistic effect; for Hesione and Ellie, it is Beethoven (III.p.158). Yet while Mangan and a visiting burglar, who have tried to save their lives, are picked off, the raid spares the other inhabitants of Heartbreak House, who have prepared with flamboyant enthusiasm for death. Unlike Mangan and the burglar they have admitted their uselessness, and so they are worth saving.

Ellie in her own way sees the value of the house. For her the revelations involve more than just the shrivelling of lies; in some of the fake glamour there is true beauty: 'There is a blessing on my broken heart. There is a blessing on your beauty, Hesione. There is a blessing on your father's spirit. Even on the lies of Marcus there is a blessing; but on Mr Mangan's money there is none' (III.p.149). (As often in the last act, she calls Hector Marcus, the alias he used when he first won her heart by telling her romantic lies.) Ellie herself goes on to admit that she does not know what this rhetoric means; but she insists 'it means something' (III.p.150). She speaks with authority. Her experience of heartbreak gives the play its title, and she in turn gives Heartbreak House its name (III.p.151). She begins the play naïve and innocent, and grows steadily in strength and insight through her encounter with the house; her growth is the play's central line of development. The play opens with Ellie asleep (in a typical Shavian joke, she has been reading Shakespeare) and it is possible to see everything that follows as her dream. We follow her as we follow Alice down the rabbit hole. She can face the truth-telling of Heartbreak House, and her reward is her spiritual marriage to Shotover, the one match achieved in the play. Her opposite number is Mangan, who is broken by the revelations about himself and the others, who regularly thinks he is going mad, and for whom the play is a descent into nightmare and death. Together they exemplify the double-edged nature of the second world as a place of confrontation with reality.

## Nightmares: *What the Butler Saw* and *A Midsummer Night's Dream*

As we follow Ellie into Heartbreak House, we follow another innocent young girl, Geraldine Barclay, into the mad world of Dr Prentice's clinic in Joe Orton's *What the Butler Saw* (1969). The play can be read as Geraldine's nightmare. The action begins with Prentice interviewing her as a prospective secretary and, it quickly becomes clear, a candidate for seduction. When Prentice asks her to strip, allegedly for a medical exam, she comments, 'I've never undressed in front of a man before'; offered an aspirin, she replies, 'No, thank you, sir. I don't want to start taking drugs' (I.pp.365–66). In the course of the play she is stripped, drugged, and treated as insane. Her identity is taken from her: she is dressed in a standard hospital gown, her hair is cut short, and she is made to impersonate Nicholas Beckett, a page from a nearby hotel, adopting his name and wearing his uniform. Nicholas, meanwhile, in a dress and a wig, impersonates her. The arrival of Sergeant Match to arrest Nicholas offers Geraldine a chance of escape, but puts her in a double bind: if she is not Nicholas, she cannot be taken away; if she is, she has to submit to a medical exam conducted by Prentice's superior Dr Rance: considering where her first medical exam led, she is right back where she started. In the space of three lines she declares, 'I'm not Nicholas Beckett' and 'I am Nicholas Beckett' (II.p.411). Finally she breaks down and confesses, 'I'm not a boy! I'm a girl!' only to find

Rance takes the truth as evidence of its opposite: 'Excellent. A confession at last. He wishes to believe he's a girl in order to minimize the feelings of guilt after homosexual intercourse' (II.p.413–14). Even in her own person she cannot make Rance believe in her sanity, since he is determined to certify her: 'Why have you been certified if you're sane? Even for a madwoman you're unusually dense' (I.p.379). Assuming the mastery in this Palace of Untruth, Rance uses the tricks of his profession to block every assertion Geraldine makes: 'She may mean "Yes" when she says "No". It's elementary feminine psychology' (I.p.382). Other characters coming into second worlds are free to adopt new identities, to Bunbury; in the mad world of the clinic Geraldine finds her identity taken from her and her sanity questioned, and every attempt she makes to tell the truth is blocked.

She is one of a number of characters caught up in a maelstrom of confusion, nudity, cross-dressing and drug-taking. To say that in the clinic the proprieties of normal life are suspended is to put it mildly. When Orton wrote, the taboo on stage nudity had not yet been broken and so Nick, Geraldine and Sergeant Match are stripped only to their underwear; when Geraldine is fully naked she is behind a screen. But Orton seems to have wanted a notional nakedness, the closest he could get to the real thing. Mrs Prentice, seeing Nick wearing underpants and a policeman's helmet, reports, 'He was nude except for a policeman's helmet' (II.p.422). (Given the bawdy meaning of 'policeman's helmet' he could be completely nude.) She keeps seeing naked men, and Rance refers to 'those manifestations of the penis which you encounter with an increasing degree of frequency' (II.p.439). Orton wrote near the beginning of a period when public nakedness was becoming a political statement, a proclamation of freedom. He himself picked up the contemporary idea that 'complete sexual licence' was 'the only way to smash the wretched civilization'.[16] Drugs were another symbol of liberation, and they too figure in the play; Orton himself took drugs, C.W.E. Bigsby speculates, 'as a retreat from public identity, as the expression of a desire to dismantle a clearly defined self'.[17] In Orton's own words, on holiday in Tangier, 'provided one spent the time drugged or drunk, the world was a fine place.'[18]

All this may suggest that the play is a liberating, Dionysiac celebration, with the clinic as a place of escape from repression, the drugs as a splendid alternative to reality, and Mrs Prentice's cry, 'Doctor, doctor! the world is full of naked men running in all directions!' (II.p.437) as an exclamation of delight. Critics have sometimes taken it that way.[19] But the drugs are tranquillizers, designed not to free the patients but to make them helpless and docile. They are instruments of the mad authority of the doctors. The naked figures who dart across the stage are driven not by sexual excitement but by panic. The overall direction is towards entrapment: '*They drag the weeping girl on to the couch and fasten her into the straitjacket*' (II.p.437). Towards the end both the play's women are trussed up in straitjackets, and as Rance activates the clinic's alarm system '*Metal grilles fall over each of the doors*' (II.p.442). As the Elizabethan stage allows a fluid sense of place, the enclosure of a modern stage set allows the clinic to become a prison.

Its role as a stage set is also quite self-conscious. The opening impression is of a conventional West End comedy set from the 1950s and earlier: '*French windows open onto pleasant gardens and shrubberies*' (I.p.363). Orton wanted to invoke 'the old theatre of reassurance'.[20] But when Rance asks why the room has so many doors, and Prentice explains it was designed by a lunatic (I.pp.376–77), we are alerted to the fact that it is also a farce set. As in other second worlds, time operates differently: the action begins in the early morning, continues unbroken, and ends in '*the glare of a bloody sunset*' (II.p.442). We have just been through a two-hour day; the time of the action is stage time.[21] The final descent of Sergeant Match through the skylight in a leopard-skin dress, making him a mock-Dionysus, is another manifestation of divinity in the second world; but it is also a literary joke recalling the origins of the theatre.[22] As the characters are trapped in a play, they are also trapped in a fiction constructed by the maddest of them, Dr Rance, who insists that Nick, who is standing right in front of him, stripped and bleeding, is Mrs Prentice's hallucination, and is unimpressed by his claim, 'If the pain is real I must be real' (II.p.443). He rewrites the natures and motives of the others to fit his own theories, and as the action approaches its climax he proclaims, 'The final chapters of my book are knitting together' (II.p.427). What is disconcerting is that the lurid pulp fiction he imagines is close to the truth. His starting point is his belief that Geraldine was sexually assaulted by her father; and Prentice, who nearly had sex with her at the beginning of the play, turns out to be her father.

In the clinic identity and even reality break down in confusion, and images of liberation become signs of entrapment. But as Arden mirrors the court and Heartbreak House mirrors England, the clinic is not a pocket of madness in a sane world. What we see in the clinic is what we would see outside, distilled and concentrated. Rance introduces himself to Prentice as a representative of Her Majesty's Government, 'Your immediate superiors in madness' (I.p.376). It is madness, all the way up; and sexual exploitation, and the abuse of power: Geraldine, thinking to escape from the doctors through arrest, imagines she would be 'safe from acts of indecency in a police station', but Prentice shakes his head: 'I wish I shared your optimism' (II.p.410). The best comfort Rance can offer her is, 'Your mind has given way. You'll find the experience invaluable in your efforts to come to terms with twentieth-century living' (II.p.438). The clinic is what Hector imagines Heartbreak House to be, an image of 'this soul's prison we call England.'

An unsuspecting viewer looking at production photos of *What the Butler Saw*, and seeing Nick and Geraldine stripped to their underwear, would imagine them as the young lovers of a sex farce, trying to get to bed with each other. In fact they have (remarkably, in view of Nick's general proclivities) no sexual interest in each other whatsoever. Theseus makes a similar mistake when at the end of the forest sequence in Shakespeare's *A Midsummer Night's Dream* (c.1595) he finds two young couples asleep on the ground, assumes 'they rose up early to observe / The rite of May' and greets them, 'Good morrow, friends. Saint Valentine is past. / Begin these woodbirds but to couple now?' (IV.i.131–32, 138–39). He imagines he is seeing the aftermath of a night of love in the woods, an escape from the city for a time of sexual licence. But as they settled for the night Hermia was careful to insist that Lysander slept at a respectable distance from her (II.ii.46–67); and Helena blocked a half-hearted threat of rape from Demetrius (who was simply trying to get rid of her) with one line: 'Your virtue is my privilege' (II.i.220). It is true that Hermia and Lysander were trying to escape the oppressive law of Athens, which threatened Hermia with death if she did not marry according to her father's wishes; but they were planning to escape *through* the woods to the house of Lysander's aunt; they did not see the woods themselves as a place of freedom, and if they had done so they would have been wrong.

For the women, as for Geraldine in Orton's clinic, it is a place of nightmare. Hermia has joked about male infidelity, promising to meet Lysander 'By all the vows that ever men have broke, / In number more than ever women spoke' (I.i.175–76). The anxiety the joke covers is suggested by her last words to him as they fall asleep in the woods, 'Thy love ne'er alter till thy sweet life end!' (II.ii.67), and her subsequent dream of Lysander watching with a smile as a serpent eats her heart. She wakes to find him gone, and when she next sees him he has fallen suddenly, totally, in love with Helena. Helena's nightmare is subtler: she gets what she wants, Demetrius's love. But it too is so sudden and so total that she rejects it as a bad joke. The mortals are the playthings of a supernatural power, the fairies who have drugged the men with love-juice, and Oberon plans for Helena not a recip-rocal, satisfying love but a mere reversal of the roles of pursuer and pursued: 'Ere he do leave this grove / Thou shalt fly him, and he shall seek thy love' (II.i.245–46). As identities in *What the Butler Saw* are fluid, one reason for Puck's misapplication of the love-juice is that to him one Athenian man looks like another. The drugs in Orton make the patients groggy and malleable, while Puck's flower releases in the men a manic, single-minded erotic energy; but in both cases the drug produces not liberty but an entrapment of the will. The one love-relationship that seems to be consummated in the forest is that of Titania and the transformed Bottom. But she too is drugged, and while she expresses extravagant affection for him he is simply polite to her. When he makes it clear that he would rather be back in Athens, her response – 'Out of this wood do not desire to go. / Thou shalt remain here, whether thou wilt or no' (III.i.146–47) – turns the wood, like Orton's clinic, into a trap. She leads him to her bower, presumably for sex, but the sensual experiences that really interest him centre on food: 'I could munch your good dry oats . . . . Good hay, sweet hay, hath no fellow' (IV.i.31–33). Coming out of the love-drug, Titania recoils: 'O, how mine eyes do loathe his visage now!' (IV.i.78).

The forest is a place not of free love but of comically misdirected, one-sided love. The pervasive references to the moon bring hints of madness, and Demetrius puns on an Elizabethan word for 'mad' when he calls himself 'wood within this wood' (II.i.192). There is also, as in *Private Lives* and *Heartbreak House*, a regression to childhood. Though Helena appeals to her pure, loving schoolgirl friendship with Hermia (III.ii.198–216), we are closer to real childishness when the women start hurling insults at each other, Hermia calling Helena 'thou painted maypole' and Helena retorting in kind: 'She was a vixen when she went to school; / And though she be but little, she is fierce' (III.ii.296, 324–25). All of this is comedy for the audience; but in the anger with which the women accuse each other – and the men – of mockery, we sense the pain from which the comedy is detaching us; it is no fun to be on the receiving end of a joke.

With an audience's (and a trickster's) detachment from the mischief he has caused, Puck calls the lovers' ordeal a 'fond pageant' (III.ii.114); Oberon promises to detach the lovers from their experience by letting them see it as a dream (III.ii.370–1); and dream and play are equated in Puck's epilogue, where the whole play becomes the audience's dream. The actors' words turn the stage into a wood, as in *Two Angry Women* they create impenetrable darkness: but Peter Quince, preparing his rehearsal, turns the wood back into a stage: 'This green plot shall be our stage, this hawthorn brake our tiring-house' (III.i.3–4). Pointing (presumably) to the actual stage and tiring-house, he uncreates illusion. Once again, the second world is consciously theatrical. It also blurs into the normal world at the end of the play. The presence of the fairies has in large measure created the wood for us; when they unexpectedly take over the stage in the last scene their words tell us they are in the palace, but our eyes may tell us we are back in the wood. Our confusion matches that of the lovers, who as they wake from their night in the forest feel suspended between dream and reality. Significantly, it is Demetrius who wonders if they are really awake: 'It seems to me / That yet we sleep, we dream' (IV.i.192–93). It is Demetrius who will be under the drug for the rest of his life. Yet the drug can also be seen as simply restoring a past reality (he used to love Helena before he switched to Hermia). Is he asleep or awake, drugged or in love? Helena's words capture the double-edged quality of the experience: 'I have found Demetrius like a jewel, / Mine own, and not mine own' (IV.i.190–91).

There is also something in the forest experience that is not to be spoken of.[23] Bottom has a recollection of being 'there is no man can tell what' (IV.i.206–7) and when he returns to his companions, he is torn between his natural garrulousness – 'I will tell you everything' – and a new reticence – 'Not a word of me' (IV.ii.29–32). The reticence wins. We hear no more of the ballad he wanted Peter Quince to write of his dream. The lovers promise to recount their dreams, but we never hear them do it, and we do not know exactly what they have told Theseus that triggers his scepticism about 'antique fables' and 'fairy toys' (V.i.3). Have they blamed their experiences on the fairies? If so, they had every right, but no reason: during the experience itself they had no evidence of the supernatural, and they never imagined it as an explanation. The men have had their loyalties inexplicably wiped clean in a moment, and just as inexplicably restored. The women have undergone betrayal and mockery; they have all fired insults and accusations at each other. Throughout the last act the men say nothing of their forest experience, and the women, who had the worst of it, say nothing at all. At the end of *What the Butler Saw* Dr Prentice advises Sergeant Match, 'we have been instrumental in uncovering a number of remarkable peccadilloes today. I'm sure you'll co-operate in keeping them out of the papers?' (II.p.448) and Match, who at this point is wearing a leopard-skin dress and holding the severed penis of a statue of Sir Winston Churchill, readily agrees. The mortals of *A Midsummer Night's Dream* are equally reluctant to discuss what for the audience has been rich comic confusion, and for them, a brush with nightmare. They may be able to distance it as a dream, an experience not in their normal lives but in the wood; but as the fairies remind us when they fill the stage as soon as the mortals leave for bed, the wood can be anywhere.

## Making the familiar strange: *Black Comedy*

It is not necessary to take a journey to find oneself in another place. An ordinary location – a city, a house, a room – can be transformed and produce the dislocations of reality we associate with Bunburying in the country and confusion in the woods. In Oliver Goldsmith's *She Stoops to Conquer* (1773) a mischievous lie by Tony Lumpkin turns Mr Hardcastle's country house into a country inn. In a relationship we shall examine more fully in Chapter Six, the mistake allows Kate Hardcastle to Bunbury without leaving home. She passes herself off as the inn's barmaid, testing the true nature of her intended husband Charles Marlow; her disguise in turn frees Marlow from the inhibitions he feels with women of his own class and lets him take the liberty of the second world to make confident sexual advances to her. Goldsmith also reveals some embarrassing truths about class when Marlow, taking his future father-in-law for an innkeeper, treats him with extraordinary rudeness, ordering him about, rejecting his menu, and ignoring his attempts at friendly conversation. (People still treat professional hosts as they would never dream of treating amateur ones.) Marlow, like Gilbert's characters, is revealing a side of his nature he would normally conceal, and when the truth comes out he is humiliated.

In Shakespeare's *The Comedy of Errors* (c.1590) Antipholus of Syracuse is surrounded by people who seem to have known him for years: he has a home and a wife, everyone knows his name, and people freely offer him merchandise (IV.iii.1–11). The trouble is, he's in Ephesus, a town he has never visited in his life before.[24] When he agrees to play along – 'I'll say as they say' (II.ii.214) – he is like one of Rance's patients agreeing to go along with the doctor's fantasy. He is also surrendering, by his own interpretation, to sorcery (IV.iii.10–11). As for him the friendliness of the strange town is eerie, for his brother Antipholus of Ephesus his home town, where he has a wife, a household, friends and business associates, is suddenly a nightmare of alienation where he is shut out of his house, arrested for debt, and locked up as a madman. For one brother, the strange becomes unsettlingly familiar; for the other, the familiar becomes strange. The key this time is a blurring of identity: the brothers, ignorant of each others' presence in the town, have the same appearance and the same name. It is the names, above all, that cause the trouble: as in Orton identity dissolves, here the names that ought to distinguish one identity from another have conflated them.

In *Black Comedy* (1965) Peter Shaffer turns an ordinary room into a second world by a simple theatrical trick. The play begins in pitch darkness, with the young sculptor Brindsley Miller and his fiancée Carol having a normal conversation, unaware of the dark. Then the record they have been listening to grinds to a stop, all the lights come on, and they start groping blindly about the set. There has been a power cut. For the characters the light–dark reversal makes the familiar strange. For the audience, once the lights come up the room becomes a stage and the play can begin. Shaffer borrowed the device from a Peking Opera scene in which a warrior and a bandit fight in pitch darkness on a fully lit stage, a scene he found 'wildly funny and wildly dangerous'.[25] He is also reproducing the conditions of English theatre up to the mid-nineteenth century: in the dark countryside of *Two Angry Women of Abingdon* or the dark rooms used for mistaken-identity sexual assignations in Restoration comedies like *The Country Wife* and *The Plain Dealer*, the characters could see nothing and the audience could see everything. The room itself has a double character, since the furnishings combine Brindsley's own playful bric-a-brac with elegant items stolen from his absent neighbour Harold (gay, fussy and insanely jealous of his possessions – the play deals unashamedly in stereotypes). After Harold's unexpected return Brindsley desperately tries to switch the furniture back, resulting in a farcical double action as characters chat obliviously while Brindsley carries furniture about, inches away from them. At one point a character sits on what he thinks is the chair he just vacated, to find it has mysteriously become a rocking chair, which tips him on the floor (p.168).

This is a critical evening for Brindsley. He is expecting the German millionaire Georg Bamberger to come and look at his work; he is also expecting Colonel Melkett, Carol's stuffy father, on the theory that if Bamberger buys some of Brindsley's work, Daddypegs (as Carol calls him) will be sufficiently impressed to permit their marriage. A favourable reaction from Bamberger could also make Brindsley's career; and for a while it looks as though the dream has come true, as a visitor with a German accent, groping about his sculptures in the dark, proclaims, 'this boy is a genius . . . . *Wunderbar!* . . . You should charge immense sums for work like this, Mr Miller' (p.188). This is Bamberger as he ought to be, except that it's not Bamberger; as Brindsley finds out after a few minutes in which he thinks he is made for life, it's Schuppanzigh from the Electricity Board, come to mend the fuse.

Another unexpected visitor is Brindsley's ex-girlfriend Clea, who enters unnoticed and sits in the dark for a long time listening to herself being insulted by Brindsley, Harold and Carol, as Brindsley plays down the true length and importance of their relationship. He then recognizes her with one touch on her bottom (p.178), and tries desperately to conceal her from the other characters. She is Brindsley's past come to life, and in sabotaging his relationship with Carol she disrupts the status quo, including his marriage plans; but the relationship she restores in its place has a lot more to it than his relationship with Carol. In *As You Like It* the restoration of the past meant the recovery of humane social values. What Clea offers is creative disruption: fun, honesty and sex. She promises to wait for Brindsley in bed, telling him that if he doesn't go along with the idea she will come downstairs and expose him. When she does come down she is wearing only a pyjama top. The second world becomes a place of sexual licence where clothes are shed and (as in a breeches part) the actress gets to show her legs. Clea also uses the licence of the second world to adopt a new identity as the cleaning lady Mrs Punnet. Speaking in '*a cockney voice of great antiquity*' she calls up incriminating memories of parties Brindsley used to hold in this room: 'Gin bottles all over the floor! Bras and panties in the sink!' (pp.193–94). On being told that Brindsley is engaged, Mrs Punnet makes her own assumptions about the lucky lady: 'Well, I never! So you've got him at last! Well, done, Miss Clea!' (p.195). By the end of the play, having set the record straight for the others about their previous relationship – in her own voice, quietly and seriously: 'Four years, in this room' (p.195) – she gets him again.

Clea has always insisted on the truth. Early in the play Brindsley describes her as 'Very honest. Very clever. And just about as cosy as a steel razor-blade' (p.145); even as they come together again he calls their previous relationship 'four years of nooky with Torquemada' (p.199). It is Clea who turns the room into a place of truth-telling as, picking up Mrs Punnet's reference to Brindsley's fondness for kinky games, she commands, 'All right! Kinky game time! . . . . Let's all play Guess the Hand!' (p.196). The others try to move away, and their fear is justified. The Colonel has already taken Clea's hand, thinking it belongs to his daughter Carol. Carol, taking Harold's hand, thinks it is Brindsley; Harold takes Brindsley's hand and identifies it correctly. Carol, at the evidence that Harold's claim is better than hers, on top of the evidence that her own father – who has made a grand display of defending her – does not recognize her, becomes hysterical.

The darkened room has already been a place where inhibitions are released. Brindsley has carelessly referred to Carol's 'monster father' to be greeted by a chilly 'Good evenin'' from the unseen Colonel (p.156). Harold's recognition of Brindsley's hand in the game is anticipated, when, thinking they are alone, he takes his hand and murmurs, 'It's rather cosy in the dark, isn't it?' (p.158). Brindsley's neighbour Miss Furnival, a prim, teetotal spinster, is given the wrong drink and gets roaring drunk. In her final hysterical breakdown she reveals that the ordinary world is for her a place of nightmare: 'Prams! Prams! Prams – in the supermarket!' (p.198). For Brindsley the nightmare is in this now strange room. Shaffer's note on our first sight of him specifies that Brindsley and the room deteriorate together: '*as things slide into disaster for him, his crisp, detached shape degenerates progressively into sweat and rumple – just as the elegance of the room gives way relentlessly to its usual near-slum appearance*' (pp.146–47). In the end the Colonel and Harold are hunting him in the dark with sharp metal prongs wrested from his own sculpture as Carol cries, 'Get him, Daddy! Get him! Get him!' (p.204) and the real millionaire arrives and falls through the trap door. But at least, as the disaster mounts, he is clinging to Clea.

As divine or supernatural interventions touch other second worlds we have examined, Brindsley's complaint that the gods are against him inspires Clea, on the stairs, to splash vodka on the people below (pp.191–92). But the real *deus ex machina* is Schuppanzigh, who at the end of the play, having fixed the fuse, proclaims, 'So! Here's now an end to your troubles! Like Jehovah in the Sacred Testament, I give you the most miraculous gift of the Creation! Light!' (p.206). He throws a switch and plunges the stage into darkness. It is the last reversal in a play full of reversals. As Clea puts it, 'It is a very odd room, isn't it? It's like a magic dark room, where everything happens the wrong way round. Rain falls indoors, the Daily comes at night, and turns in a second from a nice maid to a nasty mistress' (p.196).

This very odd room exemplifies the double-edged nature of the second world in comedy, a place of licence and nightmare, of confusion and truth-telling, and the disconcerting closeness of the second world to what passes for normal life. The price of escape, of the freedom to leave society behind, to make love or to Bunbury, is the removal of familiar landmarks – identity, old loyalties and relationships, the truths one thinks one lives by, the saving lies that keep relationships going – and a rewriting of reality that can induce panic, even the fear of madness. The anxiety can be covered by passing it off as a dream, or as someone else's idea of a joke. Characters in *The Comedy of Errors* and *A Midsummer Night's Dream* constantly assume, with varying degrees of indignation, that the others are joking. The victims of Gilbert's Palace of Truth accuse each other of joking, and themselves of dreaming (II.p.54, III.pp.69–70). There are typical points of irritation in *Black Comedy* when the Colonel asks Brindsley, 'Look, young man, are you trying to be funny?' (p.173) and calls him 'Mad as the south wind!' (p.183). If it is not comedy, it is madness. The deep abnormality of the second world leads to brushes, if only in caricature form, with the supernatural or the divine. When comedy confronts something outside the normal run of society it deals with it by becoming intensely theatrical, getting it under control through conscious artifice: the flamboyant jokes about death, the performance quality that touches so many loners. Its recurring insistence on the theatricality of the second world is of a piece with this. The lovers in the wood near Athens are acting out a pageant for Puck's (and our) amusement; Orton's clinic is a stage set, and so is Shaffer's very odd room. But the ease with which that room becomes odd, simply by a trick of the light, embodies another comic anxiety: how close the normal lies to something quite other.

# 5

# PARENTS AND CHILDREN

## Disputed authority

When in *The Importance of Being Earnest* (1895) Jack confesses, 'I have lost both my parents' (I.538) he precipitates a crisis. The news that he was 'born, or at any rate bred, in a hand-bag' (I.570) and sired by a railway ticket leaves him in a social limbo, wrecks his marriage prospects, and prompts Lady Bracknell to advise him 'to produce at any rate one parent of either sex, before the season is quite over' (I.586–87). The journey to the second world, we have seen, triggers anxiety by removing the social landmarks of identity and relationship. Among such landmarks, parents are of central importance, conferring social identity and social position. In *Twelfth Night* (c.1600) one of the first signals of Olivia's growing interest in Cesario is her question, 'What is thy parentage?' (I.v.272).

Petruchio begins his wooing of Katharine in *The Taming of the Shrew* (c.1594) by making contact at the paternal level: 'I know her father, though I know not her, / And he knew my deceasèd father well' (I.ii.100–1). Baptista confirms this: 'I know him well. You are welcome for his sake' (II.i.70). As Petruchio's madcap wooing heads for a conventional conclusion about the authority of husbands, it is grounded in an equally conventional acknowledgement of the importance of fathers. The same factor operates at a more psychological level for Katharine. Her feud with her sister Bianca seems rooted in jealousy over their father's favour (II.i.32), and the deprivation she endures at Petruchio's country house reminds her of the more civilized order she has left: 'Beggars that come unto my father's door / Upon entreaty have a present alms' (IV.iii.4–5). Petruchio plays on the fact that in the mad other world he has created for her, she wants to go home. Her reward for obedience is a return trip to her father's house; her punishment for disobedience is to have the trip put off.

Yet it is one of the well-worn conventions of comedy, and of theorizing about comedy, that parental authority is not a source of stability or comfort but an obstacle to be overcome. Northrop Frye describes 'a comic Oedipus situation' in which a young man has to defeat a rival, 'usually the father (*senex*)' to win 'the girl of his choice'; Ludwig Jekels, in a psychological reading of comedy that sees it coming out of tragedy, finds 'a mechanism of inversion' through which the guilt

94

that in tragedy is borne by the son is in comedy transferred to the father.[1] Yet in practice, as we shall see, the conflicts in English comedy are more often between fathers and daughters, reflecting the fact that daughters were more likely than sons to be coerced into marriage;[2] there are examples of son and father wooing the same girl, but not so many as Frye's generalization would suggest. More typically, the daughter wants one man and the father insists she marry another.

In the seventeenth century, according to Michael MacDonald, 'Legal practice and public opinion were firmly against forced marriages . . . and even among the aristocracy, parents were becoming more concerned about their children's happiness.'[3] The social reality seems to have been, for the most part, a sensible give-and-take between the parents' right of initiative and the children's right of refusal. Not much drama, however, can be extracted from sensible compromises, and comedy sharpens and stylizes the issue by imagining conflicts between stubbornly authoritarian parents and stubbornly romantic children. In so doing it plays on the anxiety inherent in a situation in which, though compromise was the ideal, conflict was always possible; it derives comic energy from putting the conflict in an extreme form, and formal satisfaction from a simple solution, the defeat of the parents. Alan Macfarlane sees a generational conflict on the issue of marriage, a conflict between 'individual emotion (psychology) and long-term interests (economics)', running from the middle ages to the end of the nineteenth century; he claims, 'Much of the greatest literature . . . was generated by this very tension.'[4] Legally, the balance shifted towards the parents with the Marriage Act of 1753, which tightened the conditions for a valid marriage and enforced parental consent for those under twenty-one.[5] There is, we shall see, an equivalent shift in comedy: while parents well into the seventeenth century simply have to swallow defeat, graciously or not, in the eighteenth century there is far greater respect for their rights and feelings. This is a case in which comedy seems to stay in tune with the spirit of its time, and to shift with it.

## A Midsummer Night's Dream

In earlier comedies the defeat of parental authority entails a period of confusion in which, with or without a literal journey to a second world, familiar landmarks are removed. If parents preside over normal social reality, then disrupting that reality is a useful stage towards defeating them. This is the pattern of popular comedies like Henry Porter's *The Two Angry Women of Abingdon* (c.1588) and the anonymous *The Merry Devil of Edmonton* (c.1603), in which parents who try to block the matches their children want are defeated after a good deal of confused scrambling in the dark. It is the ostensible pattern of Shakespeare's *A Midsummer Night's Dream* (c.1595), in which coercive parental authority is seen at its most extreme in the figure of Egeus, who invokes 'the ancient privilege of Athens' (I.i.41) against his daughter Hermia: if she does not bend to his will and marry Demetrius, he will have her put to death. It is Theseus who recalls the third option: she could retire to a convent. Egeus wants her obedient, or dead. Egeus is crabbed and cantankerous;

Theseus speaks in gentle, reasonable tones but in so doing he reveals the grim thinking that lies behind the law:

> What say you, Hermia? Be advised, fair maid.
> To you your father should be as a god –
> One that composed your beauties, yea, and one
> To whom you are but as a form in wax
> By him imprinted, and within his power
> To leave the figure or disfigure it.
>
> (I.i.46–51)

This is the dark side of the security that comes from having parents to guarantee one's identity: an absolute demand that Hermia can cope with only by running away.

Egeus can be brushed off as a stock type, Frye's *senex*, And even to an Elizabethan audience Theseus's view of parental power might have seemed a caricature. While the contemporary custom of children kneeling to ask their parents' blessing suggests a god-like authority,[6] in practice 'obedience' seems to have meant a due regard for parents' feelings, not the total submission Theseus asks for; the laws of Athens are not the laws of Elizabethan England.[7] After the night in the forest Theseus forgets about the law and reduces the issue to Egeus's demands, which he dismisses in a line: 'Egeus, I will overbear your will' (IV.i.178). Then Egeus himself disappears: he is missing from Act Five, and there is no reference to him. Or rather, that is the case in the Quarto texts on which most modern editions are based; in the Folio he returns to assume Philostrate's part, objecting to *Pyramus and Thisbe* as he objected to Hermia's love for Lysander. He may now seem a toothless menace, but he is still growling. And what are we to make of his invisibility in the Quarto? Does it really suggest a new world free from such authority as he represents? As Egeus is absent in Act Five, Hermia and Helena, who have had much to say for themselves earlier in the play, are completely silent. Athens is a world dominated, conventionally enough, by men. While Hermia's problem is more dramatic, we should note that the first reference to Helena is to 'Nedar's daughter, Helena' (I.i.107). The speaker is Lysander: even the younger generation think this way. When the court party finds the lovers asleep on the ground it is Egeus who helps draw them back to daylight reality by naming them, using his power to confer identity: while he gives the men their proper names, Hermia is simply 'my daughter' and Helena is 'old Nedar's Helena' (IV.i.127–29). One of the landmarks Hermia uses as she gropes her way back from dream to reality is the sight of 'my father' (IV.i.195). The women's problems have been solved, but they return in the end to the male-dominated world in which those problems began, in which their identities are conferred by their fathers, and they sit through the final act in silence. It may be that the removal of Egeus is the removal of an irritant, whose result is not to transform that world but to make it acceptable.

There is a glimpse of an alternative authority in Lysander's plan to flee to the house of his dowager aunt who 'respects me as her only son' and under whose protection 'the sharp Athenian law / Cannot pursue us' (I.i.160–63). This glimpse of a protecting maternal figure to set against Egeus is countered by Theseus's reference to the slow-waning moon, delaying his wedding night, as 'a stepdame or a dowager / Long withering out a young man's revenue' (I.i.5–6). The play debates the authority of mother figures no less than father figures (Titania's claim on the Indian boy is the issue that splits the fairy world), and Theseus's view of the malignant older woman suppressing a young man is one we shall meet again.

## Arbitrary power: *Love for Love*

Parental authority may in theory be part of the social order at which comedy aims, but it is an authority that easily turns repressive and when it does it becomes the spring that drives the comic plot, the obstacle to be overcome. When parents try to prostitute their children in mercenary marriages – Yellowhammer in Thomas Middleton's *A Chaste Maid in Cheapside* (1613), Overreach in Philip Massinger's *A New Way to Pay Old Debts* (c.1625) – they are part of the dehumanizing reduction of social life we examined in Chapter Two: children are traded as goods in the market. This comes close to literal prostitution in the case of Overreach, who prepares his daughter for meeting the man of his choice by telling her to 'kiss close' (III.ii.118) and if he shows interest to invite him to a couch. The authority such fathers abuse is (as Theseus's inital support for Egeus suggests) virtually a political one. In Samuel Foote's *The Minor* (1760) Richard Wealthy, having cast off his daughter for not marrying the man of his choice, declares, 'I consider families as a smaller kind of kingdoms, and would have disobedience in the one as severely punished as rebellion in the other' (I.p.53). This authority is set against English liberty in Susanna Centlivre's *The Busybody* (1709), where Sir Jealous Traffick keeps his daughter locked up on principles he has learned in Spain.

If fathers have a quasi-political authority, mothers have control at a physical, sexual level. Theseus's complaint about the dowager moon 'long withering out a young man's revenue' is given sexual significance through the Widow Blackacre in Wycherley's *The Plain Dealer* (1676) and Agatha Posket in Pinero's *The Magistrate* (1885). Blackacre, whose constant lawsuits show an obsession with her own power, will not allow her son Jerry financial independence, and blocks his first sexual experiments by keeping him out of the maids' garret (IV.pp.472–73).[8] Agatha Posket lies about her son Cis's age in the process of lying about her own, not just making him too young but putting him on the wrong side of puberty. Socially he is a child, but he has the body and appetites of a young man. Agatha watches in agony as other women, not knowing how indiscreet they are being, kiss and fondle him. Cis, when he learns the truth, complains, 'this is a frightful sell for a fellow . . . . I always thought there was something wrong with me' (III.i.291–93) – as though he has taken the signs of puberty for a strange disease.

Refusing to let their sons grow up, these blocking mothers deny the renewal of life. The dead father of Nancy Lovely in Susanna Centlivre's *A Bold Stroke for a Wife*

(1718) takes this denial to extremes. He has framed a will that seems to make her marriage impossible, leaving her in charge of four guardians of opposed natures, all of whom must give their consent. As a former servant of his puts it, there is more here than a refusal to let his daughter grow up: 'He hated posterity, you must know, and wished the world were to expire with himself. He used to swear if she had been a boy, he would have qualified him for the opera' (I.i.78–80).

Nancy's father is a classic instance of the dead hand held over the living. Sir Sampson Legend in Congreve's *Love for Love* (1695), in whom the figure of the blocking parent finds perhaps its fullest embodiment, is vigorously, monstrously alive. In the Hobbesian war of all against all, his vitality threatens to crush the lives around him. He sees himself as 'of a long-lived race . . . of your patriarchs, I, . . . fellows that the flood could not wash away' (V.p.297). He plays on his name – 'your Sampsons were strong dogs from the beginning' (V.p.300) – and in his rivalry with his son Valentine for the hand of Angelica he boasts so much of his continuing sexual prowess that she has to warn him, 'You'll spend your estate before you come to it' (V.p.299). His favourite oath is 'Body o' me', as in 'Body o' me, I have made a cuckold of a king, and the present majesty of Bantam is the issue of these loins' (II.p.240). The play's other old man, Foresight, is impotent in every sense, and his obsession with omens shows that the best he can do is reduce his sense of helplessness to a system. Sir Sampson is supremely confident in his own power, symbolized by his still-vigorous body.

He says of his relations with Valentine, 'What, I warrant my son thought nothing belonged to a father but forgiveness and affection; no authority, no correction, no arbitrary power' (II.pp.238–39). For an audience with fresh memories of 1688 there is political resonance in that last phrase. To the arbitrary power of the monarch is added the arbitrary power of the creator. Valentine exists because Sir Sampson, like God, chose that he should: 'Did not I beget you? And might not I have chosen whether I would have begot you or not? . . . Did you come a volunteer into the world? Or did I beat up for you with the lawful authority of a parent, and press you to service?' (II.p.243). The act of creation may be God-like (Sir Sampson, like Milton's God, is 'free / To act or not'),[9] but the language is still political. Sir Sampson is a one-man press gang. Valentine counters by seeing his life not as a product of Sir Sampson's will but as a mystery neither of them understands: 'I know no more why I came, than you do why you called me' (II.p.243). But when Sir Sampson commands him to strip to his original nakedness, Valentine makes a further claim:

VALENTINE: My clothes are soon put off; but you must also deprive me of reason, thought, passions, inclinations, affections, appetites, senses, and the huge train of attendants that you begot along with me.
SIR SAMPSON: Body o' me, what a many headed monster have I propagated!

(II.p.243)

Valentine, echoing Shylock's plea, 'Hath not a Jew hands, organs, dimensions, senses, affections, passions?' (III.i.56–57), demands the right to lead a full human life, a demand that staggers his father, who sees his son as merely a creature of his own power. His shock is compounded when Valentine's servant Jeremy claims he too has tastes and appetites: 'These things are unaccountable and unreasonable' (II.p.244). Sir Sampson is astonished not just that his son has an independent life, but that anyone does.

Boasting about his name, Sir Sampson forgot about Delilah. When Angelica defeats him and chooses Valentine, her dismissal of the old man is uncompromising: 'You have not more faults than he has virtues; and 'tis hardly more pleasure to me, that I can make him and myself happy, than that I can punish you.' When Valentine comments, 'If my happiness could receive addition, this kind surprise would make it double' (V.p.310), the kind surprise seems to be the discovery that she despises his father as much as he does. Other comedies may end with a sense of accommodation, embodying the compromises of normal social life. In Shakespeare's *The Merry Wives of Windsor* (c.1600) the Pages accept philosophically Fenton's winning of their daughter Anne and his defeat of their candidates: 'Well, what remedy? Fenton, heaven give thee joy!' (V.v.230). Old Bellair in Etherege's *The Man of Mode* (1676) has like Sir Sampson competed with his son for the same woman (Frye's comic Oedipus situation) but is positively cheerful in defeat. His line, 'Adod, the boy has made a happy choice' (V.ii.400), ends the play. Congreve himself would later soften the ending of *Love for Love*; but as he originally (and I think more truly) wrote it, Sir Sampson storms out in impotent rage: 'Oons, cullied, bubbled, jilted, woman-bobbed at last. – I have not patience' (V.p.311). In the war between the generations there is no compromise, no mercy; Sir Sampson has wanted it that way, and that is what he gets.

## Double parents

In the severity of the Sampson–Valentine conflict, in which nothing less than the nature of human life is at issue (are we just creatures of another's power, or do we have lives of our own?) Congreve probes the anxiety at the root of the common observation that the generations have different interests. He shows what generational conflict looks like stripped of its pieties and compromises: war, virtually to the death. The persistence of the heavy father convention shows the depth of this anxiety. Yet any convention this persistent becomes ripe for parody, and the parody can be a way of lifting the anxiety, as the tyrant becomes a buffoon. Two cases involve martinets who are putty in the hands of women: in Hugh Kelly's *The School for Wives* (1773) General Savage issues military commands to his son on the question of marriage, while being himself henpecked by his mistress; in Dion Boucicault's *Old Heads and Young Hearts* (1844) Colonel Rocket raps out orders to his daughter, who blithely ignores him: 'Hollo! halt – attention! (ROEBUCK *and* KATE *go out, still conversing, without apparently hearing him*)' (II.p.67).

The anxiety is also lifted, and the convention is challenged more directly, by plays that offer opposed models of parenthood, sternness and benevolence. Up to the eighteenth century the theory of parenting recommended severity, though the practice seems to have been more gentle.[10] The eighteenth century put an increasing value on parental benevolence.[11] It also brought a new consciousness of the role parents play in training their children and forming their characters; diaries of the period show a desire to find 'a happy mean between excess severity and excess indulgence.'[12] This new interest in training may account for the popularity throughout the period of comic plots borrowed from Terence's *Adelphi* (*The Brothers*). In Terence's play the stern countryman Dema raises one of his sons on strict principles while the other is raised in a more lenient and easy-going way by Dema's brother Micio, an epicurean town-dweller. Though the strictly raised son appears demure, both boys are in fact good-natured wastrels, suggesting that it does not matter which system is used, boys will be boys. English writers adapting the story generally ignore this conclusion, as they ignore the ironic twist at the end when the curmudgeonly Dema, tired of being unpopular, wins favour by forcing his brother (who has simply spent his money on himself) into expensive acts of generosity. In place of Terence's urbane irony they put a moralizing myth with elements of wish-fulfilment. As early as Thomas Shadwell's *The Squire of Alsatia* (1688), and as late as Richard Cumberland's *The Choleric Man* (1774), the stern father produces an unsatisfactory son (a Blifil-like hypocrite in Shadwell, a loutish rakehell in Cumberland), while the genial substitute father, who unlike the Terentian original is also actively benevolent, produces a good-natured gentleman. The wish-fulfilment works two ways: the softer option works better, and the substitute father is the good one, playing on the childhood fantasy of trading in one's unsatisfactory parents for an improved set.

Opposed theories of childrearing, without the motif of adoption, also figure in Henry Fielding's *The Fathers* (c.1735). Here the convention is briefly questioned, as the indulgent father seems to have raised spoiled children; but his offspring show their true virtue in the crisis of his apparent bankruptcy, while their strictly-reared opposite numbers turn nasty. There is a late variation in H.J. Byron's long-running hit *Our Boys* (1875), whose popularity attests to the continuing fascination of the theme.[13] The vulgar but good-natured Middlewick has raised his son indulgently, and the result is a warm, easy relationship between them; Sir Geoffrey Champneys has raised his son sternly, and meets coldness in return. The differences, however, are more apparent than real: in a reversion to Terence, both boys are in fact equally good-natured; Middlewick expects his generosity to produce absolute obedience (II.p.132), and Champneys is more soft-centred than he looks. The characters start to move in lock step, as both sons defy their fathers and the fathers (after each has taunted the other with the failure of his system) cut them off. Finding the boys living in poverty in London, the fathers try unsuccessfully to maintain the role of stern Roman parent but their true benevolence comes through. The play works with a double image of the father, the strict authority figure who is feared, the benevolent parent who is loved, and creates a wish-fulfilment story in which the first is a performance and the second is the reality.[14] Audiences flocked to see it.

In Elizabeth Inchbald's *Wives as They Were, and Maids as They Are* (1797) the moralizing Mandred rebukes Miss Dorrillon[15] for her extravagance. Her feelings for him puzzle her: though offended by his lectures and his generally morose character, she has a curious, instinctive affection and respect for him. She does not know he is really her father, returned in secret from India. In anticipation of the hand-game in *Black Comedy*, she finds Mandred's hand 'warmer and kinder' than her lover's (III.i.p.47). His sternness goes so far that he allows her to be arrested for debt, but his body language betrays him: '*He walks proudly across the room, then stops, takes out his handkerchief, throws his head into it, and is going off*' (IV.iii.p.58). In the end he bails her out. Here, as in *Our Boys*, the tyrant and the benevolent father are the same man.[16]

Sir Anthony Absolute, in Richard Brindsley Sheridan's *The Rivals* (1775), is a broadly comic version of the double parent. As his name implies, he insists on his own authority in a manner that recalls Sir Sampson Legend. He has happy memories of training up his son Jack: 'in their younger days, 'twas "Jack, do this" – if he demurred – I knocked him down' (I.ii.279–81). He now insists that his son marry the woman he has chosen for him, not only sight unseen but without knowing the lady's name. His view of the lady is 'Odds life, Sir! if you have the estate, you must take it with the live stock on it, as it stands' (II.i.374–76). Jack, assuming he is stuck in a conventional comic plot, imagines the lady must be 'some mass of ugliness'; fathers, after all, never know best. Sir Anthony retorts, 'the lady shall be as ugly as I choose', and goes on to construct a fantasy of a monster bride (II.i.406–14). In fact the lady is Lydia Languish, with whom Jack is already carrying on a secret courtship. His father is bullying him into marrying the woman he already loves. With this discovery tyranny becomes benevolence, and Jack turns himself into a parody of the pious, obedient children of eighteenth-century comedy, indifferent to his father's account of Lydia's true appeal so long as his father's will is done. Sir Anthony, who in his youth was 'a bold intriguer, and a gay companion' who married for love (II.i.450–51), is livid: 'Why, you unfeeling, insensible puppy, I despise you. When I was of your age, such a description would have made me fly like a rocket!' (III.i.71–73). Sheridan is writing late enough in the tradition that he has two stock conventions to parody: the blocking parents of earlier comedy and the pious, obedient children of the eighteenth century. He upends both traditions, and produces his own mischievous variation on the fantasy of the double parent, tyrannical and benevolent.

## She Stoops to Conquer

Goldsmith's *She Stoops to Conquer* (1773) develops the eighteenth-century interest in different models of child-rearing by contrasting Hardcastle's relations with his daughter Kate and Mrs Hardcastle's relations with her son Tony. Hardcastle stands for the old ways: he lives in an old-fashioned house, prides himself on his old-fashioned tastes and manners, and regales the company with old, inaccurate war-stories. He acts as a benevolent patriarch for the local community: 'Half the differences of the parish are adjusted in this very parlour' (II.i.219–20). His tastes are not Kate's – she would rather live like a fashionable woman of the town – but they have struck a balance. In the morning she pleases herself by dressing like a lady, paying and receiving visits; in the evening she pleases him by wearing a plain housemaid's dress. She has, if anything, internalized his authority: when he finds her in the plain dress though 'there was no great occasion', she comments, 'I find such a pleasure, sir, in obeying your commands, that I take care to observe them without ever debating their propriety' (III.i.10–13). Her obedience is rewarded when the dress becomes a disguise that allows her to catch her intended husband Marlow off guard and win him on her own terms.

In keeping with their compromise over dress, there is a genial give-and-take between father and daughter, quite unlike the hard work she has with Marlow. The match is Hardcastle's idea, springing from his longstanding friendship with Marlow's father. But Hardcastle is not disposed to insist on the interest of the older generation at the expense of couple's happiness: he and Kate agree to accept the possibility that it might not work out (I.i.141–47). They also agree to disagree about Marlow's modesty: Hardcastle sees it as his chief virtue, Kate as the chief stumbling block. In the end Hardcastle comes round to her way of thinking, finding Marlow's modesty excessive and encouraging him to be more open (V.i.57–59). He even tells Marlow not to be such a prude: 'girls like to be played with, and rumpled a little too sometimes' (V.i.53–54). Though she has not put it quite that way, Kate has made it clear from the beginning that part of her interest in Marlow is physical, and Hardcastle, talking man to man, sees nothing wrong with that. By the same token, Kate sees as part of Marlow's 'merit' his respect for his father's authority (IV.i.239–45). When she allows the fathers to eavesdrop on their final interview she is sacrificing the privacy lovers expect not just to comic effect but to the principle that parents have a legitimate interest in their children's affairs.

While they can acknowledge each other's interests, Kate and her father can also disagree, even argue, without souring their relations or losing their mutual respect. We see this when they compare their first impressions of Marlow, Hardcastle finding him obnoxiously impudent (Marlow thought he was an innkeeper) and Kate finding him physically attractive but maddeningly shy:

MISS HARDCASTLE:  And yet there may be many good qualities under that first appearance.

HARDCASTLE:  Ay, when a girl finds a fellow's outside to her taste, she then sets about guessing the rest of his furniture. With her, a smooth face stands for good sense, and a genteel figure for every virtue.

MISS HARDCASTLE:  I hope, sir, a conversation begun with a compliment to my good sense won't end with a sneer at my understanding?

HARDCASTLE:  Pardon me, Kate. But if young Mr Brazen can find the art of reconciling contradictions, he may please us both, perhaps.

MISS HARDCASTLE:  And as one of us must be mistaken, what if we go to make
  further discoveries?
HARDCASTLE:  Agreed. But depend on't I'm in the right.
MISS HARDCASTLE:  And depend on't I'm not much in the wrong.

(III.i.70–84)

Kate is disposed to have her own way, and Hardcastle is disposed to lecture. But when he steps out of line he accepts her correction, and in the last analysis they treat each other as equals. When at the end of the play Hardcastle assures Marlow, 'if she makes as good a wife as she has a daughter, I don't believe you'll ever repent of your bargain' (V.iii.160–62), he does not just mean, as a more conventional father might have it, that as an obedient daughter she will be an obedient wife. Rather she has shown, in partnership with her father, that she can take a relationship originally based on authority and deference, open it out, and humanize it.

In this relationship Goldsmith dramatizes the compromises of family life that comedy generally suppresses in favour of more absolute, stylized relations. If the social historians cited earlier are correct,[17] he is letting us glimpse what went on in normal life (on a good day), whatever the prevailing theories were. Mrs Hardcastle, on the other hand, is the nurturing mother turned rancid, another version of the double parent: this time there is tyranny beneath the caring. She insists on seeing Tony as an invalid in constant need of her attention (I.i.54–60). Like Widow Blackacre and Agatha Posket, she lies about her son's age, partly to preserve the fantasy of her own youth – unlike Hardcastle she has no devotion to the past, and tries to keep up with London fashions – and partly to prevent him from growing up. When he complains of having been purged and dosed all his life, there is a flash of hostility in her retort, 'Wasn't it all for your good, viper?' (II.i.591). Tony in turn sees her treatment as indistinguishable from persistent beating: 'If I'm to have any good, let it come of itself; not to keep dinging, dinging it into one so' (II.i.594–95). When he works against her in her role as blocking parent trying to stop the marriage of Constance and Hastings, he presents his disloyalty as the result of his training: 'all the parish says you have spoiled me, and so you may take the fruits on't.' Hardcastle, overhearing, finds 'morality . . . in his reply' (V.ii.137–40). There is no reconciliation of mother and son to match the harmony of father and daughter: just rebellion against a tyranny that masqueraded as benevolence.[18]

### Plotting and piety: *False Delicacy* and *The Conscious Lovers*

The resistance to parental authority dictated by the stock comic plot is complicated, especially in the eighteenth century, by a respect for parental feeling that is part of the culture. Sterling, in David Garrick and George Colman the Elder's *The Clandestine Marriage* (1766), regularly expresses natural sentiments, but in the end what interests him is money. He rejects Lovewell as a suitor for his daughter Fanny on the grounds that while 'You're a good boy, to be sure – I have a great value for you . . . . There's no *stuff* in the case, no money, Lovewell!' (I.i.p.118). When Sir John Melvil, who was to marry Fanny's older sister, proposes to marry Fanny instead, Sterling is at first indignant at the switch, protesting he is not running a slave market; but when he learns the new proposal is financially better he changes his tune: 'it is no more than transferring so much stock, you know' (III.i.p.142). We might expect a comedy to show such a character no quarter. But when at the end of the play Fanny's secret marriage to Lovewell is discovered, her chief emotion is shame at having deceived her father: 'Indeed, sir, it is impossible to conceive the tortures I have already endured in consequence of my disobedience.' He refuses at first to forgive her, for fear that 'other silly girls' will follow her example; Lovewell responds that the grief she has suffered will actually be a deterrent (V.ii.pp.166–67). The plot of the play is the deserved defeat of a blocking father; the sentiment of the play is a warning against the shame of filial disobedience.

In Hugh Kelly's *False Delicacy* (1768) the conflict of conventional plotting and pious feeling is particularly sharp. Colonel Rivers wants his daughter Theodora to marry Sidney, while she is in love with Sir Harry Newburgh and plans to elope with him. Cecil, the play's *raisonneur*, comes down on both sides of the question. He rebukes Sir Harry for his planned elopement, thinking of the feelings of the family (II.i.p.26). At the same time he admits the Colonel 'has no right to force her inclinations; 'tis equally cruel and unjust' (II.i.p.27). In that spirit, having rebuked the elopement he plans to assist it. Theodora's maid Sally, speaking from within the old comic tradition, describes the Colonel – with some justice – in terms that would apply to Egeus and Sir Sampson Legend: 'there isn't so obstinate, so perverse, and so peevish an old devil in all England'. But Theodora, who has every right to agree, takes offence: 'I would rather every thing was discovered this minute, than hear him mention'd with so impudent a familiarity by his servants' (III.i.p.37). Even as she sets out to meet Sir Harry, she is torn: 'An elopement even from a tyrannical father, has something in it which must shock a delicate mind' (IV.ii.p.60).

Colonel Rivers gets his way by playing on that delicacy. As Theodora waits for Sir Harry, he suddenly enters, with a flash of melodrama: Sally shrieks and runs off, Theodora exclaims, 'My father!' and Rivers replies, 'Yes, Theodora, your poor, abandon'd, miserable father' (IV.ii.p.61). Instead of threatening to lock her up or send her to a convent, he tells her to follow her own will, gives her the £20,000 he had promised her at her marriage, and lays on the guilt: 'Since, therefore, neither duty nor discretion, a regard for my peace, nor a solicitude for your own welfare, are able to detain you, go to this man, who has taught you to obliterate the sentiments of nature, and gain'd a ready way to your heart, by expressing a contempt for your father. Go to him boldly, my child, and laugh at the pangs which tear this unhappy bosom' (IV.ii.p.63). The upshot is that when Sir Harry comes for her she refuses to go. Urged to consider her own happiness, she replies, 'What a wretch must the woman be, who can dream of happiness, while she wounds the bosom of a father?' – at which Cecil exclaims, 'What a noble girl!' (IV.ii.p.65). To a cynical mind it would appear that Rivers has found a clever way to exercise his tyranny, and that Theodora's delicacy is an example of the false delicacy of the title. But Cecil, as the play's *raisonneur*, blocks that response with his admiration of Theodora's piety.

Plot and sentiment are in stubborn conflict. The maid Sally, who has aided the lovers in the traditional manner, threatens to give notice. The dilemma is resolved when the unwanted suitor Sidney, whose affections are otherwise engaged, declines Theodora's hand and delivers a lecture against enforced marriages. Plot and sentiment are then realigned and the Colonel, back in the wrong, is reduced to comic bluster: 'I won't put myself in a passion about it. – I'll tear the fellow piece-meal. – Zounds! I don't know what I'll do' (V.i.p.71). In the end he cools down, accepts his defeat with a good grace, and declares himself 'not only satisfied, but charm'd with Mr Sidney's behaviour' (V.i.p.79). This is, we might note, the tribute of one man to another, and Theodora gets what she wants when the men are satisfied. The high point of her own virtue has been her renunciation of her own happiness for the sake of her father.

In Sir Richard Steele's *The Conscious Lovers* (1722) the conflict, or rather the potential conflict, is between father and son. Sir John Bevil wants his son to marry Lucinda Sealand, while he has really given his heart to the orphan Indiana, whom he has taken under his protection. But the challenge Steele sets himself is not how the son will defeat the father, but how to get drama, let alone comedy, out of a father and son who refuse to offend each other. Sir John has left Bevil free to follow his own inclinations, the better to judge his character, a test he passes effortlessly (I.i.34–41). There is no financial issue to create the sort of conflict we see in *Love for Love*: Bevil has inherited a substantial estate from his mother. (Comedy's usual reliance on money to create father–son conflicts is suggested in Fielding's *The Modern Husband* [1732] when Captain Bellamour, in the middle of such a conflict, declares, 'When a father and son must not talk of money-matters, I cannot see what they have to do together' [II.ii.p.268].) Free in every respect, Bevil has inter-nalized his father's authority, maintaining the sort of relationship that in another family or another play might depend on money. As Sir John's servant Humphrey puts it, 'He is as dependent and resigned to your will as if he had not a farthing but what must come from your immediate bounty. You have ever acted like a good and generous father, and he like an obedient and grateful son' (I.i.49–53). With no implication of insincerity, 'acted' suggests that these are roles to play for their own inherent worth.

Humphrey suggests one possible source of drama: 'Well, though this father and son live as well together as possible, yet their fear of giving each other pain is attended with a constant mutual uneasiness' (I.i.145–48). This conveys the tone of the matchmaking plot: not head-on conflict but a series of delays, hints, and evasions. Lucinda wants to marry Bevil's friend Myrtle, and Bevil declares himself ready to follow his father's will 'with the assurance of being rejected' (I.ii.16). Hoping his father will read the irony, he thanks him for having arranged a prudent, mercenary match for him in contrast to his own extravagantly romantic courtship, whose upshot was grief when his beloved wife died (I.ii.63–84). It is the closest he can come to accusing him of behaving like a heavy father. He is using here a favourite device of eighteenth-century comedy: the memory of a father's wild youth creates sympathy for the indiscretions of his son. What Bevil cannot do is simply rebel.

The problem is resolved, appropriately, by the discovery that Indiana is in fact the daughter of Sealand, and therefore Lucinda's half-sister. As father–son relations are couched in the sedate language of mutual esteem, father–daughter relations (as in *False Delicacy*) are driven by emotion. When Indiana and Sealand first meet they are ignorant of their relationship, but in his presence she suddenly breaks the play's cool tone and pours out a tearful account of her sufferings, in which Sealand recognizes the story of his long-lost daughter. The discovery clears the way for Indiana's match with Bevil, on terms appropriate to the play: 'Have I then, at last, a father's sanction on my love? – his bounteous hand to give, and make my heart a present worthy of Bevil's generosity?' (V.iii.238–40). The father–son conflict, such as it was, is resolved by a father–daughter reunion; all it takes is the discovery that Indiana too has a father.

## Lost fathers

The moral authority of the father represented by figures like Sir John Bevil is blended with nostalgia when the father is dead. In George Farquhar's *The Twin Rivals* (1702) the late Lord Wouldbe stood for true generosity: 'He kept a porter, not to exclude, but to serve the poor. No creditor was seen to guard his going out, or watch his coming in. No craving eyes, but looks of smiling gratitude' (III.ii.178–81). His virtues are recalled in his older son Hermes; in his younger son Benjamin generosity degenerates into vicious prodigality. There is a more genial version of the convention in Sheridan's *The School for Scandal* (1777), when Sir Oliver Surface tests his nephews against the standard set by their late father, finding the wastrel Charles more engaging than the priggish Joseph: 'Egad, my brother and I were neither of us very prudent youths' (II.iii.29–30). Joseph loses points for the economy of selling his father's house; Charles gains points for the extravagance of buying it. Charles is in his greatest danger with his uncle when he auctions off the ancestral portraits; but his refusal to sell Sir Oliver's picture redeems him in the eyes of the original, and draws the ultimate accolade: 'How like his father the dog is!' (IV.i.116).

In such cases the dead father's moral authority is a touchstone for testing the living. Shakespeare's comedies are also haunted by lost, idealized fathers. The early scenes of *As You Like It* (c.1600) are full of memories of Sir Rowland de Boys, and other characters, beginning with his sons, are sorted into those who respect his memory and those who do not. Sir Rowland charged Oliver, as the heir, to look after Orlando;[19] Oliver has ignored his wishes, and Orlando – who for the family servant Old Adam is 'you memory of Old Sir Rowland' (II.iii.3–4) – declares, 'The spirit of my father grows strong in me, and I will not endure it' (I.i.66–68). Duke Frederick, having congratulated Orlando on winning the wrestling, chills immediately on learning his parentage: 'The world esteemed thy father honourable, / But I did find him still mine enemy' (I.ii.215–16). Rosalind counters by linking Sir Rowland to her own lost father, the banished Duke: 'My father loved Sir Rowland as his soul, / And all the world was of my father's mind' (I.ii.225–226). For Orlando the journey to Arden is not so much a venture into a new world as a homecoming; learning his identity, the Duke introduces himself: 'I am the Duke / That loved your father' (II.vii.198–99). Having come to Arden himself, the repentant Oliver plans to turn the estate over to Orlando, and the messenger who brings the news of Duke Frederick's conversion introduces himself with the name that by now has a talismanic power: 'I am the second son of old Sir Rowland' (V.iv.151).

Rosalind begins the play brooding over a banished father, but by the time she meets the Duke in the forest she has other things on her mind, and instead of the sort of father–daughter reunion Shakespeare will dramatize so movingly in *King Lear* and *Pericles*, there is what sounds like an accidental encounter: 'I met the Duke yesterday and had much question with him. He asked me of what parentage I was. I told him, of as good as he; so he laughed and let me go. But what talk we of fathers when there is such a man as Orlando?' (III.iv.33–37). Taken beyond its literal meaning, 'he laughed and let me go' suggests the Duke is ready to accept this natural change (she has laughed and let *him* go) with a grace that fathers in comedy, and life, do not always manage. In the end, however, Rosalind, returning as herself, greets the Duke and Orlando in the same words, 'To you I give myself, for I am yours' (V.iv.115), economically resolving the generational conflict and the dilemma of heroines in plays like *False Delicacy*. It is a conventional surrender to male authority, more conscious and articulate than that of the silent brides in *A Midsummer Night's Dream*. It is also a linking of relationships, like that of Kate as daughter and wife in *She Stoops to Conquer*. It implies that what we give in love is what we are, and what we are our first relationships have made us.

Shakespearean heroines show a recurring tendency to link their lovers with their fathers.[20] Portia in *The Merchant of Venice* (c.1596) is won by the terms of her father's will, and won by Bassanio, who originally came to Belmont in her father's time (I.ii.110–120). While she initially complains, 'so is the will of a living daughter curbed by the will of a dead father' (I.ii.24–26), there is in fact no conflict: she and her father choose the same man. It is Shylock's daughter Jessica, about to elope with Lorenzo, who is torn: 'Alack, what heinous sin is it in me / To be ashamed to be my father's child!' (II.iii.16–17). She hopes her elopement will 'end this strife' (II.iii.20). Her father's endorsement of her marriage takes the bitterly ironic form of money wrested from him in court. The Jessica story calls up the pain of the generational conflict the Portia story resolves.[21]

In *Twelfth Night* (c.1600) Viola's first comment on hearing the name of the local ruler is 'Orsino! I have heard my father name him.' Her next thought is curiosity about his marital status: 'He was a bachelor then' (I.ii.28–29). It is Viola's reunion with her twin brother Sebastian that resolves the romantic plot, and at the centre of their recognition scene is the shared memory of their father's death, the day Viola turned thirteen. (So presumably did Sebastian, but it is a sign of the centrality of the father–daughter relationship for Shakespeare that they both measure the loss by *her* birthday.) Not only does their reunion take place under his aegis; on the brink of marriage they recall his death, suggesting that the new life they are about to begin is an answer to that death, something offered to his memory.

### All's Well That Ends Well

Written in the shadow of *Hamlet*, and offering a darker version of the opening of *As You Like It*, *All's Well That Ends Well* (c.1603) is a comedy that initially seems to have some trouble shaking off death. It opens with the Countess, Bertram, Helena and Lafeu entering '*all in black*' (I.i.0.3) and their first talk is of Bertram's dead father. Even Lafeu's promise that the King will be a new father to Bertram is shadowed by the news that the King is mortally ill. Helena's father, a famous doctor, could have cured him, but he too is dead. In the words of the Countess, 'This young gentlewoman had a father – O, that "had", how sad a passage 'tis' (I.i.18–19).

Bertram, like Orlando, triggers memories of his father. The king's first greeting to him is, 'Youth, thou bear'st thy father's face.' But when he goes on, 'Thy father's moral parts / Mayst thou inherit too!' (I.ii.19–22) the plays divide. The King recalls the old Count's courtesy to inferiors: he 'bowed his eminent top to their low ranks' (I.ii.43). (Sir Rowland de Boys had the same virtue: when Oliver calls Adam 'you old dog' the servant retorts, 'God be with my old master! He would not have spoke such a word' [I.i.78–81].) But when the King commands Bertram to marry Helena he rejects her as being the wrong class, and does not bother to be polite about it: 'A poor physician's daughter my wife? Disdain / Rather corrupt me ever!' (II.iii.115–16). His attempt to seduce the Florentine girl Diana shows that sexually exploiting his social inferiors is another matter. Compounding fornication with impiety, he is willing (like Charles Surface selling the family pictures) to buy his pleasure with a ring he himself calls

> an honour 'longing to our house,
> Bequeathèd down from many ancestors,
> Which were the greatest obloquy i'the world
> In me to lose.
>
> (IV.ii.42–45)

In bed, he gives the ring to Helena, thinking she is Diana. It is appropriate Helena should now be its custodian, since her sense of the family tradition is sharper than his. While Bertram speaks vaguely of 'many ancestors' she is more precise, describing the passing of the ring 'From son to son some four or five descents / Since the first father wore it' (III.vii.24–25). The words 'son' and 'father' have a power for her they seem to have lost for Bertram.

She has begun, however, by leaving her own father behind:

> What was he like?
> I have forgot him. My imagination
> Carries no favour in't but Bertram's.
> (I.i.83–85)

This is her version, more harshly worded for a tougher play, of Rosalind's 'What talk we of fathers, when there is such a man as Orlando?' In her first plan to win Bertram by curing the King, she uses a remedy inherited from her father. But this gains only the formality of marriage; as though to signal the limits of parental authority, Bertram refuses her both love and consummation. Her second, successful trick is to use her own body. She cannot, like Rosalind, bring the interests of the generations together.

Nor can she recover her father, who is simply forgotten as the play goes on. What she does do is gain a mother in the Countess, who brings on stage the figure of the benevolent matriarch glimpsed beyond the borders of *A Midsummer Night's Dream*. Early in the play the Countess tells her, 'You ne'er oppressed me with a mother's groan, / Yet I express to you a mother's care' (I.iii.144–45). Offended by Bertram's treatment of Helena, she disowns him and adopts her daughter-in-law as her daughter: 'thou art all my child' (III.ii.68). At the end Helena's relationship with Bertram, though technically resolved, remains tentative, couched in 'if'-clauses, and she turns with palpable relief to her simplest, strongest bond: 'O my dear Mother, do I see you living?' (V.iii.320).

## Family reunions

The security parents represent can lead to a comic ending which is not the creation of a marriage in defiance of the older generation, but a family reunion whose main business is to bring parents and children together. The deeper satisfaction of such a reunion, hinted at in *All's Well*, is spelled out at the end of *The Comedy of Errors* (c.1590). The difficult relations of Antipholus of Ephesus and his wife Adriana are not explicitly resolved, and the prospect of marriage between Antipholus of Syracuse and Luciana is held off as something to discuss later. The main emphasis is on getting the twin brothers back with each other, and their reunion with their lost father Egeon. But the real centre of authority is the Abbess, who appears for the first time in the final scene. As his world crumbles, Antipholus of Ephesus runs to the Abbey for protection. His wife, who has been treating him as a lunatic, demands custody, and a rivalry develops between the two women as to who has the right to treat him. The Abbess rebukes Adriana for nagging her husband, and refuses to let her take him home until she herself has cured him 'With wholesome syrups, drugs and holy prayers' (V.i.104). The women's rivalry, in which the Abbess wins, is given added piquancy by the discovery that the Abbess is the twins' mother, and Adriana's mother-in-law. The sympathies of the blocking-parent plot are reversed: Antipholus escapes from a marriage that has gone wrong, and Mother will look after him.

If the mother represents nurture (a role abused by Mrs Hardcastle) the father stands for moral authority. There is a string of seventeenth-century plays based on theme of the prodigal, in which the parable of the prodigal son, though not reproduced in all its details, hovers in the background with its promise of a father–son reunion.[22] The anonymous *The London Prodigal* (c.1604) is in many ways typical. Flowerdale Senior has returned in disguise from Venice to spy on his son. Recalling his own reckless youth (a motif that will have a good run in the eighteenth century), he is at first indulgent to the young man's extravagant ways. But his patience rapidly wears thin; a merchant himself, he is particularly offended at his son's habit of running up debts. Disguised as an old servant, he challenges the youth: 'Thou hadst a father would have been ashamed', to which Flowerdale Junior replies, 'my father was an ass, an old ass' (III.iii.270–71). As punishment, Flowerdale Senior has his son arrested for debt on his wedding morning, and denounces him: if his wife were not pleading for him, 'I'd teach thee what it was to abuse thy father: / Go! Hang, beg, starve' (III.iii.276–77). Flowerdale Junior is saved and brought to repentance by the Griselda-like patience of his wife; his reward is that his father comes out of disguise and (with a brief lecture against backsliding) forgives him.

*The London Prodigal* provides the stern outlines of a story given much gentler treatment in Richard Cumberland's *The West Indian* (1771). While Flowerdale Junior is guilty of forgery, gambling, whoring and thieving, and is accused (though falsely) of murdering his wife, Belcour, a young man just arrived from Jamaica, is guilty only of the indiscretions of a naive, impulsive nature. He does not know his parentage; in fact he is the son of Stockwell, who like Flowerdale Senior is a merchant. (For plays inculcating the virtues of prudence, merchants make a useful moral centre.) Stockwell is also a Member of Parliament, and other characters look to him for protection and reassurance. When Louisa Dudley fears that Belcour and her brother Charles are about to fight a duel, a servant reassures her: 'Mr Stockwell is with them, madam, and you have nothing to fear' (V.ii.16–17). There is something in him of the humane, benevolent Deity who presided over the prosperous England of the eighteenth century;[23] a sterner God looks down on *The London Prodigal*. Not revealing his identity at first, in order to observe Belcour's character, he watches the young man with loving concern: 'What various passions he awakens in me! He pains, yet pleases me; affrights, offends, yet grows upon my heart' (III.i.137–39). His feelings are such that he has to prepare himself for their first interview as though for an ordeal: 'what a palpitation does it throw my heart into; a father's heart! 'Tis an affecting interview; when my eyes meet a son, whom yet they never saw, where shall I find constancy to support it?' (I.iv.21–25).

He has to prepare Belcour with equal care for the final revelation. The test of the young man's goodness is whether or not the virtuous Louisa Dudley, to whom he has behaved indiscreetly, will accept him. He passes the test. The moral ground established, feeling comes next. The father–daughter reunion had been the emotional high point of *The Conscious Lovers*. Cumberland had already gone further in the father–daughter reunion of *The Fashionable Lover* (1772), whose heroine is prepared for overwhelming joy as for major surgery without an anaesthetic – 'Prepare yourself – be constant. [ . . . ] Bear up' – as other characters struggle with the emotional ordeal of watching: 'I can't stand this: I wish I was any where else. [ . . . ] There, there; I'm glad 'tis over.' When she faints with joy, her father cries, 'What have I done?' (IV.iii.pp.82–83). Women were assumed at the time to be more emotionally susceptible than men;[24] but Belcour too, though he takes it like a man, has to be prepared:

BELCOUR: Have I a father?
STOCKWELL: You have a father: did not I tell you I had a discovery to make? Compose yourself: you have a father, who observes, who knows, who loves you.
BELCOUR: Keep me no longer in suspense; my heart is softened for the affecting discovery, and nature fits me to receive his blessing.
STOCKWELL: I am your father.
BELCOUR: My father? Do I live?
STOCKWELL: I am your father.
BELCOUR: It is too much; my happiness o'erpowers me; to gain a friend and find a father is too much; I blush to think how little I deserve you. (*They embrace.*)
(V.viii.103–116)

This is the happy ending to which *The West Indian* aims: not boy gets girl, but boy gets father. Cumberland orchestrates the scene quite consciously as the play's emotional climax, locating the protection, love and understanding of a long-lost parent as the hero's ultimate reward.

No convention that goes to such extremes as this can stay unparodied, and the pattern of *The London Prodigal* – the moral authority of the father leading to correction and forgiveness – was inverted almost as soon as it appeared. In John Fletcher's *Monsieur Thomas* (c.1611) the father, hearing his son has returned from his travels chaste and demure, declares 'the boy's spoiled' (I.ii.42) and decides to cut him off by marrying again. They are reconciled when every time he proposes the name of a new wife, his son claims to have slept with her. The arbitrary power of Crosswill in Richard Brome's *The Weeding of Covent Garden* (c.1633) takes the form of insisting his children go with him to the tavern. Wastrel fathers have to be reconciled with their sons in Dryden's *The Kind Keeper* (1678) and Otway's *The Atheist* (1683). In Otway's play the father submits to the son in return for a steady supply of sack, beef, beer and wenches. Middleton produces a darker parody in *Michaelmas Term* (c.1605) by the simple device of cutting the story off. A moralizing, disguised father spies on his daughter's life of sin in London; we wait for the scene of revelation, forgiveness and reconciliation; it never comes.

The surge of emotion that accompanies the family reunion is countered in *The Importance of Being Earnest* (1895) by the blandness of Miss Prism's reunion with her handbag: 'It has been a great inconvenience being without it all these years' (III.399–400). The whole tradition is – perhaps – finally sent on its way by Joe

Orton in *What the Butler Saw* (1969). Orton places a rather different value on family relations than writers like Cumberland do. Geraldine claims, 'I lived in a normal family. I had no love for my father' (I.p.382). Dr Rance boasts of having placed his whole family in a communal straitjacket: 'I've a picture of the scene at home. My foot placed squarely upon my father's head. I sent it to Sigmund Freud and had a charming postcard in reply' (II.p.442). In the play's last moments Orton uses a version of the traditional recognition token, an elephant brooch whose two halves fit together, to reveal that Geraldine and Nicholas are brother and sister, and the Prentices are their parents: when Mrs Prentice was a young woman, Prentice raped her in the linen cupboard of the Station Hotel, and left the brooch 'in part payment' (II.p.445). Other revelations accompany the main one. The previous night, Nick and Mrs Prentice had sex in the same hotel;[25] this is not quite what Frye had in mind by a comic Oedipus situation. At the beginning of the play we saw Prentice abusing his authority as an employer by trying to seduce Geraldine. When she asks why she has to lie on the couch for a job interview, he replies, 'Never ask questions. That is the first lesson a secretary must learn' (I.p.366). Now we learn that he was also abusing the authority of a father. (Nick's own deference to authority is suggested when he repeatedly addresses the older men as 'sir'.) Orton's formal parody of the comic plot entails a darker parody of comedy's view of parents as comforting authority figures.

Mrs Prentice approaches the final revelation in a state of emotional excitement: 'Oh, my heart is beating like a wild thing!' (II.p.444). But the character who is most delighted is Dr Rance, who has been planning to get a lurid book out of the events of the day. His principal theory (Geraldine was attacked by her father) is confirmed, and the news about Nick and his mother is more than he dared hope for: 'Oh, what joy this discovery gives me! . . . Double incest is even more likely to produce a best-seller than murder – and that is as it should be for love *must* bring greater joy than violence' (II.p.446). Family order has been restored after a period of confusion; far from oppressing their children's sexual natures, the parents them-selves have broken the last taboo. Forces that are so often opposed, love (at least that is what Rance calls it) and parental authority, form not a harmonious relation-ship but an unholy alliance, and a revelation of the grimmest of family secrets is greeted with cries of delight. The comic tradition of parent–child relations, with its wide range and its fundamental contradictions, implodes into a black hole. What is left is a backhanded compliment to the tradition's popularity, Rance's hope that his story will be a best-seller.

# 6

# NEGOTIATIONS

## Comedy against marriage

According to Lady Bracknell, Jack's marriage cannot take place unless he produces at least one parent. Gwendolen's condition is very different: he must be called Ernest. Lady Bracknell claims he must satisfy society; Gwendolen claims he must satisfy her. Both are setting up the sort of impediment that creates the action of a comedy by blocking a marriage, the formal end towards which the comedy aims. The blocking parent is, we have seen, less commonly a factor than might be supposed: the lovers of *A Midsummer Night's Dream* quickly find their problem is not Egeus but each other. In the confusion of the comic action parents are often a source of stability and reassurance. The action that blocks the ending and creates the comedy is more likely to be produced by the lovers themselves: there are misunderstandings to resolve, conditions to meet, conflicts to work through. In the process lovers not only fight and bargain but pretend and play-act, creating drama by means that are themselves consciously theatrical, using comedy itself to ward off the comic ending until the relationship is secure.

It is on the question of marriage that the essential conflict between laughter and the happy ending is at its most urgent, and the comic principle that the thing you desire is inside the thing you fear is clearest. Literature, fictional and non-fictional, is full of warnings of the dangers of matrimony;[1] comedy makes a specialty of such warnings. T.G.A. Nelson observes 'a tension between the forward movement of the plot, which is usually towards marriage, and the backward pull of the dialogue, which ridicules it.'[2] It is when the lovers get what they want that the drama ends, and that is just the problem. As Bellinda puts it in Congreve's *The Old Bachelor* (1693), 'courtship to marriage, as a very witty prologue to a very dull play' (V.i.p.110). Once a proposal is accepted, warns Algy in *The Importance of Being Earnest* (1895), 'the excitement is all over' (I.76); Lane has already observed that 'in married households the champagne is rarely of a first-rate brand' (I.20–21).

Marriage involves not just boredom but the day-to-day difficulty of sharing space. In Farquhar's *The Beaux' Stratagem* (1707) Mrs Sullen reports how her husband comes home drunk, staggers about breaking furniture, then 'comes flounce into bed, dead as a salmon into a fishmonger's basket; his feet cold as ice,

113

his breath hot as a furnace' and by grabbing the covers 'disorders the whole economy of my bed, leaves me half naked' (II.i.60–65). In Dryden's *Marriage-a-la Mode* (c.1672) Rhodophil says of his marriage with Doralice, 'when we are alone, we walk like lions in a room, she one way, and I another: and we lie with our backs to each other so far distant, as if the fashion of great beds was only invented to keep husband and wife sufficiently asunder' (I.i.173–77). The tightly defined space of the stage itself allows such problems to be dramatized. Left alone on stage Rhodophil and Doralice behave exactly as he has described: '*They walk contrary ways on the stage; he, with his hands in his pocket, whistling; she, singing a dull melancholy tune*' (III.i.40.1–3). The sexes have different interests;[3] the Sullens in *The Beaux' Stratagem* formally summarize their incompatibility: 'I can't drink ale with him . . . . Nor can I drink tea with her . . . . I can't hunt with you . . . . Nor can I dance with you' (V.iv.214–17). This incompatibility is combined with the difficulty of sharing space in Vanbrugh's *The Provoked Wife* (1697). Sir John Brute wants to smoke his pipe in silence; Lady Brute and Bellinda, sitting and doing needlework, insist on chatting. Their conversation turns to tobacco as one of the trials women endure in marriage, and after looking '*earnestly at 'em*' for a few moments '*He rises in a fury, throws his pipe at 'em and drives 'em out*' (III.i.41–55).

Comedy conventionally shows love as the factor that brings couples together for marriage. In our time this is the standard expectation in ordinary life as well; and social historians have ample evidence that even in earlier times, when marriages were often arranged to achieve material ends (property and social standing), affection played a key role.[4] For the patients of the seventeenth-century physician Richard Napier love was important in courtship, and (as in comedy) a frequent cause of disturbance.[5] Yet Mary Astell was not alone in warning, in her 1730 tract on the miseries of marriage from the woman's viewpoint, that 'They who marry for love, as they call it, find time enough to repent their rash folly.'[6] She is commenting on what happens not just in life but in comedies like Dryden's *Marriage-a-la Mode* and Otway's *The Atheist* (1683), where marriages contracted for love end respectively in boredom and mutual hatred.

When in Susanna Centlivre's *The Busybody* (1709) Miranda tells Sir George Airy, 'let the world see we are lovers after wedlock', she adds, ''twill be a novelty' (IV.iii.p.344). Sardonic comedies show love kept going in marriage by artifice, plot contrivance or just plain fantasy. In Jonson's *Every Man out of his Humour* (1599) Puntarvolo courts his own wife as though she were a lady he had just met, trying for romance but achieving only clockwork: 'I will step forward three paces; of the which, I will barely retire one; and (after some little flexure of the knee) with an erected grace salute her (one, two, three)' (II.ii.10–12). While Puntarvolo tries to keep romantic admiration going, the tailor Stuffe, in Jonson's *The New Inn* (1629), keeps sex exciting by taking his wife off for dirty weekends: whenever he has made a new gown he dresses her in it, and they go to a country inn in the roles of countess and footman: 'a fine species / Of fornicating with a man's own wife' (IV.iii.72–73).

Colley Cibber's *Love's Last Shift* (1696) centres on the theme of married fornication: Amanda wins back her estranged husband Loveless by disguising herself as a courtesan, making him plead for her favours, and finally surrendering with a plea that is also a promise: 'Oh! lead me to the scene of unsupportable delight; rack me with pleasures never known before, till I lie gasping with convulsive passion' (IV.iii.213–15). Afterwards, she reveals her identity by showing his name branded on her arm, as hers is on his, a sign of the physical passion that first drew them together (V.ii.169–71). She further eases his return to matrimony with a gift of £2,000.

As parents are double figures, tyrannical and benevolent, the pleasures of the whore and the virtues of the wife are combined in a single figure.[7] But while she gets her man, she loses him again in Vanbrugh's sequel, *The Relapse* (1696); and, more to the point, Cibber's own play admits a problem. When Amanda's accomplice Young Worthy predicts, 'she'll have the pleasure of knowing the difference between a husband and a lover' (I.i.438–39) he makes it clear that she can get Loveless at his sexual best only by pretending they are not married. In Shakespeare's *All's Well That Ends Well* (c.1603) Helena gets Bertram to consummate their marriage only by making him believe he is fornicating with Diana; there is a wry sadness in her recollection, 'when I was like this maid, / I found you wondrous kind' (V.iii.310–11). Such plot deceptions are internalized by Rhodophil in *Marriage-a-la Mode*, when he describes how a husband, plodding away at his nightly duties, finally achieves orgasm by thinking of another woman (IV.i.187–92). The impossibility of keeping love going in reality is summarized in Somerset Maugham's *The Constant Wife* (1927). When John asks his wife Constance, 'Do you think I can't be a lover as well as a husband?' she replies, 'My dear, no one can make yesterday's cold mutton into tomorrow's lamb cutlets' (III.p.351).

## The war between men and women

In the trials of marriage both parties suffer. But male characters (not always in comedies by male playwrights) are quick to point out how much men in particular have to lose. Marriage may cement society but it kills sociability, and a man's friendships deteriorate; Toper, in Susanna Centlivre's *The Beau's Duel* (1702), while promising to help Manly win his lady, has misgivings about the outcome: 'e'er the second bottle, you'll be calling, what's to pay? Your wife won't go to bed till you come home; this makes company uneasy' (IV.i.p.116). Vere Queckett, in Pinero's *The Schoolmistress* (1886), wants to keep up membership in his club, traditionally a place for men to escape from women;[8] his wife, who holds the purse strings, refuses the money. More seriously, Plume admits at the end of Farquhar's *The Recruiting Officer* (1706) that in giving himself to Silvia he is giving up 'my liberty and hopes of being a general' (V.vii.84–85).

The obvious answer to all this male complaining is that whatever men had to lose in marriage, women had far more. Through most of the period under discussion, the legal control men had over their wives meant that, as Susan Carlson puts it, in the traditional marriage ending 'the comic heroine usually finds love and happiness only at the price of freedom and power.'[9] Miss Montague, in Hugh Kelly's *A Word to the Wise* (1769), declares that when a man proposes marriage what he is really saying is, 'though you were born to triumph over an admiring world, I desire you will instantly appoint me the master of your fate; my happiness depends on your being a slave' (V.i.p.82). Yet, while the changes in the law that gradually produced greater freedom for women did not begin until 1870,[10] social historians argue that even before then marriages were often less authoritarian in fact than they were in theory.[11] The idea of marriage as companionship, as a partnership of equals, seems to have taken root quite early, and the goodwill and common sense that softened the theoretical power of parents seem to have been exercised here too.

But comedy conventionalizes, and dramatists are more likely to take extreme positions. As, in and around the eighteenth century, conservative comedies champion the authority of parents, in the same period we find the happy ending reinforced by images of wifely submission. Indiana in Steele's *The Conscious Lovers* (1722) gives herself to Bevil with a delighted cry: 'Oh, my ever loved! my lord! my master!' (V.iii.274–75). Even the witty and outspoken Gertrude of Shadwell's *Bury Fair* (1689) promises Wildish, 'I can obey, as well as e'er a meek, simpering milksop on 'em all; and have ever held non-resistance a doctrine fit for all wives, though for nobody else' (V.i.535–37). Elizabeth's Inchbald's *Wives as They Were, and Maids as They Are* (1797) raises the expectation that a woman playwright may see things differently: Lord Priory's authority over his wife is comically grotesque – if she does not rise by 5 a.m. he locks her in her room – and at the end, questioned about her feelings, she readily expresses her fear of him but has some difficulty expressing her love. But her final position on matrimony is, 'Not all the rigour of its laws has ever induced me to wish them abolished' (V.iv.p.78), and the other women fall in line behind her, choosing the doctrine of obedience. The play's ending denies the clear direction of its satire on male tyranny; but at least Inchbald allows her women to choose, accepting the code as an act of their own wills.

For other writers there is no choice: female obedience is a matter not of convention but of nature. At the end of *The Provoked Husband* (1728), Colley Cibber's completion of an unfinished work by Vanbrugh, Lady Townley learns the folly of gadding about the town, submits to her husband's authority, and gives a lecture on marriage: 'To make it mutual, Nature points the way: / Let husbands govern, gentle wives obey' (V.ii.388–89). Nature returns as an old-fashioned matriarch in Henry Arthur Jones' *The Case of Rebellious Susan* (1894), when Sir Richard Kato lectures not just the erring Elaine Pybus but the women of England in general for the folly of social activism: [12]

> that wise, grim, old grandmother of us all, Dame Nature, is simply laughing up her sleeve and snapping her fingers at you and your new epochs and new movements . . . . Go home! Go home! Nature's darling

woman is a stay-at-home woman, a woman who wants to be a good wife
and a good mother, and cares very little for anything else.

(III.p.154)

The appeal to nature, an appeal we have also seen in plays that defend the caste
system, is of course a way to make convention look like inescapable reality; and we
shall see later how more sceptical comedies tackle that form of thinking. The
outspoken heroines of Renaissance comedy are allowed some racy protests about
wifely obedience. Beatrice in Shakespeare's *Much Ado About Nothing* (c.1599) asks,
'Would it not grieve a woman to be overmastered with a piece of valiant dust? To
make an account of her life to a clod of wayward marl?' (II.i.56–58). Crispinella in
John Marston's *The Dutch Courtesan* (c.1604) complains, 'To hear this word *must*! If
our husbands be proud, we must bear his contempt; if noisome, we must bear with
the goat under his armholes' (IV.i.31–33). Both women are on their way to
marriage, but are allowed a period of licence to protest at the conditions before
accepting them.

Comedy accumulates evidence that the marriage at which it aims is not just a
harmony of lovers but a conflict of opposing interests, a conflict writers like
Cibber and Jones resolve by the woman's surrender. In the longer comic tradition
of which English stage comedy is a part, the battle of the sexes is a recurring
theme. It is sometimes literal, as in the siege of the Acropolis in Aristophanes'
*Lysistrata*, or James Thurber's cartoon sequence *The War between Men and Women*
(which includes 'The Fight in the Grocery' and 'Capture of Three Physics
Professors').[13] This comic literalness finds its way into English drama. In the battle
between the forces of Roister Doister and Christian Custance in Nicholas Udall's
*Roister Doister* (c.1552), the women's weapons include distaff, broom, skimmer and
firefork. In Thomas Dekker's *The Honest Whore, Part Two* (1604) the patient linen-
draper Candido and his newly married wife prepare to settle the power relations
within their marriage through a physical fight, in which his weapon is a yard
(bawdy pun intended) and hers is an ell.

But Dekker stops the fight and teaches a lesson. Demanding the right to strike
the first blow, the wife kneels instead, declaring, 'I disdain / The wife that is her
husband's sovereign' (II.ii.108–9). It is a paradigm of conventional comedy: an
entertaining conflict, and then the wife willingly submits. One of the play's male
characters argues such conflict is inevitable, and can have only one ending: 'You
know, that a woman was made of the rib of a man, and that rib was crooked. The
moral of which is, that a man from the beginning must be crooked to his wife'
(I.iii.111–13). Shaw reverses the power relations in *Man and Superman* (1905),
having Jack Tanner submit to capture by Ann Whitfield. But if he is unconventional in one way he is conventional in another, appealing to nature, explaining the
battle of the sexes not through Genesis but through his own pseudo-science in
which the man serves the Life Force by thinking and creating while the woman
serves it by breeding. Woman's purpose, Tanner warns Octavius, 'is neither her
happiness nor yours, but Nature's. Vitality in a woman is a blind fury of creation

. . . . Of all human struggles there is none so treacherous and remorseless as the struggle between the artist man and the mother woman' (I.pp.64–65). The comedy of the play stems from Ann Whitfield's relentless pursuit of Tanner: intelligent and articulate, he is no match for her instinctive cunning, and the ending is her victory. But as Ian Clarke has pointed out, Shaw's view of women as essentially child-breeders is not that different from the doctrine preached in *The Case of Rebellious Susan*, and Tanner's analysis of the battle of the sexes is 'little more than traditionalist bachelor's counsel suffused with sexist gender stereotyping.'[14]

When comedy intellectualizes sexual conflict, as in Dekker and Shaw, it can simply revert to traditionalist doctrine, and the effect in Shaw in particular is stultifying. There is a freer view of gender roles in less pretentious plays, where the audience is not lectured but entertained by the skill and inventiveness of the combatants. Dion Boucicault's *London Assurance* (1841) is a typical case. Grace Harkaway values her independence, and when she becomes attracted to Young Courtly she ensures that she both wins him and keeps an edge over him. His courtship involves play-acting as he adopts a double identity: Augustus Hamilton, the role in which he first attracts her; and a caricature of himself as a shy young man. As himself, he tests her feelings by announcing the death of Augustus Hamilton. Knowing what he is up to, she leads him on by pretending to faint (he cries 'Huzza!' [IV.196]); she then comes to and feigns complete indifference. Their relations are summarized at the end of Act Four, when, not knowing she is hiding behind a curtain, he declares, 'I will bend the haughty Grace' and on his exit she emerges from hiding to ask, 'Will you?' (V.425–27). The roles of Grace and Courtly are not determined by nature; they are performers free to use their own skill to work out their own relationship. *London Assurance* takes a route taken by many English comedies before it, using comic role-playing as the means by which men and women, in marriage or on their way to it, jockey for power.

## Performing marriages: *The Taming of the Shrew* and *The Woman's Prize*

The struggle between Katharine and Petruchio in Shakespeare's *The Taming of the Shrew* (c.1594) not only looks one-sided but seems to get increasingly brutal as the play goes on. The snappy wit-combat of their first meeting shows them closely matched at the level of language, and may even suggest they enjoy sparring with each other. But once they are married, and he has a husband's power over her, he uses it to subject her to a physical ordeal. She arrives at his house dirty, cold and hungry; she is denied food and sleep, and instead of consummating the marriage he preaches 'a sermon of continency to her, / And rails, and swears, and rates' (IV.i.171–72). The result of this treatment, which Petruchio compares to falcon-taming and which has analogies in modern brainwashing techniques, is that she is left bewildered and disoriented: she 'Knows not which way to stand, to look, to speak, / And stands as one new risen from a dream' (IV.i.173–74).

This bewilderment is the state Petruchio has been trying to create all along. To see Katharine as waking from a dream is to draw the analogy with Christopher Sly in the Induction, who is told that he is really a lord and has only been dreaming he was a tinker (Induction.ii.79–80). As the Lord and his servants impose a new, false identity on Sly, Petruchio uses deception to transform Katharine, insisting she see herself through his eyes as 'passing courteous, / But slow in speech, yet sweet as springtime flowers' (II.i.242–43), reporting a fake version of their first conversation that turns it from a fight to a love scene, and presenting her actual resistance as an amusing performance: ''Tis bargained twixt us twain, being alone, / That she shall still be curst in company' (II.i.302–3). Their very first encounter is a confrontation over her name:

PETRUCHIO
> Good morrow, Kate, for that's your name, I hear.

KATHARINA
> Well have you heard, but something hard of hearing. They call me Katharine
> that do talk of me.

PETRUCHIO
> You lie, in faith, for you are called plain Kate, And bonny Kate, and some-
> times Kate the curst . . . .

(II.i.182–86)

He goes on for several more lines bombarding her with the word 'Kate', insisting on his authority to rename her. In their phrasing both of them implicitly agree that identity is socially conferred (your name is what others call you) and his initial aim is to change how she appears to the world. His ultimate aim, however, is to change the way she appears to herself – by one interpretation, releasing her from the stereotyped role of shrew;[15] by another, forcing a new, artificial identity on her as the Lord does to Sly.

At the end of the play her father Baptista thinks Petruchio has succeeded, and offers 'Another dowry to another daughter, / For she is changed, as she had never been' (V.ii.118–19). In fact she is so completely conceived in terms of performance that there is something cryptic, even finally unreadable, about both her first appearance and her apparent transformation. Her counterpart in the anonymous *The Taming of a Shrew* (c.1592) reveals her inner thoughts even as she publicly resists marrying Petruchio:

> But yet I will consent and marry him,
> For I methinks have lived too long a maid,
> And match him too, or else his manhood's good.

(v.40–42)

Shakespeare's Katharine offers no such policy statement. We cannot be sure how much real desire for marriage lies behind her jealousy of Bianca, how much attraction to Petruchio lies behind her resistance. (There are equivalent questions about

Petruchio: how much real brutality lies behind his play-acting? Is he really aiming to make Katharine a slave or a partner?)

When Petruchio imposes his perception of reality on her, denying even her right to tell the time – 'It shall be what o'clock I say it is' (IV.iii.191) – and arbitrarily renaming the sun and the moon, her capitulation includes a mental reservation he does not seem to notice:

> Then, God be blessed, it is the blessèd sun.
> But sun it is not, when you say it is not,
> And the moon changes even as your mind.
> What you will have it named, even that it is,
> And so it shall be so for Katharine.
>
> (IV.v.18–22)

He may rename the sun and the moon, but he cannot rename her. Yet the question remains, how important is this resistance? Is it a last pathetic gesture, or the sign of a stubborn core of reality he cannot touch? Her final lecture on wifely submission, though it offers the usual arguments from nature (women's bodies are 'soft, and weak, and smooth' [V.ii.169]), has also the quality of a public performance whose clearest aim is to give Katharine an edge over the other women by shaming them and winning public approval for herself.[16] There is a gap between the theory she presents and the indignities we have seen her suffer. She insists that women have a good bargain in marriage, since the husband

> for thy maintenance commits his body
> To painful labour both by sea and land,
> To watch the night in storms, the day in cold,
> Whilst thou liest warm at home, secure and safe . . . .
>
> (V.ii.152–55)

We have seen her at home, cold, hungry and kept awake, and we have no sense of Petruchio as a hard-working provider. But Katharine herself shows no awareness of this irony; is this a case of successful brainwashing, or is she covertly signalling her knowledge that the role she is now playing is a fake?

How far Katharine is tamed, and how far she is happy, are questions provoked not just by modern resistance to the play's overt values but by a cryptic quality in the text itself, in which the sense of performance provokes us to speculate about an underlying reality but offers no certain answers. The play is clearer about Bianca, and Bianca offers an alternate model. When Biondello calls her Lucentio's 'appendix' (IV.iv.104) he is underestimating her. Dealing with rival suitors disguised as schoolmasters, she keeps (like Petruchio) her own control of time: 'I'll not be tied to hours nor 'pointed times / But learn my lessons as I please myself' (III.i.19–20). When Lucentio woos her under the guise of translating a passage from Ovid, she responds with her own translation, symbolically insisting on her

120

right of interpretation as Petruchio has insisted on his right to rename the sun. When Lucentio rebukes her for losing his bet for him, her reply is sharp: 'The more fool you, for laying on my duty' (V.ii.133). The play ends not with Petruchio's statement of victory, 'being a winner, God give you good night!' but with final statments by the losing husbands, Hortensio's 'Now go thy ways. Thou hast tamed a curst shrew' and Lucentio's ''Tis a wonder, by your leave, she will be tamed so' (V.ii.191–93). Hortensio's relationship with his widow is a cartoon outline, and his statement is simple. But Lucentio has gone from romantic adoration to the first stages of sex (as they 'kiss and court' Tranio calls Bianca's behaviour 'beastly' [IV.ii.27, 34]) to a stunned realization that he has just married a woman with a mind and will of her own. There is something flat and bewildered about his line as, struggling with his own shock, he seems to find Petruchio's victory unreal.

It is also worth noting that the first submissive wife we meet in the play, who refuses even to be called by a proper name, and who fits Petruchio's theory perfectly – 'My husband and my lord, my lord and husband, / I am your wife in all obedience' (Induction.ii.104–5) – is Bartholomew the page, fake wife to the fake lord Christopher Sly. As in Caryl Churchill's *Cloud 9* (1979), where the obedient Betty of Act One is played by a man to show she has adopted a male view of women, this model of wifely obedience is a performance constructed by a young male acting on orders from an older male, the Lord. We are alerted to the fact that Katharine and the other women are also boys following a script by a male playwright; against the appeal to nature we can set the awareness of theatre, with an attendant suspicion that the sexual hierarchy the play depicts is not natural but constructed.[17]

This at least is a possibility Shakespeare's text leaves open. John Fletcher uses the awareness of performance more overtly in *The Woman's Prize; or The Tamer Tamed* (1611), in which a husband who tamed his first wife marries a new wife, who tames him. The fact that the husband is called Petruchio is an invitation to think of Shakespeare's play, and like the Sly induction but more economically, introduces a metatheatrical level from the beginning. Fletcher's characters are more explicitly presented as role-players; though the action is a non-stop combat between them, neither is a natural fighter. Petruchio was once 'the still Petruchio' but his first wife, a scold, 'turn'd his temper, / And forc'd him blow as high as she' (I.i.37, 19–20). Maria's cousin Bianca fears that her 'modesty, and tenderness of spirit' (I.ii.57) will make her knuckle under to Petruchio. Instead she does what he did in his first marriage: against the grain of her nature she turns herself into a fighter. He has been fixed in the role of bully he first adopted as an expedient, and her job is to snap him out of it without herself becoming fixed in the role of shrew.

She opens her campaign in a sequence that recalls the mock warfare of *Lysistrata* and *Roister Doister*. Like Shakespeare's Petruchio she refuses to consummate her marriage, but she goes much further. With her fellow women she barricades herself in her bedchamber. In the comic siege that follows boarders are repelled with full chamberpots, and there are jokes about 'women's trenches' (I.iv.23) and men who are 'too old to stand' (I.iii.286). An army of women, including veteran rebels against male bureaucracy who have established bear-baiting and alehouses in defiance of the authorities (II.iv.68–74), marches to relieve the defenders. Their captains 'Dance with their coats tuckt up to their bare breeches, / And bid the kingdom kiss 'em' (II.vi.39–40). Through this carniva-lesque comedy, battle lines are drawn not just between Maria and Petruchio but between men and women. Bianca invokes a certain kind of feminist history, recalling

> All the several wrongs
> Done by imperious husbands to their wives
> These thousand years and upwards . . . .
> (I.ii.121–23)

Petruchio's fellow men blame all their troubles on Eve (II.iii.2–7). Maria, like Katharine but in a very different spirit, presents her transformation as a lesson: 'Maids that are made of fears and modest blushes, / View me, and love example' (I.ii.77–78). Petruchio, gathering his allies, warns them, 'Gentlemen, stick to me. You see our freehold's touch'd' (I.iii.279–80).

In the early scenes the protagonists, surrounded by crowds of men and women, seem fixed in an essential, age-old antagonism. But in the later scenes they are more on their own, and their relationship opens out. Shakespeare's Petruchio combined physical abuse with mind-games; Maria concentrates on mind-games. When Petruchio feigns illness she has him locked up as a plague-victim; when he threatens to go on his travels she gives him a mock-heroic send-off – 'Go far: too far you cannot' (IV.v.160); and when he pretends to die she delivers an insulting speech over his coffin that provokes him (in a parody of the funeral-into-wedding scenes of other Jacobean comedies) into popping up indignantly. In every case she matches performance with counter-performance. Through all this he sees 'some-thing / Certain I married her for, her wit' (IV.ii.225–6). She makes it clear from the beginning that she married him willingly, and still wants him. To his reply, 'Death, this is a riddle: / I love ye, and I love ye not,' she replies it is a riddle he must answer through 'your own experience' (I.iii.164–67). As the one who has set the riddle she holds the power, and the experience he undergoes is the demonstration that she can beat him at every turn. In the end, having made her point, she herself declares the game over:

> I have done my worst, and have my end, forgive me;
> From this hour make me what you please: I have tam'd ye,
> And now am vow'd your servant.
>
> (V.iv.44–46)

Earlier she demanded, 'Are we not one piece with you, and as worthy / Our own intentions, as you yours?' (III.iii.99–100), and the Epilogue goes on to claim the play's purpose was 'To teach both sexes due equality' (7). In the light of this claim

Maria's submission will disappoint most twentieth-century readers as it presumably relieved the conservative elements in Fletcher's audience. But Maria has submitted only after demonstrating that nothing in nature dictates this submission; it is her choice, and she decides when to make it. The characters themselves are constructed from layers of performance: beneath the obvious deceptions they create is the deeper role-playing of quiet natures pretending to be aggressive fighters. As the play shows an act of submission while denying submission is natural, it indulges in the battle of the sexes while denying that men and women are naturally bound to fight.

## The Man of Mode

The combatants in Shakespeare and Fletcher are working out their power relations just before and just after marriage. Harriet and Dorimant in Etherege's *The Man of Mode* (1676) start further back, negotiating the terms on which a marriage can take place – if it takes place at all. For both of them, what is natural is freedom, and what is important is the power that comes with freedom. Dorimant enjoys his power over women, his ability to satisfy his desires and frustrate theirs: 'the devil's in it, there has been such a calm in my affairs of late, I have not had the pleasure of making a woman so much as break her fan, to be sullen, or forswear herself, these three days' (I.i.191–94). As he compels Bellinda to make an assignation with him, he seems to be hypnotizing her:

DORIMANT:  Be sure you come.
BELLINDA:  I sha' not.
DORIMANT:  Swear you will.
BELLINDA:  I dare not.
DORIMANT:  Swear, I say!
BELLINDA:  By my life, by all the happiness I hope for –
DORIMANT:  You will.
BELLINDA:  I will.
DORIMANT:  Kind.

(III.ii.69–77)

It is a simple contest of strength, and she loses. It is also important to Dorimant to keep his youthful independence, symbolized by persistent infidelity; as he puts it, taunting his cast-off mistress Loveit, 'Constancy at my years? 'Tis not a virtue in season' (II.ii.179).[18]

We see him mesmerizing Bellinda into a fixed stillness, like a snake hypnotizing a bird. Harriet's keynote is constant movement. At her first entrance she is struggling with a maid who is trying to set her hair in order; at her second she is pulling a reluctant Young Bellair on to the stage. After their first meeting, Dorimant complains, 'she has left a pleasing image of herself behind that wanders in my soul. It must not settle there' (III.iii.121–23). At their second meeting, like

123

Petruchio rewriting Katharine's personality, he tries to get control of her shifting moods. Piqued by her declaration, 'My eyes are wild and wand'ring like my passions, and cannot yet be tied to rules of charming', he commands, 'Put on a gentle smile and let me see how well it will become you' (IV.i.110–11, 120–21). She refuses. When he offers to show off her beauty at court she declines to be analyzed, 'to be taken in pieces, have all my features examined, every motion censured' (IV.i.128–29).

As Dorimant's fascination with Harriet becomes so compelling he starts to think of marriage, he saves face by claiming he is interested in her estate, which will repair the ruins of his (IV.iii.182–83; V.ii.265–66). But this is for public consumption; when alone he makes it clear that his real interest is in her. Harriet too is more attracted than she dares admit: 'I feel as great a change within, but he shall never know it' (III.iii.61). She keeps her edge over him by mockery. She mimics him, behind his back and to his face (I.i.63–64, III.iii.95–98); declining to have her own performance analyzed, she has analyzed his and can reproduce it. Through the later scenes Dorimant seems to lose ground steadily.[19] He himself confesses, 'I love her and dare not let her know it. I fear sh'as an ascendant o'er me and may revenge the wrongs I have done her sex' (IV.i.139–41).

At the beginning of their final scene he holds what looks like a powerful advantage: Harriet faces an unwanted marriage with Young Bellair, and Dorimant can offer to rescue her by marrying her himself; she does not know as he does that Bellair is married and she is perfectly safe. Even here, however, she keeps the edge, meeting his professions with mockery – 'Play the dying fop and make the piece complete, sir' (V.ii.96) – and setting conditions. She has always been inclined to impose tests on him. At their first meeting she challenges him: 'To men who have fared in this town like you, 'twould be a great mortification to live on hope. Could you keep a Lent for a mistress?' At his impudent reply, 'In expectation of a happy Easter' (III.iii.78–81), with its implicit pun on resurrection and plain erection, she threatens to break off the conversation; he has presumed too far. But this, in effect, is the challenge she issues again by imposing on him a trial period of boredom in the country, in 'a great, rambling, lone house that looks as it were not inhabited, the family's so small. There you'll find my mother, an old lame aunt, and myself, sir, perched up on chairs at a distance in a large parlour, sitting moping like three or four melancholy birds in a spacious volary. Does not this stagger your resolution?' (V.ii.379–84). (There is a story that the Earl of Rochester, commonly supposed the model for Dorimant, said to a dog who bit him, 'I wish you were married and living in the country.'[20]) This is a real test of commitment; Lady Mary Wortley Montagu observed that in the restricted life of the country most couples grew tired of each other.[21]

Harriet has another, even more crucial test for Dorimant, and it is bound up in his country ordeal: can he bear to be laughed at? When she mockingly demands a public declaration of love and he refuses, afraid of losing face, she retorts, 'When your love's grown strong enough to make you bear being laughed at, I'll give you leave to trouble me with it. Till when, pray forbear, sir' (IV.i.166–68). To be on the

124

receiving end of mockery is to endure a loss of power; as he inflicts this on Loveit, Harriet inflicts it on him. Even in the play's last moments she tests his endurance. He makes a serious romantic declaration, 'The first time I saw you, you left me with the pangs of love upon me; and this day my soul has quite given up her liberty', and she complains, 'This is more dismal than the country' (V.ii.385–88). In a comedy in which having the right, cool style is a sign of power, his style is wrong; and these are the last words she addresses to him in the play.

Her mockery also implies a scepticism about his profession of fidelity, his claim (typically male, as we have seen) that he will lose his freedom in marriage. The scepticism is justified: through the last scene he spends some time mending his fences with Bellinda and Loveit. Like Katharine hanging on to her version of her name, he is trying to keep some of his old life in reserve. But if this means that Harriet's hold on him at the end is something less than complete, it also makes the idea of their marriage more convincing; this is still the real Dorimant, not a cardboard penitent.[22] And his clinging to freedom is something Harriet herself has anticipated, even accepted. When he offers not just to renounce friendship and wine but to 'sacrifice to you all the interest I have in other women' she cuts him off: 'Hold! though I wish you devout, I would not have you turn fanatic' (V.ii.136–38). Even in allowing his freedom she keeps her edge, correcting his style and letting him know she has his measure.

## Passing the test

In putting Dorimant through an ordeal, Harriet is following a very old story convention: the hero must gain the heroine through a trial that proves his worth. This test confirms her power over him, even as she prepares to surrender that power in marriage. At times the seeming arbitrariness of the test – you must pick the right casket, your name must be Ernest – has a quality of folk tale. But the tests of comedy are never purely arbitrary. Given the finality of marriage, it was common and sensible advice that a woman should be very careful in her choice of partner.[23] Gwendolen revealingly calls Ernest the only 'really safe name' (II.427). Yet safety is not her only concern: she rejects the alternative Jack offers: 'No, there is very little music in the name Jack . . . . It does not thrill. It produces absolutely no vibrations' (I.420–22). As Loveless in *Love's Last Shift* is offered the security of a wife and the delights of a courtesan, Gwendolen wants both safety and romance.

The heroine of Henry Medwall's *Fulgens and Lucrece* (c.1497), praised in the prologue for her 'inestimable prudence' (I.101), subjects her suitors to what amounts to a job interview, in which each must defend his way of life. She picks the low-born but virtuous Gaius, who offers modest sufficiency, over the aristocratic Cornelius, who offers wealth and liberty and claims to be 'brent in love's fire' (I.331). Unlike Gwendolen she does not demand an ideal: she takes the best that is on offer, and passes up the vibrations.[24] In Shakespeare's *Love's Labour's Lost* (c.1594) the King of Navarre and his three lords have broken a vow of three years' study and abstinence in order to court the Princess of France and her three ladies.

At the end of the play their marriages are deferred until they have undergone a modified version of the original ordeal, a year of fasting and contemplation. Marriage means promise-keeping, and having broken one promise they have to show they can keep another. In *Much Ado About Nothing* (c.1599) Beatrice's condition for accepting Benedick's love – 'Kill Claudio' (IV.i.288) – is so shocking that at first he refuses, and it may seem to have nothing to do with his potential as a husband. But it has everything to do with it: he has defined himself through the world of male camaraderie; given the way his friends have treated Hero, can he reverse his loyalties and commit himself to Beatrice and *her* loyalties?

There is a fundamental prudence in all these tests, a need to play for safety. On the other hand, Gwendolen's need for vibrations is anticipated by Lydia Languish in Sheridan's *The Rivals* (1775): a patroness of the circulating libraries, she demands the imprudence of romance. She insists on eloping with Ensign Beverley, against her aunt's wishes, thereby losing most of her fortune. When she learns that Beverley is really Jack Absolute, and the match is approved by the older generation, this should be an ideal fusion of prudence and romance, lover and husband. But as Cecily in *Earnest* has constructed a romantic courtship in her diary, and insists the rules should be followed – 'It would hardly have been a really serious engagement if it hadn't been broken off at least once' (II.500–1) – Lydia misses the narrative: 'There had I projected one of the most sentimental elopements! – so becoming a disguise! – so amiable a ladder of ropes! . . . and such paragraphs in the newspapers!' (V.i.150–55). Her head turned by reading, she wants to be read about; it is another variation on the baby-novel exchange, in which Lydia insists on being seen as a literary subject. Mrs Malaprop speaks more acutely than usual when she demands that Lydia forget Ensign Beverley: 'illiterate him, I say, quite from your memory' (I.ii.178–79). Yet while the mockery of Lydia's book-bound fantasy is easy, her rejection of Jack's attempt to make the prudent match look romantic – 'Pshaw! – what signifies kneeling, when you know I *must* have you?' (IV.ii.178–79) – shows she has a point. Robbed of her fantasy, she has been robbed of her initiative. Sheridan balances her female silliness with the male silliness of Faulkland, who sets conditions for Julia that are not so much unsatisfied as unsatisfiable, the fault lying with his own genius for tying himself in psychological knots. He demands total love from her, while assuming that since he cannot deserve it he can never have it (I.ii.121–27). He frets about her health, then is distressed to learn that her health is perfect, since this shows a want of feeling (II.i.164–66). When he tests her feelings by pretending he is involved in a dangerous quarrel Julia finally loses patience: 'After such a year of trial – I might have flattered myself that I should not have been insulted with a new probation of my sincerity, as cruel as unnecessary!' (V.i.90–92). As some couples try for endless romance Faulkland wants endless testing, and the result is that he nearly loses her.

The man's right to set conditions is not only accepted but internalized by Letitia Hardy in Hannah Cowley's *The Belle's Stratagem* (1780). Though the title recalls Farquhar, the real model is *She Stoops to Conquer*. Letitia's father has arranged that she will marry Doricourt, whom she has not seen since childhood. At their first meeting both are disappointed: he by a certain tameness in her manner, she by his evident lack of enthusiasm. She takes it as her responsibility to provide the missing spark: 'The woman that has not touched the heart of a man before he leads her to the altar has scarcely a chance to charm it when possession and security turn their powerful arms against her' (III.i.p.443). In effect she imposes a test on herself, and passes it by role-playing. She adopts a new identity as a brilliant woman of the town, encountering Doricourt at a masquerade and dazzling him with her wit and vivacity. In the end, having revealed her double identity as the modest girl he is supposed to marry and the brilliant woman he desires, Letitia puts herself in Doricourt's hands: 'You see I *can* be anything; choose then my character – your taste shall fix it. Shall I be an *English* wife? – or, breaking from the bonds of Nature and Education, step forth to the world in all the captivating glare of foreign manners?' (V.v.p.484). Having passed the test of her own role-playing versatility, she is now testing his nature and preferences, and the patriotic slant in her language tells the answer she wants. He seems at first to give the choice back to her – 'You shall be nothing but yourself' (V.v.p.484) – but goes on to accuse himself of 'a strange perversion of taste' in rejecting her first quiet appearance, and delivers a lecture in praise of modest English wives (V.v.p.485). Having proved she can be anything, she really needs to know if he can love the woman she originally was, and he passes the test.

The role-playing so many couples use to work out their relationships has to be abandoned in the end: for the comedy to finish and the marriage to take place, the masks have to fall. Congreve goes further in *Love for Love* (1695), in which Angelica tests Valentine, he responds by role-playing, and role-playing turns out to be not a useful interim stage but a series of mistakes. Angelica has to be careful in her choice of partner: she has 'a considerable fortune in her own hands' (p.215), and Valentine, destitute after a life of profligacy and therefore likely to marry her for the wrong reasons, is not to be taken on trust. Angelica is canny: when Sir Sampson Legend proposes to her, her first words are 'Let me consult my lawyer' (V.p.299). Her strategy is to keep her feelings concealed; Valentine complains she is 'harder to be understood than a piece of Egyptian antiquity, or an Irish manuscript' (IV.p.295). Part of his difficulty is he does not even know what test she wants him to pass, and he keeps getting it wrong. He hopes his poverty will draw her sympathy (I.p.217); when that fails, he tries feigning madness, hoping pity will draw a confession of love from her. She almost takes the bait, but catching a wink and a smile between his confederates realizes it is a trick, and pulls back (IV.p.275). He then appeals to the principle of comic structure: they have passed through the traditional period of confusion and deception, and surely it is time for the happy ending: 'The comedy draws toward an end, and let us think of leaving acting and be ourselves' (IV.p.292). But his timing is wrong; he is making this appeal at the end of Act Four of a five-act play.[25] He further spoils his chances by revealing that his feigned madness was designed to cheat his father, who wanted him to sign over his right of inheritance: Angelica accuses him of being mercenary (IV.p.293).

Valentine seems to think he has to prove himself as a comic hero, by his cleverness at role-playing and financial intrigue. What is really at stake is not his ability to win but his ability to lose. As the fortune-hunter Bassanio wins Portia by picking the casket marked 'Who chooseth me must give and hazard all he hath' (II.vii.16), Valentine wins Angelica by submitting to financial ruin. In each case a rich woman is assured that while she is marrying a man who needs her money (and who will legally get it all) he is capable not just of taking everything but of surrendering everything. Sir Sampson seems on the brink of marrying her, and Valentine at last prepares to surrender his right of inheritance: 'I never valued fortune but as it was subservient to my pleasure; and my only pleasure was to please this lady. I have made many vain attempts, and find at last that nothing but my ruin can effect it.' Angelica exclaims, 'Generous Valentine!', tears the bond that obliges him to sign, and at last confesses her feelings: 'here's my hand, my heart was always yours, and struggled very hard to make this utmost trial of your virtue' (V.p.310). He has passed the generosity test, but the effect is more hard-edged than in comedies like *The West Indian* and *Money*. What matters to Angelica is not Valentine's general benevolence but his generosity to *her*. Angelica is canny, right to the end.

## She Stoops to Conquer

Jacqueline Pearson notes that '*Love for Love* was the most popular of Congreve's comedies with women in the audience.'[26] It exemplifies a classic pattern: the woman, with the most to lose in the legal realities of marriage, maintains control in the action of the comedy. Valentine's response to Angelica's final revelation is 'on my knees I take the blessing' (V.p.310). The tests we have examined are mostly conducted by women – the one man who tries his hand at testing, Faulkland, makes a mess of it – and they give them an authority in the theatre that, in theory at least, they did not have in life. Kate Hardcastle, in Oliver Goldsmith's *She Stoops to Conquer* (1773), needs all her authority and all her role-playing skill, since her prospective husband Marlow is a very tough proposition indeed. He has to be not just tested but virtually taken apart and remade. His own relations with women are radically split, a problem he blames on a limited upbringing in colleges and inns, leaving him tongue-tied with women of his own class while 'impudent enough' with women of the servant class: 'They are of *us* you know' (II.i.90–92). Coming from a man's world, he can deal only with women who belong to that world. When he summarizes his dilemma, 'I'm doomed to adore the sex, and yet to converse with the only part of it I despise' (II.i.140–41), we see his problem, and Kate's: tongue-tied adoration holds out no hope of a relationship, but neither does impudence with those one despises. He gets lost on his way to Hardcastle's house because, anticipating a stock twentieth-century joke about men, he cannot bring himself to ask directions: 'I am unwilling to lay myself under an obligation to everyone I meet, and often stand the chance of an unmannerly answer' (I.ii.84–86). He hates, in other words, to be placed at a disadvantage, to lose control. And, as part of the prickly temper he shows throughout the play, he hates to be laughed at.

When Hardcastle first describes Marlow to her, Kate is delighted to hear he is handsome but chills at the news that he is bashful and reserved. Yet she thinks education will cure him, and is itching to get to work: 'can't he be cured of his timidity, by being taught to be proud of his wife? Yes, and can't I – but I vow I'm disposing of the husband, before I have secured the lover' (I.i.154–57). When she learns he has another side with lower-class women, she shows another side herself: 'An odd character, indeed. I shall never be able to manage him' (I.i.181–82). This second Marlow will need not encouragement but control. The Marlow who has to be taught is the first one she meets. Their initial interview is a disaster. So frozen with shyness he does not even look at her, he gabbles out broken clichés, leaving her to complete his sentences and even his thoughts. She tries to teach him: when he declares he has 'studied . . . to deserve' ladies' favours she replies, 'that some say is the very worst way to obtain them' (II.i.435–36). As he starts stammering about want of courage, she encourages him to go on talking, like someone telling a drowning man to go on waving (II.i.472–77). She emerges from the interview, however, feeling there is something there – 'He has good sense, but then so buried in his fears, that it fatigues one more than ignorance' (II.i.490–92) – and she goes on to talk of teaching him confidence.

The next Marlow she meets has confidence to burn, and she approaches him very differently. In the plain dress that makes him take her for a barmaid, she plans not to educate him but to get under his defences:

In the first place, I shall be *seen*, and that is no small advantage to a girl who brings her face to market. Then I shall perhaps make an acquaintance, and that's no small victory gained over one who never addresses any but the wildest of her sex. But my chief aim is to take my gentleman off his guard, and like an invisible champion of romance examine the giant's force before I combat.

(III.i.241–47)

Bringing her face to market, she is about to meet the sexual Marlow, for whom she is the goods on display, and she is frank about the necessity of physical attraction; she has already examined him from this viewpoint, and is satisfied. He is also an adversary to combat, not only because a man's interest in sex is a threat to an unmarried woman, but because with a prospective husband there are power relations to establish. In between these two statements, she expresses the simple hope that she will get to know him.

As the goods on display she is so successful she has to fight him off when he demands a kiss: 'I'm sure you did not treat Miss Hardcastle that was here a while ago in this obstropalous manner' (III.i.308–10). This provokes him into boasting of his popularity with London women: 'At the Ladies Club in town, I'm called their agreeable Rattle' (III.i.320–21). There was no conversation at their first meeting, but rattle is not conversation either. He goes on to give a false name, and he gets touchy when he thinks she is laughing at him. In both cases he is trying to keep an edge of superiority; she is, after all, one of the class of women he despises. When he next meets his friend Hastings he makes a crude boast of a sexual conquest below stairs, moderated only by the admission that if the girl has virtue (which he evidently doubts) he would be the last to corrupt it (IV.i.37–59). Kate has now seen, not a Marlow who is making progress, but an equally unsatisfactory extreme, a vain chatterbox who thinks of himself as a ladies' man.[27]

We might expect Kate in her management of Marlow to try for a happy medium between the extremes, warming the sentiment and cooling the hormones until she makes him worth having. But for all her talk of educating the one Marlow and controlling the other, both of them are essentially dead ends. Instead she turns herself into a different character again, and draws out a third Marlow who is not so much a combination of the originals as something new. By the time of their third interview he has learned the house is not an inn, but he now takes Kate to be a poor relation of the family, and apologizes for his behaviour. The cheeky barmaid becomes a pathetic woman living in the house on sufferance, and anxious not to offend: 'I'm sure I should be sorry to affront any gentleman who has been so polite, and said so many civil things to me. I'm sure I should be sorry (*pretending to cry*) if he left the family upon my account.' For Marlow the tears are a breakthrough: 'By heaven, she weeps. This is the first mark of tenderness I ever had from a modest woman, and it touches me' (IV.i.215–22). For the first time he encounters a woman who is not to be put on a pedestal or backed into a corner, but who has feelings for him, and could be hurt. He declares an attraction to her, coupled with a regret that 'the difference of our birth, fortune, and education, make an honourable connection impossible; and I can never harbour a thought of seducing simplicity that trusted in my honour, or bringing ruin upon one, whose only fault was being too lovely.' Kate responds, aside, with a cry of delight that echoes Angelica's discovery of the true Valentine: 'Generous man! I now begin to admire him' (IV.i.224–30). By the end of the scene she has determined to keep him.

Goldsmith seems to have strayed into the sentimental manner he claimed to despise. But the poor relation is a fake, and so are her tears; her account of his politeness and civility at their last meeting has an irony he does not notice; and her later account of the current interview has the witty malice Marlow saw in the eye of the barmaid (III.i.279). Kate tells Marlow's father that his son behaved 'As most professed admirers do. Said some civil things of my face, talked much of his want of merit, and the greatness of mine; mentioned his heart, gave a short tragedy speech, and ended with pretended rapture' (V.i.106–9). This is as exaggerated and unfair as it is witty; Kate is still pretending. But by parodying Marlow's fine sentiments she is not only keeping her own guard up; she suggests that, satisfying though they are as proof of his character, his sentiments are no more a basis for marriage than anything else he has offered her. In their final meeting he *does* mention his heart and gives a short tragedy speech about the conflict between love and duty (V.iii.15–21), to which she responds by accusing him of pretended rapture, claiming that only the vulgar consideration of money separates them.

Thus challenged, he goes down on his knees: 'Does this look like security? Does this look like confidence? No, madam, every moment that shows me your merit, only serves to increase my diffidence and confusion' (V.iii.64–66). The born-again Marlow is veering back into the tongue-tied fool of the first interview; at this point the fathers emerge from hiding and Marlow makes the discovery (equivalent to the shock Lydia Languish gets) that the woman he loves (and whose name he has never learned) is the woman he was supposed to marry. He has been led from terror of Kate Hardcastle to making a pass at a barmaid to pitying a poor relation to throwing himself at the feet of a desirable woman who turns out to be – Kate Hardcastle. What looked like a line of progress has turned out to be a circle; he is back where he started, and his response is not romantic delight but, 'Oh, the devil' (V.iii.81).

The comedy is not over, any more than it was for Valentine in Act Four. Kate has managed him, educated him, drawn out his true worth, and now, instead of helping him consolidate a new, integrated personality combining sentiment, sexual warmth and generosity, she breaks him apart into his original components, and laughs at him: 'In which of your characters, sir, will you give us leave to address you? As the faltering gentleman, with looks on the ground, that speaks just to be heard, and hates hypocrisy; or the loud confident creature, that keeps it up with Mrs Mantrap, and old Miss Biddy Buckskin, till three in the morning? ha! ha! ha!' (V.iii.88–93). The most important test is still to come, and it is Harriet's test on Dorimant: can he bear to be laughed at? The stage direction, '*They retire, she tormenting him, to the Back Scene*' (V.iii.99.1), shows her in relentless pursuit of this last aim, not keeping romance going into marriage, but keeping comedy going. It is Hardcastle who has to push them together so that the play can end.

But Marlow's final reference to 'my little tyrant here' (V.iii.154) may be the first glimmering of a sense of humour, showing progress on the final front. And Hardcastle offers hope of another kind: 'as you have been mistaken in the mistress, my wish is, that you may never be mistaken in the wife' (V.iii.165–66). The logic of this may well be, *because* you have been mistaken in the mistress, you will never be mistaken in the wife. Laughter is not just the means by which Kate keeps contol over Marlow. Through the medium of comedy, everything that could make their marriage difficult – shyness, bullying and sloppy sentiment on his part, mockery and deception on hers – has been worked through. They have now had every chance to misunderstand and offend each other, in a variety of ways. Their marriage has been protected not so much by testing and mutual examination as by inoculation.

### Facing reality: *The Way of the World*

In *As You Like It* (c.1600) Jaques advises Touchstone to get 'a good priest that can tell you what marriage is' (III.iii.78–79). In that spirit Rosalind uses their mock courtship to get Orlando past romantic adoration and tell him what marriage is. It will change both of them as naturally as the weather changes: 'men are April when they woo, December when they wed. Maids are May when they are maids, but the sky changes when they are wives' (IV.i.140–42). She promises not to be faithful and obedient but jealous, noisy, capricious and wayward. There will be clashes of temperament exacerbated by the proximity of marriage: 'I will weep for nothing, like Diana in the fountain, and I will do that when you are disposed to be merry; I will laugh like a hyena, and that when thou art inclined to sleep' (IV.i.146–49). This is her parody of the promises of the marriage service. She may be letting Orlando know what he is in for; or, as with the inoculation of Kate and Marlow, she may be getting trouble out of the way by using comedy to face it now.

The provisos of realistically minded couples have the same function: they face what marriage will be, or could be, dealing with trouble before it happens, either heading it off or ensuring that when it comes they can face it. Celadon and Florimell in Dryden's *Secret Love* (1667) expect that after a year of passion their love will die a natural death, and they take each other on the condition that they will confess when it happens and not pry into each other's affairs; they will be, if not faithful, at least honest. Their one concession to fantasy is that they will call each other not Husband and Wife but Mistress and Gallant, a sad little game that will make the honesty palatable (V.i.538–76). In Sir Charles Sedley's *Bellamira* (1687) Merryman and Thisbe, both given to the company of their own sex, face the problem that men and women have different interests, and decide how they will cope. Each demands some sacrifices. He is a drinker, and she warns him, 'I must have no morning draughts, no qualms that keep off dinner till three o'clock, . . . no noisy fools to disturb the whole street with loyal catches and senseless huzzahs.' He retorts, 'I have some provisos to offer too, in order to our future peace and quiet: I will have none of your gaming ladies to keep you up at cards till I am ready to go out in the morning, so that we have scarce time for the great end of matrimony' (III.p.30). Both of them think of the practical business of getting through a day, finding time for dinner and sex when they are on different schedules. To compensate for these demands each makes concessions: he promises to forswear jealousy, and she allows him some nights to drink with his friends. Their practical demands and compromises show them getting ready for the give-and-take of marriage, confronting the difficulties with frankness and good humour. Here, as in *As You Like It*, traditional jokes about the problems of marriage are co-opted in the service of building an honest working relationship.

In the proviso scene between Mirabell and Millamant in Congreve's *The Way of the World* (1700) the theatrical role-playing we have seen elsewhere is kept to a minimum: the comedy they use is a comedy of frankness, working out their relationship by facing all the things that could go wrong. There is a special problem for Millamant. She knows that marriage for her means loss of power, that she will 'dwindle into a wife' (IV.p.380). Power matters to her as it does to Dorimant. So long as Mirabell is courting her she can string him along, torment him and (like Angelica) keep him guessing. She can even keep time at bay: 'One's cruelty is one's power, and when one parts with one's cruelty, one parts with one's power, and when one has parted with that, I fancy one's old and ugly' (II.p.349). Claiming she will get old by losing her power (not lose her power by getting old) she is trying to pretend the realities of time are not inexorable – as in *Earnest*, where it is always nearly seven. The reality is conveyed by her first entrance, where Mirabell expects to see her 'full sail, with her fan spread and her streamers out, and a shoal of fools for tenders' and is startled to find her accompanied only by Witwoud and Mincing. As Witwoud puts it, she has walked as fast through the crowd 'As a favourite in disgrace, and with as few followers.' When she snaps at him, 'truce with your similitudes' (II.p.347) it may not be just the similitudes that irritate her. She is already losing her power.

Yet marriage will mean not a consolidation of her power but a final surrender of it. Strong-willed heroines like Rosalind, Angelica and Kate Hardcastle are compensated by the power they have in the play, and there is no Act Six in which they have to face the subordination of marriage. The play ends with the woman still triumphant and the man, very often, on his knees. Congreve is franker. The proviso scene, as critics frequently insist, puts more serious limits on Millamant than it does on Mirabell.[28] Yet to be a spinster in this society was to be 'peripheral' and 'functionless'.[29] She has a choice between dwindling into a wife and dwindling into nothing. Her solution, at first, is to give in without appearing to give in. She seems to make her marriage conditional: 'I'll never marry, unless I am first made sure of my will and pleasure.' Yet when it comes to the point she goes from outright refusal to implicit acceptance: 'I can't do it, 'tis more than impossible – Positively, Mirabell, I'll lie a-bed in a morning as long as I please' (IV.p.379). There is in that last statement no 'if' clause: somewhere between the words 'impossible' and 'positively' she has decided to marry him; everything that follows is a statement of what she will do *when* they are married. At the end she makes her surrender explicit – 'Well, you ridiculous thing you, I'll have you' (V.pp.381–82) – but she erases the moment when it actually happens. Her role-playing, such as it is, is her pretence that she has been making conditions. He can read her code: after he has made *his* conditions she declares, 'I hate your odious provisos', and he replies, 'Then we're agreed' (V.p.381).

Her provisos include a confrontation with one function of time, the dying of love in marriage. Her solution is not to keep love going by public displays of affection – 'don't let us be familiar or fond, nor kiss before folks' – but, 'let us be as strange as if we had been married a great while, and as well bred as if we were not married at all' (IV.p.379). She anticipates *Earnest*, where Algy objects to married couples who flirt, washing their clean linen in public. The public coldness she proposes instead can be read as a pre-emptive strike, getting control of the death of love by presenting it as a performance, beneath which there may be real coldness (then there is no pretence) or real affection, which the performance protects from being frittered away. She is particularly against terms of endearment: 'I won't be called names. . . . as wife, spouse, my dear, joy, jewel, love, sweetheart and the rest of that nauseous cant' (IV.p.379). There is a grim example of what she means earlier in the play when the Fainalls greet each other – 'My dear . . . . My soul' (II.p.341) – and an icy chill comes off the stage.[30] Congreve had already shown the language of affection reduced to subhuman noises by Fondlewife in *The Old Bachelor* (1693): 'Poor Cocky, kiss Nykin, kiss Nykin, ee, ee, ee' (IV.i.p.82). Alan Ayckbourn, specialist in showing dysfunctional marriages, has a wife call her husband 'Jumjums' (*Absent Friends* [1974], I.p.113). Millamant is justified not just on grounds of taste but on the evidence of what such marriages are really like.

Mirabell's contribution to the war with time is simpler; he warns her off the premature use of cosmetics: '*Item*, I article that you continue to like your own face, as long as I shall' (IV.p.380). As she wants no artificial endearments, he wants no artificial parody of eternal youth; he has seen Lady Wishfort. He knows what time will do, but he wants to control her response to it. In this respect he is treading on a female preserve. This is a sensitive area, and while they both make demands about space hers are particularly concerned with privacy.[31] She demands 'To have my closet inviolate; to be sole empress of my tea-table, which you must never presume to approach without first asking leave. And lastly, wherever I am, you shall always knock at the door before you come in' (IV.p.380). In that last demand she may be thinking of his attitude to the space they are currently in. It was established as a closed room by Sir Wilfull Witwould's awkward attempts to get out of it. Though Mirabell has entered it by her permission – earlier in the scene, after some hesitation, she agreed to see him (IV.p.375) – he comes in without knocking and sees the room as an enclosure he has successfully broken into: 'Do you lock yourself up from me, to make my search more curious? Or is this pretty artifice contrived, to signify that here the chase must end and my pursuit be crowned, for you can fly no further' (IV.p.378). In Steele's *The Funeral* (1701) Campney locks himself and Harriet in a room to make her declare her feelings, and she responds by running around it like a trapped animal. Towards the end of Shaw's *Pygmalion* (1914) '*Eliza goes out on the balcony to avoid being alone with Higgins. He rises and joins her there. She immediately comes back into the room and makes for the door*' (V.p.131). All three plays use stage space to show a man's insistence on invading a woman's privacy. But Mirabell goes on to talk about the ultimate invasion of Millamant's space: '*Item*, when you shall be breeding . . . . I denounce against all strait-lacing, squeezing for a shape, till you mould my boy's head like a sugar-loaf' (IV.pp.380–1). Again he is concerned with her body, and again he wants realism: when she is pregnant she should look pregnant. Having asserted proprietary rights in a way that makes questions of legal property pale by comparison,[32] he then concedes dominion over the teatable, provided she sticks to female drinks, tea and coffee, and to female gossip.

The different interests of the sexes are shown in the company they keep, and here each tries to control the other. She refuses to 'converse with wits that I don't like, because they are your acquaintance, or be intimate with fools, because they may be your relations' (IV.p.379–80). While other comedies complain that marriage kills sociability, she is aware of the opposite problem: each partner brings baggage in the way of obnoxious friends and idiotic relatives. He in turn allows her general acquaintance, but denies her a 'sworn confidante, or intimate of your own sex' (IV.p.380). Behind this lies male jealousy of female friendship, and of the way women (as in *The Woman's Prize*) gang up on men. As he claims to control her makeup and her body, he denies her intimacy with anyone but himself.

Frankness is the keynote throughout the scene. They are frank about the problems of sharing space, the fear of what time will do, the conflict between his demand for power and her demand for privacy. The only appeal to nature they make is to the reality of the body. Her response to the word 'breeding' – 'Ah! Name it not' (IV.p.381) – plays in modern productions as mock coyness about sex; in its time it could also have expressed a real fear of the dangers of pregnancy and childbirth, a fear women confided to their diaries.[33] There is no pretence that marriage will always be romantic, or that laughter will see them through. What makes the scene an anticipation – perhaps even a portrayal – of a valid working marriage is just this frankness, this refusal to pretend. Its pattern of give-and-take is also important, and the simple fact that they are talking with each other. Congreve stresses the latter point by following the proviso scene with the wonderfully inarticulate proposals Millamant gets from Petulant and Sir Wilfull (IV.pp.383, 385). He stresses the give-and-take by the contrast with Fainall. While Mirabell and Millamant negotiate, Fainall tries to set the terms of his marriage by making arbitrary demands that will give him total power.[34]

Mirabell and Millamant have ignored property in favour of personal relations. In the Fainall marriage, personal relations are dead and property is all there is to talk about: 'Next, my wife shall settle on me the remainder of her fortune not made over already, and for her maintenance depend entirely on my discretion' (V.p.399). He is stymied by the revelation that before her marriage his wife conveyed her estate in trust to Mirabell. While Mirabell and Millamant have been frank about their provisos, Mrs Fainall's was a secret kept even from the audience. The Fainall marriage (and Mirabell bears responsibility for this) was a fraud from the start, and the play ends on a note of warning:

> From hence let those be warned, who mean to wed,
> Lest mutual falsehood stain the bridal bed;
> For each deceiver to his cost may find,
> That marriage frauds too oft are paid in kind.

> (V.p.408)

Falsehood and deception – in the comic form of role-playing – have been the staple of marriage negotiations in many of the comedies we have looked at. Even Rosalind, trying to face the truth, does it through Ganymede. Congreve ends his comedy with a warning against the means of comedy itself, when they are brutally reduced as they are by the Fainalls. His central couple uses a different kind of comedy, basing their marriage on the risk of honesty, not denying all those jokes against marriage but facing the truth that lies behind them, and, by the wit through which they express that truth, using comedy to control it.

# 7

# COMEDY AGAINST ITSELF

## Against laughter

If Millamant and Mirabell took too seriously the factors they confront in the proviso scene – his invasion of her liberty, her inevitable ageing, the dying of love – they might well decide not to get married at all. It is comedy that allows them to control these fears, trivializing them just enough to make them endurable. But in reminding themselves of these things, mocking each other in the process, they are playing a potentially dangerous game. If they were not kept steady by their underlying need and desire for each other, their relationship could well break down. Comedy helps, but only if comedy itself is kept under control. It is widely recognized that there is something destructive in laughter: it 'would seem to require the obliteration of a something or somebody.'[1] Even the person being made to laugh, who might expect to share the superiority of the joker, may end up sharing the discomfort of the victim. It is significant that while it is conventional to think of the pleasures of laughter, uncontrolled laughter is a physical ordeal. Peter Shaffer records that on the opening night of *Black Comedy* (1965) a 'stern-looking middle-aged man' fell into the aisle 'and began calling out to the actors in a voice weak from laughing, "Oh stop it! Please stop it!"'[2] Shaffer was of course delighted. The humorist Stephen Leacock goes further, reporting that during one of his lectures a red-faced man keeled over from laughter and there were calls for a doctor: 'my heart beat high with satisfaction. I was sure that I had killed him.'[3] Like Ben Jonson's promise in the Prologue to *Volpone* to rub the audience's cheeks with salt, this reveals (jokingly, so as to get under our defences) that the entertainer who makes us laugh is in some way out to get us. The joker has control not just over his victim but over his audience.

Jonson's critical jottings in *Timber* include the statement, borrowed from Aristotle, that the moving of laughter is a fault in comedy. Steele's epilogue to *The Lying Lover* (1704), echoing Hobbes, offers a reason: 'Laughter's a distorted passion, born / Of sudden self-esteem, and sudden scorn.'[4] For comedy to attack laughter seems like a contradiction in terms; but we have seen elsewhere that comedy feeds on contradictions. It derides marriage and works towards marriage; it mocks the solitary figures who stand apart from their fellows, yet uses their perspective on the world. Given this tendency to self-contradiction, it is natural that comedy should turn against itself, attacking its own procedures. Laughter, in so far as it is derisive and aggressive, works against the concord the comic ending tries to create; and so comedy attacks laughter.

In Shakespeare's *Love's Labour's Lost* (c.1594), laughter is destructive. The women taunt and humiliate the men who are courting them, and the courtship goes nowhere. The men in their turn taunt and humiliate the actors in the show of the Nine Worthies, which breaks up in disorder. When in the newly serious atmosphere produced by the death of the Princess's father (this death cannot be laughed off) the women set trials for the men as a test of their seriousness in love, Rosaline demands that Berowne learn the limits of wit, its failure to cope with real suffering: she orders him to jest a twelvemonth in a hospital. When he protests that it is impossible 'To move wild laughter in the throat of death' she retorts, 'Why, that's the way to choke a gibing spirit' (V.ii.845–88). She herself has such a spirit, and her command can be seen as a last grim joke against Berowne, a joke by which comedy destroys itself.

The misgivings about wit that are argued explicitly in *Love's Labour's Lost* are dramatized more subtly and pervasively in *Much Ado About Nothing* (c.1599). Beatrice and Benedick not only use wit aggressively, keeping each other at bay, but attack each other's wit, knowing how much pride each has invested in it. In a society that conventionally saw silence as a virtue in women, Benedick insults Beatrice by calling her 'my Lady Tongue' (II.i.262); knowing the importance of male camaraderie to him, Beatrice dismisses Benedick as 'the Prince's jester, a very dull fool' (II.i.131). She accuses him of a fragile ego: if he doesn't get his laughs he sulks, 'then there's a partridge wing saved, for the fool will eat no supper that night' (II.i.142–44). Her attacks on him are more searching than his attacks on her, and in the trick devised by Don Pedro to bring them together (using his wit against theirs, he has them eavesdrop on conversations that make them believe they are in love with each other) Beatrice is made ashamed of her gibing spirit – 'So turns she every man the wrong side out . . . . Sure, sure, such carping is not commendable' (III.i.68–71) – while Benedick, whose touchiness about Beatrice's gibes shows how much he hates being laughed at, is inured against his friends' mockery: 'I may chance have some odd quirks and remnants of wit broken upon me, because I have railed so long against marriage. But doth not the appetite alter?' (II.iii.231–34). Each has a certain pride invested in keeping the edge in wit-combats, and in each that pride is broken as Beatrice learns not to be a mocker and Benedick learns not to let the fear of mockery control his life.

When Beatrice accuses Benedick of 'devising impossible slanders' (II.i.132) this suggests a link between the malice of wit and the machinations of the play's villain Don John, whose impossible slander of Hero leads Claudio to denounce her for unchastity at what was supposed to be their wedding. The shock of Claudio's attack, like the death of the King of France in *Love's Labour's Lost*, produces a new, serious atmosphere in which wit is out of place. Having, so far as they know, killed Hero, Don Pedro and Claudio make an appalling attempt to keep the old jocular camaraderie going, and call on Benedick to entertain them. But he has come on Beatrice's orders with a challenge, and he confronts Claudio with the words, 'You are a villain. I jest not' (V.i.145). It takes them some time to realize he is serious. By the end of the play the wit has returned, and it now eases the transition to the ending by letting Beatrice and Benedick come together without losing face. Benedick's 'Come, I will have thee, but by this light I take thee for pity' (V.iv.91–92) is the equivalent of Millamant's 'I'll endure you' (IV.p.381). Wit has been restored; but only after it has been examined for its malicious, destructive side, and temporarily surrendered.

The lovers of *Much Ado* and *The Way of the World* use comedy to control the discomfort they feel in coming together, knowing what they are surrendering in the way of pride and freedom. We have seen that the control of anxiety is an important part of comedy's business. But even this use of wit comes under attack in Tom Stoppard's *The Real Thing* (1982). In the first scene Max responds to the discovery of his wife's apparent adultery with lines like, 'I notice that you never went to Amsterdam when you went to Amsterdam. I must say, I take my hat off to you, coming home with Rembrandt place mats for your mother. It's those little touches that lift adultery out of the moral arena and make it a matter of style' (I.i.p.13). We have seen how much in comedy depends on having the right style. But this turns out to have been a scene in a play written by Henry, whose own wife Charlotte denounces it as a fake: 'You don't really think that if Henry caught me out with a lover he'd sit around being witty about place mats? Like hell he would. He'd come apart like a pick-a-sticks. His sentence structure would go to pot, closely followed by his sphincter' (I.ii.p.22). Like Beatrice attacking Benedick, Charlotte uses wit against wit. In the second act Henry goes further: fearing his new wife Annie is betraying him he declares against wit, parodies it, then comes out with a flat, serious statement: 'I don't believe in debonair relationships. "How's your lover today, Amanda?" "In the pink, Charles. How's yours?" I believe in mess, tears, pain, self-abasement, loss of self-respect, nakedness' (II.ix.p.72). He demonstrates what he means when, left alone, he calls out to the unseen Annie, 'Oh, please, please, please, please, *don't*' (II.xi.p.79).

Henry's references to Charles (*Blithe Spirit*) and Amanda (*Private Lives*) turn his speech into a Noël Coward parody, and as such it is unfair. When in *Private Lives* (1930) Elyot learns that Amanda has had affairs with other men, he has no witty comeback: he exclaims, 'Oh, God!' and '*looks down miserably*'. Amanda tells him '*gently*' 'You mustn't be unreasonable, I was only trying to stamp out the memory of you' (II.p.217). It is a quiet, serious moment. They then start to attack each other through wit, but it is an angry, hurt wit, nothing debonair about it. Coward, no less than Stoppard, is aware that there are times when comedy is no help at all.

There are times when it even fails to entertain. If the function of comedy is to make the audience stop laughing, part of its mechanism needs to be a control valve that shuts off the laughter, not just before it becomes destructive but before it becomes tedious. Jonson has a habit of running a joke into the ground, keeping his fools on display long after we have got the point. In *Epicoene* (1609), perhaps with a touch of self-mockery, he admits it. Truewit expresses relief when Tom Otter finally leaves the stage: 'His humour is as tedious at last, as it was ridiculous at first' (IV.ii.149–50). The danger in comedy's dependence on repetition is admitted in Susanna Centlivre's *The Beau's Duel* (1702), when Bellmein complains of the fop Sir William Mode, 'Pox on him, I'm weary of him, there's no variety in him' (II.i.p.79). Even the best comedies need in the end to listen to the plea of Shaffer's victim, 'Oh, stop it! Please stop it!' At the performance I saw of the famous 1964 National Theatre production of *Hay Fever*, directed by Coward himself, the first two acts had the audience helpless with laughter, but the third act passed in near-silence: the audience was laughed out.

The twin dangers of malice and exhaustion can work together: when a joke runs too long, its potential cruelty comes too much to the surface. This is what happens in the gulling of Malvolio in *Twelfth Night* (c.1600). Malvolio misinterpreting Maria's letter, fancying himself in complete control, is funny; it is not just modern squeamishness that finds Malvolio locked in a dark room, begging for light, ink, and paper, not so funny. Even Sir Toby complains, 'I would we were well rid of this knavery' (IV.ii.67–68). When the joke winds down the hostility it embodies keeps going. Fabian calls for an ending: 'How with a sportful malice it was followed / May rather pluck on laughter than revenge' (V.i.365–66). Malvolio's reply, 'I'll be revenged on the whole pack of you!' (V.i.378), blocks both the laughter and the possibility of ending.

## Wit and good nature: *The School for Scandal*

Does laughter have to be malicious, or can it be allied with good nature? Hazlitt claimed Shakespeare was disabled as a writer of comedy by his lack of ill nature; Bergson argued that since laughter corrects by humiliating it cannot be kind-hearted.[5] The issue is debated explicitly in Sheridan's *The School for Scandal* (1777). Maria claims, 'wit loses its respect with me when I see it in company with malice', to which Lady Sneerwell replies, 'there's no possibility of being witty without a little ill nature. The malice of a good thing is the barb that makes it stick' (I.i.152–59). Sir Peter Teazle has a similar debate with Lady Teazle. He claims, 'true wit is more nearly allied to good nature than your ladyship is aware of.' Sir Peter's position was standard eighteenth-century thinking, and it is tempting to take it as the position of the play.[6] But when Lady Teazle replies, 'True, Sir Peter. I believe they are so near akin that they can never be united' (II.ii.156–59), we have to notice that while Sir Peter, like Maria, has made a flat statement Lady Teazle has made a joke. She finds a witty way of defending her position; he does not; we know which character will get the laugh.[7] Maria is willing to sacrifice laughter if necessary: 'If to raise malicious smiles at the infirmities or misfortunes of those who have never injured us be the province of wit or humour, Heaven grant me a double portion of dullness!' (II.ii.194–97). It is a common complaint that Maria is the dullest character in the play.

Sir Peter gets laughs by betraying his own principle, in his witty – and malicious

– attack on the scandalmongers: 'no person should be permitted to kill characters or run down reputations, but qualified old maids and disappointed widows' (II.ii.169–71). He hits where it hurts. Lady Sneerwell had her reputation wounded in her youth; by her own admission this is why she indulges in scandal, and it may explain why she is unmarried. The other scandalmongers are also single. (Lady Teazle, the exception, is not a true member of the group, and eventually they turn on her.) Lady Sneerwell is currently frustrated in her love for Charles Surface. When she responds to Sir Peter's gibe, 'Go, you monster!' (II.ii.172), we see the truth of her own statement that the malice of a good thing is the barb that makes it stick. Sir Peter's wit also has a hard edge in his bitterness about his own marriage. When Rowley claims, 'I'm sure your lady, Sir Peter, can't be the cause of your uneasiness', he retorts, 'Why, has anybody told you she was dead?' (I.ii.24–26). Like Lady Sneerwell, he can lash out when he has been hurt.

His marriage is his principal source of pain, and on that subject he has none of the resilience against laughter Benedick claims. He is more like the characters of Coward and Stoppard, who find that against the hurt of betrayal comedy is no help. He asks Rowley not to tell Sir Oliver Surface that his marriage is in trouble, 'For I should never be able to stand Noll's jokes' (I.ii.83). When the screen falls in Joseph Surface's apartment, revealing Lady Teazle behind it, Sir Oliver and all London (not to mention the audience) can have a grand laugh at Sir Peter's expense. Sir Oliver gives the laughter free rein for a while – 'I never laughed more in my life, I assure you' – then tries unsuccessfully to restrain himself, while Sir Peter makes a lugubrious attempt to be a good sport:

SIR OLIVER:  But, come, come, it isn't fair to laugh at you neither, my old friend, though, upon my soul, I can't help it.
SIR PETER:  Oh, pray don't restrain yourself on my account. It does not hurt me at all. I laugh at the whole affair myself. Yes, yes, I think being a standing jest for all one's acquaintance a very happy situation.

(V.ii.201–17)

There is no sense that the laughter is helping Sir Peter bear his misfortune; it is simply one more stage in his ordeal. And the audience is likely to have Sir Oliver's problem, knowing its laughter is unkind, and unable to stop.

Laughter does not heal. The fear of being laughed at threatens for a while to block Sir Peter's reconciliation with his wife: 'when it is known that we are reconciled, people will laugh at me ten times more.' Rowley, implicitly accepting Lady Sneerwell's equation of laughter with malice, replies, 'Let them laugh and retort their malice only by showing them you are happy in spite of it' (V.ii.248–51). Benedick embraces marriage by staring down mockery: 'I'll tell thee what, Prince: a college of wit-crackers cannot flout me out of my humour. Dost thou think I care for a satire or an epigram?' (V.iv.99–101). Sir Peter will have to do the same. In the play's final moments one last malicious joke about the Teazle marriage is raised, indulged, and then allowed to die. Lady Sneerwell's exit line is directed against her former pupil:

LADY SNEERWELL: You too, madam! Provoking insolent! May your husband live these fifty years. *Exit*
SIR PETER: Oons! what a Fury!
LADY TEAZLE: What a malicious creature it is!
SIR PETER: Hey! Not for her last wish?
LADY TEAZLE: Oh, no!

(V.last.197–202)

In Lady Teazle's 'Oh, no!' the malice is dismissed, and the joke along with it. The laugh dies. Defeated in the intrigue, Lady Sneerwell may be said to have won the debate: the only way to remove malice from laughter, it seems, is by the sort of operation that kills the patient.

## No offence: *The Conscious Lovers*

Sheridan does not openly vindicate Lady Sneerwell, for to do so would require the play to apologize for its own comedy. By a sleight of hand he keeps the audience so amused they may not notice that the views of the sympathetic characters are at odds with the play's practice. It is the play's private joke against itself. Less sophisticated comedies are more openly apologetic. The prologue to Nicholas Udall's *Roister Doister* (c.1552) approaches the audience with an air of defensive anxiety, assuring us it offers 'mirth with modesty . . . / Wherein all scurrility we utterly refuse / Avoiding such mirth wherein is abuse.' The play's brand of mirth, we are assured, is good for us: comedy is a medicine which taken according to instructions 'prolongeth life and causeth health'. But even after this assurance the anxiety persists: 'As we trust no good nature can gainsay the same; / Which mirth we intend to use, avoiding all blame' (1–14). Udall is presumably assuring the audience that his comedy will not be the scatological, anarchic and subversive comedy of the vices of the morality plays. But as the assurances are repeated over and over, the worry about guilt by association mounts. This early in its history, English comedy seems to be apologizing for itself. The characters of comedy can register a similar anxiety. Comic intrigue can have its cruel side, and the characters of Hannah Cowley's *The Belle's Stratagem* (1780) worry about the deceptions they practice on each other: ''tis inhuman to conceal his happiness' (V.iii.p.476); 'hang it, to impose upon a poor fellow at so serious a moment! – I can't do it' (V.iv.p.477). They seem reluctant to behave like characters in a comedy.

In his admiring prologue to Sir Richard Steele's *The Conscious Lovers* (1722) Leonard Welsted urges the audience to support the play's campaign 'To chasten wit, and moralize the stage' (28). Steele in fact seems determined to chasten comedy itself, a determination that goes so far the play threatens to disable itself not just as comedy but as drama. By Steele's own account the scene in which Bevil persuades his friend Myrtle not to fight a duel with him was the play's *scene-à-faire*: 'the whole was writ for the sake of the scene in the fourth act, wherein Mr. Bevil evades the quarrel with his friend' (Preface, p.437). If drama is action, there is something perversely anti-dramatic in making a play's crucial scene one in which an action is prevented. Bevil himself, torn between his desire to marry Indiana and his refusal to offend his father (who wants him to marry Lucinda) is forced into the role of comic intriguer, and plays it with reluctance: 'let me resolve upon – what I am not very good at, though it is – an honest dissimulation' (I.ii.18–19). The sentence fights its own forward movement, and completes itself only with the assurance that the dissimulation is honest. Lucinda's lover Myrtle, in order to head off her marriage to Cimberton, disguises himself as Cimberton's elderly uncle. When in the play's last moments he reveals himself, there is a general cry of 'Mr Myrtle!' The small flash of comic excitement is dampened a bit by the formality of 'Mr'; it is dampened further when Myrtle apologizes for behaving like a character in a comedy: 'And I beg pardon of the whole company that I assumed the person of Sir Geoffry, only to be present at the danger of this lady's being disposed of, and in her utmost exigence to assert my right to her' (V.iii.317–22). In the event his disguise was unnecessary, and he seems relieved.

In another delaying tactic, Myrtle joins with Bevil's servant Tom to impersonate the lawyers Bramble and Target, offering contradictory legal opinions on whether Cimberton's uncle should be a party to the negotiation of his marriage. The scene recalls Jonson's *Epicoene* (1609), in which Otter and Cutbeard, disguised as lawyers, argue about the impediments to Morose's marriage, and the impediments to those impediments; but while Jonson's scene draws its energy from the unstoppable torrent of legal jargon, Steele's embodies impediment itself: Target has a bad stammer. Bevil, proposing that Tom impersonate Target, comments, 'All his part will be to stutter heartily, for that's old Target's case. Nay, it would be an immoral thing to mock him, were it not that his impertinence is the occasion of its breaking out to that degree' (II.i.109–13). *Qui s'excuse, s'accuse*; Steele actually compounds the offence, as Bevil calls attention to the cruelty of the comedy then complacently justifies it on moral grounds. Steele's critics attacked him 'for exposing to laughter an object of pity'.[8] He himself is much more comfortable when he is evoking not the laughter of ridicule but what Indiana, approving Bevil's courtesy to his inferiors, calls 'a smile of approbation' (II.ii.273–74). *The Conscious Lovers* is Steele's 'counter-statement' to Restoration comedy;[9] the dressing-plate Bevil presents to Indiana as a token of his esteem is as far as it could be from Horner's china. But there is some justice in Hazlitt's observation that Steele is squeamish about comedy itself, 'as if writing a comedy was no very creditable employment'.[10]

## Against closure

*The Conscious Lovers* is an example of what Susan Carlson has called comedy's 'collision course with itself'.[11] The social consolidation implied by the conventional happy ending is at odds with the destructive spirit of laughter. While Sheridan manages to give both their due, Steele dampens the laughter in favour of the smile of approbation. More commonly, it is the ending that suffers. The happy ending is, as John Creaser puts it, 'compatible neither with the bitterness of mocking laughter nor with the sadness at human realities which pervade the genre. The happy ending is a conscious unreality.'[12] According to Walter Kerr, 'The happy endings of comedy are no more than mere pretenses. Or rather they *are* more. They are frauds.'[13] Anne Barton suggests that it is not so much its happiness that makes the comic ending fraudulent as its claim to *be* an ending: 'an ephemeral moment of happiness [poses] as a permanent state.'[14] When the self-awareness of comedy leads it to question its own devices, closure itself comes under attack.

As *The Conscious Lovers* sets itself against Restoration comedy, there are comedies that question the way other comedies end, and in so doing question the whole notion of ending. Thomas Southerne's *The Wives' Excuse; or, Cuckolds Make Themselves* (1692) centres on the marriage of the Friendalls. Mrs Friendall is an attractive and intelligent woman on whom several of the play's men, with Lovemore in the lead, have designs; Friendall, a pretentious dilettante, a coward, an an unfaithful husband, is ripe for cuckolding. The servants whose gossip about their masters opens the play assume he will be cuckolded. Friendall himself, when the case is put to him by Wellvile (who is writing a play called *The Wives' Excuse; or, Cuckolds Make Themselves*) insists, not knowing the case is his own, 'She must make him a cuckold' (III.ii.248). The play's own subtitle implies the deed will be done. The fates of husbands like Pinchwife in Wycherley's *The Country Wife* (1675) and Sir Davy Dunce in Otway's *The Soldiers' Fortune* (1681), who get the horns they deserve, point the way. But Southerne sabotages the expectations of libertine comedy.[15] Everyone has reckoned without Mrs Friendall herself. She rejects the advances of Lovemore, knowing her husband is worthless but citing her own self-respect (IV.i.139–41) and refusing to submit to a dramatic cliché: 'that honourable opinion of our sex, that, because some women abuse their husbands, every woman may' (IV.i.130–32).

This in itself sounds like closure: she has made her decision and preserved her virtue. But this is Act Four. In Act Five, as though to deny the audience any kind of satisfaction, she apologizes to Lovemore for refusing him, no longer asserting her self-respect but blaming herself for inertia: ''tis the fault of my heaviness, perhaps, that can't be transported into the woman you'd have me' (V.iii.83–84). Nor does her self-denial heal her marriage, as in a more complacent comedy it might have done. In the aftermath of the discovery of Friendall on the couch with Witwoud, the Friendalls separate. But this is not a full solution either; as Mrs Friendall complains, 'I must be still your wife, and still unhappy' (V.iii.347). It is her last utterance in the play, and it denies the whole notion of a happy ending through marriage. More fundamentally, her last two words, 'still unhappy', deny comedy's claim to solve its characters' problems. Lovemore's comment, 'What alteration this may make in my fortune with her, I don't know; but I'm glad I have parted 'em' (V.iii.348–49), suggests, through the openness of 'I don't know', that he may still have a chance. Southerne leaves his characters in limbo, denying both the closure of a comic revenge and the reassurances of marriage and virtue rewarded.

The endings of Henry Arthur Jones's comedies *The Case of Rebellious Susan* (1894) and *The Liars* (1897) take one of the routes Southerne refuses. The heroines are stuck with worthless husbands (one is an adulterer, the other a bore) and are tempted by younger, more interesting men. But, at the urging of a worldly-wise *raisonneur* who speaks for the stability of society and the horrors of social disgrace, the women stay with their husbands, making Mrs Friendall's sacrifice but, unlike her, keeping their marriages intact and winning the promise that their husbands will be more attentive in future. Somerset Maugham's *The Circle* (1921) takes the Jones formula and twists it. Elizabeth is married to the humourless Arnold Champion-Cheney, who is too busy with politics to be bothered with her. She is attracted by Teddie Luton, a young businessman on leave from Malaya. In Jones' plays, the young man is sent out to the empire (New Zealand in one case, Africa in the other) to save him from adultery and find a more useful direction for his energies. Maugham reverses that movement, as a sign of other reversals to come.

Two factors seem to be moving the play towards Jones's type of ending. Years ago Arnold's mother Lady Kitty ran off with Lord Porteous, and when they appear his elderly sullenness and her pathetic caricature of youthful charm are an awful warning against romantic adventure. Ostracized by society, they have suffered the fate against which Jones's *raisonneurs* warn his heroines. Maugham's own *raisonneur*, Arnold's father Clive, on the principle that only forbidden fruit is desirable, contrives a trick to keep Elizabeth from bolting. On his father's advice, Arnold offers to let Elizabeth divorce him and promises her an allowance of £2,000 a year. This is the technique Colonel Rivers used on his daughter in *False Delicacy*; in the face of such generosity she cannot possibly run away.

But when Elizabeth asks, 'How can I accept such a sacrifice?' Teddie replies, in effect, quite easily (III.pp.259–60). When she claims that in renouncing him she is giving up her last chance of happiness he retorts, 'But I wasn't offering you happiness . . . . I daresay we'd fight like cat and dog, and sometimes we'd hate each other . . . . I offer you unrest and anxiety. I don't offer you happiness. I offer you love.' Within moments she is in his arms: 'You hateful creature, I absolutely adore you' (III.p.261). Porteous, who has warned them against elopement, declares, 'You're damned fools, both of you, damned fools. If you like you can have my car.' Teddie cheerfully admits he was going to steal it anyway (III.p.262). The play ends with the lovers on the road, heading not for the happiness of the traditional comic ending but for unrest and anxiety, and Clive, not knowing what has happened, congratulating himself on the success of his scheme to preserve his son's marriage. As he bursts into hearty laughter, Kitty and Porteous join in, and the play ends with all three '*in fits of laughter*' (III.p.264). Instead of indulging laughter, then letting it end as marriage solves the problems, the play ends with a broken marriage, and laughter directed against the character who thought he had saved it.

To end a play by sending characters out on to the road is in itself a challenge to conventional comic closure, in which characters are supposed to settle down,

144

dwindling into wives and husbands. Noël Coward is particularly fond of having characters creep off with suitcases at the end of a comedy. In *Hay Fever* (1925) the guests who have endured a mad weekend amid the theatricalized emotions of the Bliss family '*creep downstairs, with their bags, unperceived by the family*' (III.p.179) and silently make their escape. *Private Lives* (1930) ends with Victor and Sibyl in the middle of a flaming row, as Amanda and Elyot, also unseen, '*go smilingly out of the door, with their suitcases*' (III.p.254). For Coward, the closed ending denies the impermanence that is the real condition of life. For Edward Bond it implies the acceptance of an unacceptable society and denies the possibility of political change. At the end of *The Sea* (1973) Willy, about to leave town with Rose, has a last visit with Evens on the beach, and gets his marching orders: 'Go away. You won't find any more answers here. Go away and find them. . . . you must still change the world' (viii.pp.64–65). Rose comes to collect Willy, and he turns to her: 'I came to say goodbye, and I'm glad you –' (viii.p.65). On that broken sentence the play ends; or rather, refuses to end. To have Willy and Rose settle down would induce the complacency Bond wants to avoid. In Bond's own words, 'it is for the audience to go away and complete the sentence in their own lives.'[16]

Bond and Coward in their different ways speak for the restlessness of the twentieth century; but they are using the medium of a genre that has its own built-in restlessness. The technical incompleteness Bond creates in a single sentence Sir John Vanbrugh creates in the action of *The Relapse* (1696). He begins by overturning the happy-ever-after ending of Cibber's *Love's Last Shift* (1696). Loveless and Amanda are seen enjoying the married bliss in which Cibber left them. They declare, 'let it be forever' (I.i.40), but before long Loveless has deceived Amanda with her friend Bellinda. She, in the meantime, fights off a seduction attempt by Worthy. Vanbrugh's handling of the ensuing action is a subtler act of sabotage than his device of overturning Cibber's ending. Amanda learns she has been betrayed, but never learns who the woman was. Loveless never learns she was tempted and stayed faithful. The situation seems to call out for a showdown, a confrontation, recriminations, and either defiance or repentance. Nothing happens. (A student of mine reported that reading the play for the first time she thought she had skipped a scene.) The marriage is neither decisively broken nor decisively healed. Worthy, rejected by Amanda, undergoes a repentance he himself sees as transient: 'How long this influence may last, heaven knows' (V.iv.160). The play ends with a dialogue between Cupid and Hymen that celebrates promiscuity and declares, 'For change, we're for change, to whatever it be' (V.v.112); and with Young Fashion's statement about his marriage to Hoyden, 'now perhaps the bargain's struck for life' (V.v.266). In Miss Prism's three-volume novel, 'The good ended happily, and the bad unhappily. That is what fiction means' (II.54–55). In *The Relapse* virtue is unrewarded, vice unpunished, and nothing ends.

Endings are inherently artificial, and the metatheatrical awareness that comes to the surface when the audience realizes the play is nearly over can be used to mock that artifice. In Frederick Reynolds's *The Dramatist* (1793) the stage-struck title character Vapid accompanies the reconciliation of the lovers with enthusiastic applause for its stage effect – 'There's light and shade! there's a catastrophe!' (V, unpaginated) – making the point that such things happen only in the theatre. A different kind of metatheatrical joke, calling attention to a standard plot contrivance by upending it, comes near the end of John Maddison Morton's *Box and Cox* (1847):

BOX: ... You'll excuse the apparent insanity of the remark, but the more I gaze on your features, the more I'm convinced that you're my long-lost brother.
COX: The very observation I was going to make to you!
BOX: Ah, tell me – in mercy tell me – have you such a thing as a strawberry mark on your left arm?
COX: No!
BOX: Then it is he! *They rush into each other's arms.*

(p.198)

Ordered endings offer consolation, reconciliation, family reunion; they deny the Hobbesian war of all against all that comedy depicts when wit combats are in full swing. Conventionally the dance symbolizes comedy's final harmony; it plays this role in comedies as different as *As You Like It* and *The Man of Mode*, But at the end of Alan Ayckbourn's *Absurd Person Singular* (1972) the symbol of harmony becomes a symbol of aggression. A dance, combined with musical chairs and a game of forfeits, is the means by which Sidney Hopcroft, a fussy little man whose social rise has been played off against the deterioration of the other characters, celebrates his power over them. Fun becomes torture. As the participants have to cope, variously, with an apple under the chin, a spoon in the mouth and a pear on the spoon, an orange between the knees, and a tea-cosy on the head, Sidney, in hysterical excitement, urges them on: 'Dance. Dance. Come on. Dance. Dance. Dance' (III.p.101). The comedy of ridicule has invaded the ending, perverting the traditional image of harmony. Ayckbourn was not the first to do this. Though we do not know what staging Wycherley had in mind, we see the spirit of ridicule invade the image of the harmony of marriage when near the end of *The Country Wife* he calls for '*a dance of cuckolds*' (V.p.361).

## Marriage refused

The dance usually suggests marriage's role as symbol and supporter of the larger order of society. The sheer number of couples can suggest general public happiness, not just private satisfaction, and marriage ought to imply hope for the future. In Northrop Frye's reading of the comic ending, 'a new social unit is formed on the stage ... the audience witnesses the birth of a renewed sense of social integration.'[17] Yet recent critics have dismissed Frye's view as having more to do with romance than comedy, and as too dependent on the fabricated anthropology of *The Golden Bough*.[18] For the couples themselves marriage, the end of the play, is the end of their story. That is just what they worry about as the men contemplate losing their freedom and the women contemplate dwindling into wives. In practice the very nature of drama blocks the sense of renewal: there is no ready way a dramatist can take the novelist's privilege of glancing into the future that lies beyond the weddings, naming and numbering the children as Dickens (for example) is fond of doing. In a stage comedy a marriage is an ending.

It is an ending some characters resist. The dance of cuckolds at the end of *The Country Wife* is preceded by a general, formal declaration against marriage, allowing only one exception:

ALITHEA:  There's doctrine for all husbands, Mr Harcourt.

HARCOURT:  I edify, Madam, so much, that I am impatient till I am one.

DORIMANT:  And I edify so much by example I will never be one.

SPARKISH:  And because I will not disparage my parts I'll ne'er be one.

HORNER:  And I, alas, can't be one.

PINCHWIFE:  But I must be one – against my will to a country wife, with a country murrain to me.

MRS PINCHWIFE:  (*Aside*) And I must be a country wife still too I find, for I can't like a city one be rid of my musty husband and do what I list.

(V.p.360)

This reads like a parody of the survey of couples, with good wishes for each (and warnings for Touchstone and Audrey), that Hymen and Jaques offer at the end of *As You Like It,* The repetition of the play's title in the speeches of Pinchwife and Margery adds a metatheatrical self-consciousness: as the play moves towards its end, it is making its final statement. And in that statement the two characters who are actually married feel trapped.

We saw in the last chapter how often comedy, through incidental jokes and the onstage depiction of bad marriages, declares against the institution that gives it its formal ending. The logical conclusion would be for comedy to resist that final formality, to refuse to end with marriage. And many comedies, as part of the general resistance to closure we have examined, do just that. Nor do we have to wait for the free-thinking twentieth century. At the end of the anonymous *The London Prodigal* (c.1604) two of Sir Lancelot Spurcock's three daughters are married. The third, Delia, described as 'your wisest daughter' (V.i.446), vows to stay single, citing 'the cares and crosses of a wife, / The trouble in this world that children bring' (V.i.465–66). Her refusal is based on general common sense. The principal women of Thomas d'Urfey's *The Richmond Heiress* (1693) end the play by rejecting Frederick, who has courted both of them; mercenary and disloyal, he is simply not worth marrying, and both women choose a single life instead. Being involved in a comic intrigue does for Modely at the end of William Whitehead's *The School for Lovers* (1762); far from winning Araminta, his gift for deception leads her to mistrust him, and to turn him down. Rather than glossing over the men's imperfections for the sake of the standard ending (as Shakespeare can be accused of doing in *Two Gentlemen of Verona, All's Well That Ends Well* and the Claudio–Hero

147

plot of *Much Ado*) plays like these raise the frank question, is this man worth marrying? They give an equally frank answer.

The non-marriage ending can also be tied in to questions of form. In Alan Ayckbourn's *The Norman Conquests* (1973) Tom, who complains that he can't tell jokes because he forgets the ending, makes a hash of proposing to Annie: he suggests they 'come together more or less on a permanent basis. Temporarily at least.' When she asks if he means marriage, he replies, 'Yes. . . . And no.' She replies, 'I'll see', and there the matter rests (*Round and Round the Garden*, II.ii.pp.23–24). Besides the comment on modern marriage, which still uses the language of a permanence it no longer possesses, Ayckbourn is making a formal point: marriage is an ending, and Tom is bad at endings. The compression of dramatic form is also a factor. As the audience senses the approach of an ending, the metatheatrical awareness that is never far from the surface of comedy becomes activated, and we are aware of how little time there is left. *Love's Labour's Lost* (c.1594) is explicit about this, as the women, not trusting the men, hold them off for a year of trial:

BEROWNE

> Our wooing doth not end like an old play;
> Jack hath not Jill. These ladies' courtesy
> Might well have made our sport a comedy.

KING

> Come, sir, it wants a twelvemonth and a day,
> And then 'twill end.

BEROWNE

> That's too long for a play.
> (V.ii.864–68)

In Fielding's *The Fathers* (c.1735) two marriages are held off beyond the end of the play. In one case the man's proposal is so sudden and unexpected the woman bursts out laughing (not a good start). While one observer comments that the events of the day 'might furnish out a good subject for a comedy' another objects that 'a catastrophe would be wanting; because you know it is a constant rule, that comedies should end in a marriage' (V.v.p.88). It is, we have seen, no such thing; but Fielding's metatheatrical joke depends on the claim that he is overturning tradition.

The rejection of marriage and the theatrical demand for a decisive ending come together in the convention of the happy divorce. The denouement of Jonson's *Epicoene* (1609) builds with mounting tension to the breaking of the marriage of Morose with the title character, who, in a final metatheatrical joke, proves to be a boy. But the convention is not fully in place here; Jonson is too committed to the comedy of aggression to let Morose show any delight at his release. He has merely been fooled, and he walks silently off the stage. For a truly happy divorce we turn to Thomas Shadwell's *Epsom Wells* (1672), described in its own epilogue as 'A play without a wedding' (1), in which the Woodlys lead up to their divorce with a mock proviso scene (V.i.878–906) and celebrate it as though it were a wedding, with music and dancing; and to Farquhar's *The Beaux' Stratagem* (1707) where the Sullens, working together in perfect harmony, make a cheerful impromptu ceremony out of their decision to part:

SULLEN: These hands joined us, these shall part us – away.
MRS SULLEN: North.
SULLEN: South.
MRS SULLEN: East.
SULLEN: West – far as the poles asunder.
BELLAIR: Begar the ceremony be vera pretty.

(V.iv.232–37)

In a literal sense the most we can be seeing in *Epsom Wells* and *The Beaux' Stratagem* is a private agreement to part, common enough and sometimes called divorce,[19] but not divorce itself. The couples are not free to remarry. What the endings really show is comedy's formal intention to make its characters happy, and to celebrate that happiness with images of festivity. As in *Absurd Person Singular* the comedy of aggression transforms the image of the dance, so here the desire for happiness transforms the anti-marriage ending, making the separation of a couple as upbeat and cheerful as the joining of one. The air of unreality that touches more traditional happy endings is strongly present here. When in *The Beaux' Stratagem* Archer declares, 'Consent is law enough to set you free' (V.iv.274), he identifies the ending as a wish-fulfilment fantasy. The audience is bound to reflect, if only it were that simple. Comedy simplifies and stylizes the hard work of parting, no less than it does the hard work of joining.

## Open and shut: Shaw's revision of *Pygmalion*

Bernard Shaw's *Pygmalion* (1914) ends with one of the notable non-marriages of English comedy, that of Henry Higgins and Eliza Doolittle. The expectation that the principal male and female characters will come together belongs to what Shaw in his postscript to the 1916 printing of the play calls the 'reach-me-downs of the ragshop in which Romance keeps its stock of "happy endings" to misfit all stories' (p.141). (For Romance we might well read Comedy.) Higgins and Eliza are kept apart by many factors, including his mother fixation – no other woman, he claims, can come up to her – and his view of the teacher–pupil relationship as ruling out any erotic entanglement: 'teaching would be impossible unless pupils were sacred' (II.p.51). From Eliza's point of view, the power Higgins has to remake her is a source of discomfort between them; Shaw claims in the postscript that 'Galatea never does quite like Pygmalion: his relation to her is too godlike to be altogether agreeable' (p.157). She bitterly resents the way he has used her as a guinea pig and left her with no clear future. Lovers in other plays can make power a matter of negotiation within a larger relationship; the Higgins–Eliza relationship is too much a matter of pure power, and the power runs all one way.

The play follows comic tradition in its pervasive scepticism about marriage. Alfred Doolittle, on his wedding day, speaks of being 'turned off [hanged]' (V.p.129). Higgins, with a variation on the Sullens' agreement to go to opposite points of the compass, sees men and women as having incompatible wills: 'One wants to go north and the other south; and the result is that they both have to go east, though they both hate the east wind' (II.p.50). He tempts the naïve flower girl with childish fantasies of romantic marriage (II.p.45), and his suggestion that the transformed Eliza might settle her future by marrying is not much better: 'Most men are the marrying sort (poor devils!); and youre not bad-looking: it's quite a pleasure to look at you sometimes' (IV.p.106). In other words, she is a pretty face who could capture a fool. Eliza retorts that he has turned a flower girl not into a duchess but into a prostitute: 'I sold flowers. I didnt sell myself' (IV.p.107). At moments like these the play seems to set itself not just against an Eliza–Higgins marriage, but against the whole institution.

Yet Higgins's view of Eliza in the last scene, after she has walked out on him, is not simply one of indifference and condescension; it is remarkably confused. He declares, 'I can do without anybody' (V.p.133), and admits he misses her; having let her fetch and carry things for him, he claims to despise her for it. Having claimed a Svengali-like power over her, he is at first outraged and then delighted at the independence she shows in threatening to set up on her own as a language teacher. When she defies him, he calls her 'damned impudent slut', then praises her defiance as the result of his teaching: 'By George, Eliza, I said I'd make a woman of you; and I have' (V.p.138). He offers to take her back 'For the fun of it' (V.p.135) in a relationship either of them could end at will. Yet the offer of a free, open partnership is contradicted when Eliza tells him that Freddy Eynsford Hill 'writes to me twice and three times a day, sheets and sheets' and Higgins explodes: 'Damn his impudence!' (V.p.135). The freedom he offers Eliza does not, it seems, include freedom to receive the attentions of another man. He may not want to marry Eliza, but the idea that anyone else might makes him angry.

There are suggestions through the play that their relation is not just that of teacher and pupil. Higgins has to disclaim any sexual interest in Eliza more insistently than he would do if it were simply not an issue. During her fight with him on the night she wins his bet, Eliza takes off a ring he has bought for her and hurls it into the fireplace: the image, inescapably, is of breaking an engagement. From the beginning, the play's interpreters picked up these hints, and moved towards the hand-me-down romantic ending. During the first run, to Shaw's fury, Beerbohm Tree took to throwing roses at Mrs Patrick Campbell at the end of the play.[20] The romantic endings of the 1938 film and of *My Fair Lady* were made, respectively, without Shaw's knowledge[21] and over his dead body. In fact Shaw, as he originally wrote the play, had left matters open. His refusal to let Higgins and Eliza marry was part of a general refusal to close off the story, a rejection not just of this particular ending but of any ending. In the original conclusion of Act Four, after triumphing over Higgins with a mocking pantomime of his exit, Eliza drops to her knees and searches for the ring she had thrown away. She is still looking for it as the curtain falls. For all her disdain for Higgins, she is keeping her options open. In the original ending of Act Five, Higgins behaves as though Eliza has accepted his offer of a continuing partnership, and is prepared to fetch and carry once again. He tells her to buy him a ham, a Stilton Cheese, a tie and a pair of gloves; she sweeps out with a disdainful 'Buy them yourself.' When Mrs Higgins offers to buy them instead, Higgins replies, '*sunnily*', 'Oh, dont bother. She'll buy em all right enough' and the play ends as he '*rattles his cash in his pocket; chuckles; and disports himself in a highly self-satisfied manner*' (V.p.306).[22] Between his confidence and her defiance, their relationship remains unresolved.

The price Shaw paid for this openness was, inevitably, the suggestion that Higgins and Eliza might have a future together; evidently he decided, watching performers take that option, that the price was too high. He began the process of closure in the postscript to the 1916 printing, in which he makes definite what the play leaves as a possibility: Eliza marries Freddy. Something like a comic ending is restored, though on unconventional terms. As a work of prose fiction, the postscript can look beyond the play to tell the story of the marriage, a shapeless chronicle of life going on as Eliza and Freddy struggle to make do. To that extent Shaw is still resisting closure. Shaw revised the play for the 1941 Penguin edition, partly as a reflection of the 1938 film and partly as a strong reaction against it. In this revision, now the best known version of the play, doors that were originally left open are shut. At the end of Act Four Eliza now finds the ring and '*considers for a moment what to do with it. Finally she flings it down on the dessert stand and goes upstairs in a tearing rage*' (IV.p.109). Her rejection of Higgins, which the original version left in doubt, is now decisive. New material is added that strengthens her relationship with Freddy, including a scene in which they run through the streets together, stopping for frequent embraces. Higgins ends the play with a new speech: 'she's going to marry Freddy. Ha! ha! Freddy! Freddy!! Ha ha ha ha ha!!!!! (*He roars with laughter as the play ends*)' (V.p.140). As always when a play ends with a laugh, something is wrong. The marriage is now seen as definite, and provides the closure Shaw originally denied. But the laugh, which has the manic quality of the 'Dance. Dance. Dance' of *Absurd Person Singular*, greets that marriage with a burst of mockery through which Higgins releases his anger at Eliza for throwing herself away. The collision between laughter and the happy ending is at its strongest here, as laughter turns on marriage and rends it.[23]

### Anti-comedy: *Measure for Measure* and *Woman in Mind*

There must be a point, we may fairly assume, where the self-destructiveness of comedy produces not a comedy full of piquant contradictions but a play that can no longer be a comedy, one in which the genre is so torn by its own contradictions that it can no longer function. Plays like *Much Ado About Nothing* and *The Beaux'*

151

*Stratagem* clearly do not go that far; but what of *The Wives' Excuse, The Conscious Lovers, What the Butler Saw*, even *Pygmalion*? There is a kind of play, I think, that – without using comic devices to utterly non-comic ends, as *Othello* uses the handkerchief – becomes an inversion of comedy, an anti-comedy, one in which the outlines of the genre appear but light and shade are reversed to create a negative image. Determining which plays go that far is a tricky matter; any of those I have just listed might conceivably qualify, but all are more or less debatable. I have chosen to end with two plays, written in different periods and radically different in character, that seem to me clear enough to illustrate the principle.

Shakespeare's *Measure for Measure* (c.1604) was published in the Folio among the comedies, but its difficult relation to the genre has sent critics searching for qualifying adjectives, 'dark' and 'problem' being the favourites. There is in fact plenty of laughter in the play, but in the long run that laughter is suppressed by authority. The play's official clown, the bawd Pompey (called 'Clown' in the Folio, though editors prefer to use his proper name) is at first irrepressible. Up before the magistrates, he confuses the court, defies the law, and when asked, 'What do you think of the trade, Pompey? Is it a lawful trade?' cheerfully replies 'If the law would allow it, sir' (II.i.224–26). Arrested and imprisoned, he simply gets a new job as assistant executioner. But his new employer the Provost cuts off his role as clown: 'Come, sir, leave me your snatches, and yield me a direct answer' (IV.ii.6–7). Pompey continues to joke, but his role fades in Act Four and by Act Five he has vanished from the play. The play's other compulsive joker is Lucio, who plays a positive role in getting Isabella to plead for her brother's life, and whose gossip about the absent Duke (which he shares unwittingly with the disguised Duke himself) is wickedly funny. But Lucio's fundamental coldness, in his cynical refusal to bail Pompey and his even more cynical treatment of Kate Keepdown (a prostitute he gets with child and abandons), suggests the underlying inhumanity of laughter; and at the end of the play Lucio, whose persistent heckling through the finale resists the Duke's attempt to create an ordered ending, is the only character who is not forgiven but punished. His slanders offend the Duke, but his real crime is that he has made the audience laugh at a point where they should stop laughing. As the laws of Vienna suppress sex, the laws of the play seem designed to suppress laughter.

In his role as assistant executioner Pompey jokes about death: his greeting to his first client, 'Pray, Master Barnardine, awake till you are executed, and sleep afterwards' (IV.iii.32–33), plays with the traditional idea of death as sleep, and makes death itself sound less than final. Comedy's traditional resistance to death appears in jokes like these, in the plotting of Claudio's return from apparent death, and in Barnardine's wonderfully simple solution to the death penalty: told to come and be executed, he just says no. Yet the play as a whole, far from laughing off death, is terribly, compulsively serious about it. The Duke is at his most eloquent in his long speech to Claudio recommending death over life (III.i.4–41), though his argument is essentially negative: he offers not a hope of happiness beyond the grave, but a catalogue of the misery of life. When Claudio declares he is willing to die rather than let his sister Isabella surrender her virginity to save him, he makes death sound like marriage: 'I will encounter darkness as a bride, / And hug it in my arms' (III.i.84–85). Isabella in turn offers what for her is the ultimate accolade: 'There spake my brother! There my father's grave / Did utter forth a voice. Yes, thou must die' (III.i.86–87). Once again a Shakespearean comedy is touched by memories of a lost father; this time his memory presides approvingly not over his daughter's marriage to a man but over his son's marriage to death. If the plotting of the play aims at saving Claudio, the thinking of the characters aims at his death. When he himself pleads for life it is in a sudden panic that he later regrets (III.i.116–38, 173–74). In the end he reappears alive, but silent, making his restoration to life seem less than complete.

The plot machinery includes the story of Angelo's betrayal and desertion of Mariana. Isabella, hearing the couple's story, has her own view of how it should end: 'What a merit it were in death to take this poor maid from the world! What corruption in this life, that it will let this man live!' (III.i.233–35). That is the solution of tragedy; they should both die. The Duke instead imposes the solution of comedy: having substituted Mariana for Isabella in Angelo's bed he orders their marriage. But 'impose' and 'order' are the key words. Angelo, his crimes exposed, demands the only ending he can see for himself: 'Immediate sentence then and sequent death / Is all the grace I beg' (V.i.381–82). Marched off to marriage, he continues to beg for death.

Marriage, love, sex, the renewal of life: the play's plotting endorses these things but its language works against them. Claudio has consummated his marriage with Juliet while their legal position is still shadowy, and she is pregnant. Lucio sees this as natural healthy fertility – 'her plenteous womb / Expresseth his full tilth and husbandry' (I.iv.43–44) – but Claudio's own image is of eating rat poison (I.ii.128–30). Sex and death, connected in the traditional pun on death as orgasm, are literally connected in Vienna, where fornication carries the death penalty.[24] Lucio's punishment at the end of the play is to be whipped, hanged, and married to Kate Keepdown. The Duke lets him off the first two punishments but insists on the third; Lucio sees no difference: 'Marrying a punk, my lord, is pressing to death, whipping and hanging' (V.i.533–34). Kate Keepdown never appears, and we never get her views on being married as a punishment for her husband. Mariana is on stage when Angelo, newly married to her, continues to insist on death; her reaction, if any, is buried in silence.

Marriage as the death penalty, consummation as rat poison, and a groom who would rather die: the play brings four couples together (the same number as *A Midsummer Night's Dream* and *As You Like It*) but it hardly seems to celebrate the results. Moreover, the three principal characters who are pushed towards marriage are all established from the beginning of the play as natural loners who would rather withdraw from the world. (We may add Lucio as a fourth, given his views on marriage, his trickster's freedom of movement – he deals with all social levels – and the detachment that lies behind his wit.) The Duke, going into disguise, disclaims any romantic motive – 'Believe not that the dribbling dart of love / Can pierce a complete bosom' (I.iii.2–3) – and insists he has 'ever loved the life removed' (I.iii.8).

Isabella is first seen about to enter one of the strictest of orders, the Poor Clares; she complains the rules are not strict enough. Drawn out of the convent to plead for Claudio's life, she goes with palpable reluctance, and on Angelo's first refusal tries to withdraw and head back to the convent. Angelo, noted for his austerity, takes office with palpable reluctance, suggesting he would rather study the law than enforce it, and finding himself attracted to a woman for the first time in his life, is torn by self-disgust. These are the characters the play pushes into marriage.

There is some question as to whether Isabella will go. The Duke, having proposed marriage, then withdraws: 'But fitter time for that' (V.i.505), and in his last speech predicts he will ask her again – later (V.i.546–48). Not only does she give no answer; the question itself keeps receding, until her marriage with the Duke, like the marriages in *Love's Labour's Lost*, is held off beyond the end of the play, with no assurance that it will take place at all. She owes him her brother's life, and there is evidence that they esteem each other, but throughout the play he has guided and manipulated her, and while it was all for her good his relation to her, like Higgins' to Eliza, may be too godlike to be agreeable.

*Measure for Measure* preserves the traditional form of comedy, with the multiple-marriage ending. But its imaginative drive towards death is more clear and compelling than its drive towards marriage, and in that way it reverses the normal impulses of comedy and problematizes its form. Alan Ayckbourn's *Woman in Mind* (1985) engages not so much with the traditional plot structure as with the traditional means by which comedy has allowed its characters to evade social integration: the perspective of the loner, and the escape to a second world. It is a play of detachment and withdrawal, in which the pain and anxiety comedy normally controls are felt so acutely the control persistently breaks down.

While *Measure for Measure* ends with problematic marriages, the starting situation of *Woman in Mind* is a marriage that is a complete disaster. Susan drudges for her husband Gerald and her sister-in-law Muriel, taking no satisfaction in it and getting nothing in return. Whatever love there may have been in the marriage has died long ago, and when she comments that she and Gerald have 'known each other rather a long time' he responds, 'it sounds like an appalling accusation' (I.p.25). We are deep into the waste land of which couples in other comedies, on their way to marriage, sometimes catch worrying glimpses. Even the food is terrible: one of the play's running gags concerns Muriel's attempts at cooking. Her *omelette aux fines herbes* made with Earl Grey tea evokes the comic misery of this play as cucumber sandwiches and muffins evoke the engaging triviality of *Earnest*.

Susan escapes into a world of her imagination, in which an alternative family – who appear on stage – shower her with love and appreciation, she has a beautiful affectionate daughter instead of a grimly withdrawn son, and her husband Andy is a brilliant cook, producing salmon with 'his own special mayonnaise', summer pudding and peach sorbet (I.p.35). In the real world Gerald, a vicar, is labouring at a parish history; in the alternate world Susan is a famous historical novelist. The alternate world is not a place one journeys to, like the Forest of Arden; like the very odd room in *Black Comedy* it occupies the same space as the normal world. Susan enters it without leaving her garden; it is the garden itself that changes, growing in size and acquiring a pool and a tennis court. The alternate world follows tradition in being consciously theatrical: it parodies the tennis-and-champagne ambience of commercial West End comedies of the 1950s and earlier, the ambience Orton evokes in the set of *What the Butler Saw*. Susan's brother Tony at one point plays tennis with a glass of champagne in his hand (I.p.14).

Initially a place of escape, the second world becomes increasingly a place of nightmare. It involves a surrender of daylight identities and relationships; this leads to an unsettling of all identity in a sequence in which characters start to speak each other's lines and Susan feels her own identity broken and redistributed: 'Oh God, I'm everywhere. What am I doing everywhere . . . It's like not . . . (*Slowly*) . . . Not being – anywhere' (II.p.64). Entering the second world is looking into a mirror, since it reflects her own needs and fantasies; and as she looks into that mirror her reflection breaks and dissolves. She begins to lose control of her dream family: Andy speaks her thoughts before she can utter them herself (II.p.63), and the others start to ignore her, carrying on conversations without her (II.p.88). At this point the two worlds begin to blend, as dream versions of her real family enter the second world, and the two husbands greet each other, with sinister enthusiasm, as old friends (II.pp.87–88). This is more alarming than the interplay of court and forest in *As You Like It*: Susan's dream of escape is becoming an inescapable nightmare version of her reality. Supernatural powers sometimes appear in the second world, if only in parody form. Here Susan has sex with Andy on the lawn during a thunderstorm, and declares as she surrenders, 'Oh, dear God! I'm making love with the Devil' (II.p.76).

The second world produces a wedding, but it too is scrambled into nightmare. Susan's dream daughter Lucy is about to be married, but the groom, to Susan's horror, turns out to be her real son Rick (Lucy then dissolves into Rick's wife Tess) and even before this happens the wedding itself becomes a horse-race. Susan's brother Tony reports 'I've just been having a snoop round the brides' enclosure. Our Lucy looks as good as any of them, I must say . . . . She's in peak condition, she's free of injuries, and, of course, the going'll suit her' (II.p.84). Besides the sexual joke (brides are ridden) we may reflect that couples who marry in traditional comedy have won a game and beaten off the competition: Lucy's wedding takes the idea literally.

Susan's cry of protest, 'Where's my wedding? What's happened to the wedding I was promised?' (II.p.86), reminds us that the whole second world, wedding and all, is a projection of her needs. Susan is one of those loners whose perspective governs the play, in this case quite literally. Ayckbourn tells the reader the ground rules from the beginning, and the theatre audience should catch on quickly: '*Throughout the play, we will hear what she hears; see what she sees. A subjective viewpoint therefore and one that may at times be somewhat less than accurate*' (I.p.9). Like other loners at odds with their worlds she has a misanthrope's attacking wit. During the sequence in which she imagines having sex with the devil she is in reality going through the house inflicting comic punishments. In an echo of the judgment on bad poetry in

Jonson's *Every Man in his Humour* (death by fire) she burns the manuscript of Gerald's parish history. Quoting its climax, he lets us hear what the world has lost: 'And finally, what lessons are there to be learnt from the past 600 years of parish history? For is it not the duty of the present to learn from the past in order to prepare for the –' (II.p.78). But he is being punished for more than his writing: when he demands, 'What terrible, nameless, unmentionable thing can I possibly have done to you?' Susan replies, 'Married me?' (II.p.78). Her revenge on Muriel plays on Muriel's obsessive belief that her late husband is trying to contact her from beyond the grave; Muriel thinks of her friend Enid, whose late fiancé wrote on her ceiling, 'LOVE ... ENID ... ETERNALLY' (I.p.30). Susan, who has been constantly irritated by her family's sexual inhibitions, produces her own version of love triumphing over death, writing on Muriel's ceiling, 'KNICKERS OFF, MURIEL' (II.p.80).

But while Susan's perspective is the source of the play's malicious laughter, we are aware from first to last of the pain of her solitude. Each act begins and ends with her voice moaning in a blackout. The play's final note is Susan's *'last despairing wail'* (II.p.92). Characters in other second-world comedies think they are going mad, but the audience, watching the action objectively, knows they are only confused. Susan really is having a mental breakdown, and the play takes us right inside it. Her isolation from other people is conveyed at the beginning as she comes round, having knocked herself out by stepping on a garden rake (we never see the cruel visual comedy; we just get the pain) and Bill, the doctor, is speaking to her: 'Wo! Won't spider slit up pikelet!' (I.p.9). The breakdown of her consciousness has led to a scrambling of language that blocks her contact with other people. When Dogberry declares that comparisons are odorous or Mrs Malaprop calls Lydia as headstrong as an allegory on the banks of Nile, the fun for the audience lies in decoding the scrambled message, as it can do quite easily. This is comedy's problem-solving function, in miniature. But Ayckbourn's audience, with just one chance to listen to Bill's speech, may well be as confused as Susan, not knowing any more than she does that he is really saying, 'Whoa! [or is it No?] Don't try to sit up quite yet.' The decoding becomes easier as the scene goes on, and the gibberish fades into normal language. Bill's first clear word is 'Susan'. (I.p.10). But at the end of the play Susan, trapped in hallucination, finds even the dream characters deserting her. She pleads with them not to leave her alone, and tries to assert her identity: 'Tone show, fleas. Fleas, tone show. December bee? Choose 'un. December choosey. December bee? December bee?' (II.pp.91–2). (Don't go, please. Please, don't go. Remember me? Susan. Remember Susie. Remember me? Remember me?) As she tries to make contact her own language scrambles, and there is no response.

Shakespeare works against the story of comedy, in a play whose impulse to death is stronger than its impulse to marriage, and whose marriages are subject to protest, silence and deferral. He challenges the comic ending. Ayckbourn probes the sources of laughter: detachment, hostility and pain. Working against the communal focus of comedy and even the normal practice of drama, the play locks the audience into the consciousness of a single character, one whose relationships are horrible and whose isolation is painful. The play, especially in Susan's counter-attacks on her family, still gets laughs. But it shows us all too clearly where those laughs come from. In its normal practice comedy expresses anxieties in order to control them; here the control weakens, and the expression is what registers. We are left, in Bergson's image, with the bitter aftertaste of the sea-foam of laughter. We see what it means to be dislocated from the social world; to return to the image that began our discussion of comedy's control in Chapter One, a real baby in a real handbag would suffocate.

# CONCLUSION

The baby in the handbag is a comic image of social dislocation. It is cut off from social ties, and therefore has no name, no identity. Even its being deposited in the cloakroom of a railway station implies insecurity. Railway stations are places of transition; no one lives there. The absurdity of the image keeps us at a distance from the problem; this is the detachment of comedy. At the same time the problem is solved: Jack gets his family, his identity, the marriage he wants. The fact that the play takes the trouble to solve the problem implies that the anxiety it causes is at some level real. And yet the solution, dependent on bizarre coincidence and shot through with formal parody, has its own absurdity. The solution is unreal. The play, by admitting that, paradoxically guarantees its own honesty as a play: if we were asked to believe the ending seriously, we would fight it. But the unreality of the solution means that the anxiety remains unsatisfied, leaving business for other comedies. As Wilde declared in another context, 'All art is quite useless.'[1] Neither laughter nor the happy ending truly solves the problems comedy poses.

The forms of comedy are bound up with the forms of society: the structures of family and marriage, the business of material exchange and social display. The persistent double-edged nature of comedy's effects shows its double attitude to those structures; we have noted the difficulty of deciding whether *The Importance of Being Earnest* questions society so radically as to leave our faith in it shaken, or so playfully as to leave that faith intact. The proviso scene in *The Way of the World* is precariously balanced between the need for marriage and resistance to it. Mirabell and Millamant take the difficulties of marriage just seriously enough to talk their way through them, and just lightly enough not to be stymied by them. The use of role-playing to give the woman authority in the marriage negotiations of other comedies suggests that her empowerment is a brief period of licence before her inevitable submission; but the wit and intelligence she displays during that period make the submission seem doubly regrettable. At the same time, while reacting against the structures of society, comedy keeps close to them, needing the reassurances of order, security and identity they provide. Its double attitude to marriage is of a piece with its double attitude to parents, to the social business of display and marketing, to loner figures and to places of escape. It is by constant self-contradiction that comedy keeps itself alive.

It also survives because it poses fundamental questions about living in society. Its tension between detachment (embodied in laughter) and community (embodied in the happy ending) is the fundamental tension of social life: the need to live one's own free life, and the need to live it with others. But no organism can survive long without adapting, and comedy adapts. Though this has not been a chronological survey, having seen how different periods have been distributed under the headings of our discussion, we may make some suggestions about comedy's response to historical change. There is a heavy concentration of loners of various kinds in Restoration comedy, as though in this period the pressures of social life in a concentrated community sharpened the need for privacy. At the same time the escape to the second world in this period takes the relatively attenu-ated form of sexual adventure in the park, as though society so presses upon the characters that other places are hard to imagine. The second-world convention almost vanishes in the comedy of the eighteenth century, where the acceptance of social accommodation is unusually high; as that acceptance drops in the twentieth century, the other place returns. Scenes of negotiation between lovers cluster thickly in Renaissance and Restoration comedy, but thin out as the decline of public space keeps men and women apart and the increasing distance between stage and audience works against the close-up playing that makes scenes of negoti-ation interesting. The plays that show comedy establishing its ground rules, displaying the tactics by which it controls anxiety and keeps its detachment, cluster in the nineteenth and twentieth centuries. It is as though the form, aware of its age, is becoming retrospective and self-conscious. In the twentieth century, comedy's lack of interest in parent–child relations reflects the decreasing authority of parents in society; its lack of interest in marriage negotiations reflects a society in which marriage is neither as inevitable nor as binding as it used to be.

Given the connection between comedy and the structures of marriage and the family – and most of this study's debt to social history has been in this area – the perceived weakening of those structures in the late twentieth century raises ques-tions about comedy's future. The survival, if only in outline, of the multiple-couple ending in *The Real Thing*, and the rethinking of the boy-gets-girl image at the end of *Cloud 9*, where Betty embraces Betty, may appear in retrospect not fresh versions of a still-vigorous tradition but a last look back at it just before its death. It is too early to be sure. The tradition I have surveyed has been dominated (though not monopolized) by male playwrights working in a male-dominated society. In the late twentieth century all that is changing. In *Women and Comedy: Rewriting the British Theatrical Tradition* Susan Carlson argues that the linear structures of traditional comedy represent a male perspective; she opposes to this tradition contemporary comedy by women, often worked out collectively, expressing their values and breaking free of traditional structures.[2] This may well be where the future of comedy lies. Some of the conventions I have discussed may adapt to the conditions of the future, and survive. I have argued for the persistence of this genre up to the late twentieth century. But the most recent play I have discussed, Ayckbourn's *Woman in Mind*, shows how readily the self-questioning that helps comedy survive can become self-destructive. In that play a manuscript written by a man (Gerald's parish history), arguing (with typical reliance on linear structure) that it is the duty of the present to learn from the past in order to prepare for the future, is not lost in exchange for a baby but summarily burned – by a woman. The woman herself is in the middle of a breakdown, suggesting the terror of life without structure; yet the structures society makes available to her are intolerable. This dark version of comedy's self-contradiction leads in this case to paralysis; as to what it portends for the future, the most one can say, in the words of a much older comedy, is that what's to come is still unsure.

# NOTES

## INTRODUCTION: FIVE CENTURIES OF A GENRE

1 Brian Corman, *Genre and Generic Change in English Comedy 1660–1710* (Toronto, Ont.: University of Toronto Press 1993), p.3.

2 David Perkins, *Is Literary History Possible?* (Baltimore, MD, and London: Johns Hopkins University Press 1992), p.115.

3 Martin Butler, *Theatre and Crisis 1632–1642* (Cambridge: Cambridge University Press 1984; repr. 1987), pp.156–57; Christopher K. Brooks, 'Marriage in Goldsmith: The Single Woman, Feminine Space, and "Virtue"', *Joinings and Disjoinings: The Significance of Marital Status in Literature*, ed. JoAnna Stephens Mink and Janet Doubler Ward (Bowling Green, OH: Bowling Green State University Popular Press 1991), pp.19–35.

4 David Perkins, op. cit., p.131.

5 On the continuing popularity of plays written between 1695 and 1710, see Shirley Strum Kenny, 'Perennial Favorites: Congreve, Vanbrugh, Cibber, Farquhar, and Steele', *Modern Philology*, 73 (1976), S4–S11. See also Robert D. Hume, *The Rakish Stage: Studies in English Drama, 1660–1800* (Carbondale and Edwardsville, IL: Southern Illinois University Press 1983), pp.10–11.

6 Mark S. Auburn, 'Theatre in the Age of Garrick and Sheridan', *Sheridan Studies*, ed. James Morwood and David Crane (Cambridge: Cambridge University Press 1995), pp.17–18.

7 Eric Rump, 'Sheridan, Congreve and *The School for Scandal*', *Sheridan Studies*, op. cit., pp.58–70. On Sheridan's general debt to earlier drama, see Mark S. Auburn, ibid., pp.36–37.

8 *The Orton Diaries*, ed. John Lahr (London: Methuen 1986), pp.107, 140–41.

9 John Lahr, *Prick up your Ears* (New York: Knopf 1978; repr. New York: Vintage Books 1987), p.97.

10 William Hazlitt, *Lectures on the English Comic Writers* (1818), intro. R. Brimley Johnson (London, New York and Toronto, Ont.: Geoffrey Cumberlege, Oxford University Press 1907; repr. 1951), pp.1, 4.

11 Henri Bergson, 'Laughter' (1900), in *Comedy*, ed. Wylie Sypher (Garden City, NY: Doubleday 1956), pp.67, 84, 97. Of the many theories about why we laugh, Bergson's has been perhaps the most durable, but it has not gone unchallenged. George McFadden argues that Bergson seems to be calling for pliable accommodation to the social order rather than freedom, and that his own thinking shows mechanical rigidity: *Discovering the Comic* (Princeton, NJ: Princeton University Press 1982), pp.113–14.

12 Henri Bergson, ibid., p.190.

13 Walter Kerr, *Tragedy and Comedy* (New York: Simon & Schuster 1967), p.29.

14 Arthur Koestler, *The Act of Creation* (London: Hutchison 1964), p.51.

15 Alice Raynor, *Comic Persuasion: Moral Structure in British Comedy from Shakespeare to Stoppard* (Berkeley, CA, and London: University of California Press 1987), p.3; T.G.A. Nelson, *Comedy: An Introduction to Comedy in Literature, Drama, and Cinema* (Oxford and New York: Oxford University Press 1990), p.2; Susan Purdie, *Comedy: the Mastery of Discourse* (Toronto, Ont. and Buffalo, NY: University of Toronto Press 1993), p.116.

16 George Meredith, 'The Idea of Comedy and the Uses of the Comic Spirit' (1877), in *Comedy*, ed. Wylie Sypher, p.46; Henri Bergson, op. cit., p.150.

17 Michael MacDonald, *Mystical Bedlam: Madness, Anxiety, and Healing in Seventeenth-Century England* (Cambridge: Cambridge University Press 1981), pp.41, 88, 99–100.

18 Ibid., pp.111, 274.

19 Peter Laslett, *The World We Have Lost Further Explored* (London: Methuen 1983), pp.88, 158.

20 Peter Laslett, *Family Life and Illicit Love in Earlier Generations* (Cambridge: Cambridge University Press 1977), p.113.

21 John Habakkuk, *Marriage, Debt and the Estates System: English Landownership 1650–1950* (Oxford: Clarendon Press 1994).

22 Lawrence Stone, *Uncertain Unions: Marriage in England 1660–1753* (Oxford: Oxford University Press 1992).

23 Donatus, quoted in *Theories of Comedy*, ed. Paul Lauter (Garden City, NY: Doubleday 1964), p.31. This fine anthology is currently out of print, a problem some enterprising publisher should address.

24 Peter L. Berger and Thomas Luckmann, *The Social Construction of Reality* (Garden City, NY: Doubleday 1966), p.29.

25 Robert Bechtold Heilman, *The Ways of the World: Comedy and Society* (Seattle, WA, and London: University of Washington Press 1978), p.7.

26 Harold Perkin, *Origins of Modern English Society* (London and New York: Routledge & Kegan Paul 1969; repr. 1985), p.280; G.J. Barker-Benfield, *The Culture of Sensibility: Sex and Society in Eighteenth-Century Britain* (Chicago, IL, and London: University of Chicago Press 1992), pp.37–103. Stuart M. Tave has pointed out the difference between the Restoration theory of comedy, which emphasized ridicule, and the nineteenth century theory, which emphasized good nature; see *The Amiable Humorist: A Study in the Comic Theory and Criticism of the Eighteenth and Early Nineteenth Centuries* (Chicago, IL: University of Chicago Press 1960), p.viii.

27 For a warning against the over-simple application of labels, with a specific application to the late seventeenth century, see Robert D. Hume, ' "The Change in Comedy": Cynical Versus Exemplary Comedy on the London Stage, 1678–1693', *Essays in Theatre*, 1 (1983), pp.101–18. On the falsifications entailed in the narrative form of literary history, see David Perkins, op. cit., pp.29–51.

28 David Perkins, op. cit., p.155.

29 T.G.A. Nelson, op.cit., p.48; Eric Bentley, *The Playwright as Thinker* (New York: Harcourt Brace 1946; repr. New York: Meridian Books 1955), p.107; J.L. Styan, *The Dark Comedy* (2nd edn, Cambridge: Cambridge University Press 1968), p.297.

30 On Shakespeare's isolation from the urban tradition, see Anne Barton, *Essays, Mainly Shakespearean* (Cambridge: Cambridge University Press 1994), pp.304–5.

31 Ralph A. Houlbrooke, *The English Family 1450–1700* (London and New York: Longman 1984), p.253.

32 Linda A. Pollock, *Forgotten Children: Parent–Child Relations from 1500 to 1900* (Cambridge: Cambridge University Press 1983), pp.140, 271.

33 Kathleen M. Davis, 'Continuity and Change in Literary Advice on Marriage', *Marriage and Society: Studies in the Social History of Marriage*, ed. R.B. Outhwaite (London: Europa Publications 1981), pp.58–80. In an essay in the same collection, Christopher N.L. Brooke declares himself 'a little in rebellion against the whole conception of novelty

and change: for what is striking is the way in which different attitudes can live together' ('Marriage and Society in the Central Middle Ages', pp.18–19).

34  J.C.D. Clark, *English Society 1688–1832* (Cambridge: Cambridge University Press 1985), p.64.

35  I have not spent time on the pros and cons of an author-based survey. Suffice to say that author-based criticism is already plentiful, and a survey of this kind would block the more extensive view I want to take of the genre itself.

36  On the importance of parks in particular, see Anne Barton, op. cit., pp.350, 366–72.

37  Michael G. Ketcham, 'Setting and Self-Presentation in the Restoration and Early Eighteenth Century', *Studies in English Literature*, 23 (1983), p.405.

38  On the declining importance of the park in eighteenth century comedy, see Anne Barton, op. cit., p.376; on the general question of the decline of the public self, see Richard Sennett, *The Fall of Public Man* (New York: Alfred A. Knopf 1977).

39  Ann Clark, *Women's Silence, Men's Violence* (London and New York: Pandora Press 1987), pp.117, 121.

40  Colin McDowell, *Dressed to Kill: Sex Power and Clothes* (London: Hutchinson 1992), p.57.

41  Mark Girouard, *The Victorian Country House* (New Haven, CT, and London: Yale University Press 1979 (revised edn)), pp.16, 28–29, 34–38.

42  On direct address in the Renaissance theatre, see Alexander Leggatt, *Jacobean Public Theatre* (London and New York: Routledge 1992), pp.76–88. On the Restoration, see Peter Holland, *The Ornament of Action* (Cambridge: Cambridge University Press 1979), p.29. Holland draws a generic distinction – tragedy preserved a sense of illusion and separated stage and audience, while comedy used direct address – that has been questioned by Judith Milhous and Robert D. Hume, *Producible Interpretation: Eight English Plays 1675–1707* (Carbondale and Edwardsville, IL: Southern Illinois University Press 1985), p.65. On acting straight to the audience in early Victorian theatre, see Michael R. Booth, *Theatre in the Victorian Age* (Cambridge: Cambridge University Press 1991), p.125.

43  Robert D. Hume, *The Rakish Stage: Studies in English Drama, 1660–1800*, op. cit., p.218.

44  Michael R. Booth, op. cit., p.84.

45  Ibid., p.71.

46  Michael Goldman, *Shakespeare and the Energies of Drama* (Princeton, NJ: Princeton University Press 1972), p.4.

47  Geoffrey Squire, in *Dress Art and Society 1560–1970* (London: Studio Vista 1974) points to the popularity of epicene figures in Elizabethan art (p.58). But from the second quarter of the seventeenth century the fashion for increasingly low-cut dresses removed any ambiguity about the wearer's sex (p.84).

48  Some ambiguity remained: Mrs Kent played Young Fashion in Vanbrugh's *The Relapse* (1696), giving a heterosexual subtext to the homosexual advances he receives from old Coupler, reversing the effect of *As You Like It*. There were some performances with all-female casts: see Elizabeth Howe, *The First English Actresses: Women and Drama 1660–1700* (Cambridge: Cambridge University Press 1992), pp.57–58.

49  Elizabeth Howe, op. cit., p.35.

50  Katharine Worth, *Sheridan and Goldsmith* (New York: St Martin's Press 1992), p.29.

51  Sheridan got to this point by careful revision; in earlier versions the lady was not so innocent. See *The Origins of The School for Scandal*, ed. Bruce Redford (Princeton, NJ: Princeton University Library 1986), pp.98–104, 128.

52  Ian Donaldson links these two plays, and several others, as examples of what he calls 'the discomfiture of the judge': *The World Upside-Down: Comedy from Jonson to Fielding* (Oxford: Clarendon Press 1970), pp.2–4. Here and elsewhere I have felt free to include in a discussion of comedy a play commonly called a farce. The border between the genres is permeable, and many plays (including *The Comedy of Errors* and *What the Butler*

*Saw*) carry dual passports. It is worth recalling that Horace Walpole called *She Stoops to Conquer* 'the lowest of all farces' (Katherine Worth, op. cit., p.92).

## 1 GETTING CONTROL

1  Christopher Fry, 'Comedy', *Tulane Drama Review*, 4 (1960), p.78; Walter Kerr, *Tragedy and Comedy* (New York: Simon & Schuster 1967), p.31.

2  August Wilhelm von Schlegel, *Lectures on Dramatic Art and Literature* (1808), trans. John Black, in *Theories of Comedy*, ed. Paul Lauter (Garden City, NY: Doubleday 1964), p.338; Allan Rodway, *English Comedy: Its Role and Nature from Chaucer to the Present Day* (London: Chatto & Windus 1975), pp.20–21.

3  Jocelyn Powell, *Restoration Theatre Production* (London: Routledge 1984), p.189.

4  William Hazlitt, *Lectures on the English Comic Writers* (1818), intro. R. Brimley Johnson (London, New York and Toronto, Ont.: Geoffrey Cumberledge, Oxford University Press 1907; repr. 1951), p.15.

5  In a similar reduction to the material, Dromio of Ephesus, in Shakespeare's *The Comedy of Errors* (c.1590), complains that the beatings he receives make him feel like a human football: 'If I last in this service, you must case me in leather' (II.i.84).

6  Seriously religious people do not fare well in comedy. Jokes about Puritans and Methodists abound, and *New Men and Old Acres* (1869), by Tom Taylor and Augustus William Duborg, includes a young lady with an Oxford-Movement enthusiasm for fasting that is deflated by the heroine, who prefers 'fish and a cutlet' (III.p.306).

7  For analogues, see R.B.Parker, introduction to the Revels edition (London: Methuen 1969), pp.xxix–xl. Parker failed to find examples among the *lazzi* of the Commedia dell'arte, though he was certainly right to look; in 1995 I saw a version of the gag in the Pantomime Theatre in the Tivoli Gardens, Copenhagen. For links with *Secunda Pastorum* and Swift's *A Modest Proposal*, see William W.E. Slights, 'The Incarnations of Comedy', *University of Toronto Quarterly*, 51 (1981), pp.16–22.

8  The letter is quoted in *Plays by Henry Arthur Jones*, ed. Russell Jackson (Cambridge: Cambridge University Press 1982), p.15. The relevant passage in the play is at II.p.129. Enough ambiguity remained that William Archer 'came away from the theatre with a strange feeling that he had heard one thing and understood another' (p.15).

9  Ian Clarke, *Edwardian Drama: A Critical Survey* (London and Boston, MA: Faber & Faber 1989), pp.44–48. Characteristically challenging the convention while preserving it, Noël Coward gave the role of *raisonneur* to a woman in his 1924 drama *The Vortex*,

10  Clarke, ibid., p.43.

11  On Jones's own conservatism, including his belief that women were physiologically nearer to children than men were, see Clarke, ibid., pp.27–28, 44.

12  Jose Harris, *Private Lives, Public Spirit: A Social History of Britain, 1870–1914* (Oxford: Oxford University Press 1993), p.74.

13  Joel H. Kaplan and Sheila Stowell, *Theatre and Fashion: Oscar Wilde to the Suffragettes* (Cambridge: Cambridge University Press 1994), p.37.

14  The significance of 'dressed up' is suggested by Kaplan and Stowell, who point out that in the original production Susan's dresses got finer as she became more submissive (ibid., p.36).

15  Zvi Jagendorf, *The Happy End of Comedy: Jonson, Molière, and Shakespeare* (Newark, DE: University of Delaware Press; London and Toronto, Ont.: Associated University Presses 1984), pp.155–56.

16  Frances Gray, *Noël Coward* (London: Macmillan 1987), p.177.

17  See Michael Neill, ' "Feasts Put Down Funerals": Death and Ritual in Renaissance Comedy', *True Rites and Maimed Rites: Ritual and Anti-Ritual in Shakespeare and his Age*, ed.

Linda Woodbridge and Edward Berry (Urbana and Chicago, IL: University of Illinois Press 1992), pp.47–74.

18  Arthur Koestler, *The Act of Creation* (London: Hutchison 1964), p.47.

19  As Michael Billington points out, the play judges its characters by examining their very different attitudes to death. See *Stoppard: the Playwright* (London and New York: Methuen 1987), pp.88–89.

20  Mark Girouard, *Life in the English Country House* (New Haven, CT, and London: Yale University Press 1978), p.300; Clive Aslett, *The Last Country Houses* (New Haven, CT, and London: Yale University Press 1982), pp.55–57; John Habakkuk, *Marriage, Debt and the Estates System: English Landownership 1650–1950* (Oxford: Clarendon Press 1994), pp.649–60.

21  See, respectively, F.M.L. Thompson, *The Rise of Respectable Society: A Social History of Victorian Britain, 1830–1900* (London: Fontana Press 1988), pp.58–59; and Jose Harris, op. cit., p.26.

22  *The Letters of Oscar Wilde*, ed. Rupert Hart-Davis (New York: Harcourt Brace 1962), p.425.

23  Ibid., p.439.

24  Alan Sinfield, ' "Effeminacy" and "Femininity": Sexual Politics in Wilde's Comedies', *Modern Drama*, 37 (1994), pp.34–35. Sinfield offers a corrective to arguments like those of Christopher Craft, 'Alias Bunbury: Desire and Termination in *The Importance of Being Earnest*', *Representations*, 31 (1990), pp.19–46.

25  Richard Ellmann, *Oscar Wilde* (first published London: Hamish Hamilton 1987; repr. Harmondsworth: Penguin 1988), p.403.

26  *The Letters of Oscar Wilde*, op. cit., p.504.

27  Ibid., p.465.

28  Leonore Davidoff, *The Best Circles: Society Etiquette and the Season* (London: Croom Helm 1973), p.40.

29  *Complete Works of Oscar Wilde*, intro. Vyvyan Holland (London and Glasgow: Collins 1948; repr. 1983), p.351.

30  Ibid., p.352. On Gribsby's double name, which is not in the version printed in the Collins edition, see the New Mermaid edition of *The Importance of Being Earnest*, ed. Russell Jackson (London: Adam & Charles Black; New York, W.W. Norton 1988), p.112.

31  *The Letters of Oscar Wilde*, op. cit., p.778.

32  Ellmann, op. cit., p.399.

33  Ibid., p.398.

34  Christopher Craft, op. cit., pp.28–29.

35  Leonore Davidoff, op. cit., pp.54–56; *The Letters of Oscar Wilde*, op. cit., pp.168–69.

36  *Complete Works of Oscar Wilde*, op. cit., p.1039.

37  Roger B. Henkle, 'The Social Dynamics of Comedy', *The Sewanee Review*, 90 (1982), p.213. According to Sinfield, Wilde's comedies generate such mixed responses that deciding whether they are 'progressive or reactionary is . . . not an appropriate project' (op.cit., p.46).

38  Ellmann, op. cit., p.406.

## 2  WATCHING SOCIETY

1  Jean-Christophe Agnew, *Worlds Apart: The Market and the Theater in Anglo-American Thought, 1550–1750* (Cambridge: Cambridge University Press 1986), p.10.

2  Ibid., p.79.

3  Geoffrey Squire, *Dress Art and Society 1560–1970* (London: Studio Vista 1974), p.84.

4  *The Diary of Samuel Pepys*, ed. Robert Latham and William Matthews, VIII (London: G. Bell & Sons 1974), p.463.

5  Peter Holland, *The Ornament of Action* (Cambridge: Cambridge University Press 1979), p.229. On the levee in English comedy, including its social and literary contexts, see Emrys Jones, 'The First West End Comedy', *Proceedings of the British Academy* 68 (1982), pp.215–58.

6  Simon Callow, *Being an Actor* (Harmondsworth: Penguin 1995 (revised edition)), p.54.

7  Harold Perkin, *Origins of Modern English Society* (London and New York: Routledge & Kegan Paul 1969; repr. 1985), p.176. See also J.C.D. Clark, *English Society 1688–1832* (Cambridge: Cambridge University Press 1985), pp.90–91.

8  Thomas Dekker has the linen-draper Candido deliver a long speech in defence of the citizen's flat cap, and of the whole idea of socially coded dress, in *The Honest Whore, Part Two* (1605) (I.iii.26–71).

9  Sheridan himself had suffered from gossip: his secret marriage to Elizabeth Linley involved him in two duels, his injuries were exaggerated in the press, and many other details were slanderously distorted. See Katharine Worth, *Sheridan and Goldsmith* (New York: St Martin's Press 1992), pp.22–23.

10  *The Origins of The School for Scandal*, ed. Bruce Redford (Princeton, NJ: Princeton University Library 1986), p.164.

11  Ralph A. Houlbrooke, *The English Family 1450–1700* (New York and London: Longman 1984), pp.65–66; G.J. Barker-Benfield, *The Culture of Sensibility: Sex and Society in Eighteenth-Century Britain* (Chicago, IL, and London: University of Chicago Press 1992), p.190. Houlbrooke points to the advantage of the market from the children's point of view: they could actually meet each other, and their parents could take their wishes into account. Barker-Benfield stresses the complaints of contemporary moralists at the commercializing of human relations.

12  See, for example, Dion Boucicault, *London Assurance* (1841), II.255–65; and T.W. Robertson, *Society* (1865), II.ii.p.63.

13  The Allwit–Whorehound arrangement had its parallels in reality, as reported in church court records. See Martin Ingram, *Church Courts, Sex and Marriage in England, 1570–1640* (Cambridge: Cambridge University Press 1987), pp.283–84.

14  Pennyboy junior, the newly rich prodigal of Ben Jonson's *The Staple of News* (1626), has a similar levee of tradesmen, but he lacks Evelyn's sardonic insight into the way he is being exploited.

15  On the play's equation of personal and financial relations, see Lars Engle, ' "Thrift is Blessing": Exchange and Explanation in *The Merchant of Venice*', *Shakespeare Quarterly* 37 (1986), pp. 20–37.

16  Harold Perkin, op. cit., pp.38–39, 43.

17  On the growth of pride in English liberty after 1688, and the contrast with French oppression, see J.A. Sharpe, *Early Modern England: A Social History 1550–1760* (London: Edward Arnold 1987), pp.347–48.

18  Derek Jarrett, *England in the Age of Hogarth* (London: Hart-Davis, MacGibbon 1974; repr. Frogmore: Paladin 1976), claims that the constitution which appeared to guarantee liberty actually ensured subordination (p.14). On the question of women, Mary Astell's 1730 tract *Some Reflections upon Marriage* (New York: Source Book Press 1970) asks, 'if *all men are born free*, how is it all women are born slaves?' (p.107). On the other hand, Alan Macfarlane, *Marriage and Love in England: Modes of Reproduction 1300–1840* (Oxford and New York: Blackwell 1986), argues that women had more liberty in practice than they did in law (pp.288–89).

19  John Lahr, *Prick up your Ears* (New York: Knopf 1978; repr. New York: Vintage books 1987), p.134.

20 'A Satyr on Charles II', *The Complete Poems of John Wilmot, Earl of Rochester*, ed. David M. Vieth (New Haven, CT, and London: Yale University Press 1968), p.60.

21 *The Orton Diaries*, ed. John Lahr (London: Methuen 1986), p.237.

22 John Lahr, *Prick up your Ears*, op. cit., p.152.

## 3 LONERS

1 Robert Bechtold Heilman, *The Ways of the World: Comedy and Society* (Seattle, WA, and London: University of Washington Press 1978), p.14; Henri Bergson, 'Laughter' (1900), in *Comedy*, ed. Wylie Sypher (Garden City, NY: Doubleday 1956), pp.147, 150.

2 Peter L. Berger and Thomas Luckman, *The Social Construction of Reality* (Garden City, NY: Doubleday 1966), p.48.

3 Eric Rothstein and Frances M. Kavenik, *The Designs of Carolean Comedy* (Carbondale and Edwardsville, IL: Southern Illinois University Press 1988), p.169. Harold Weber notes Lucy's defiance of social and dramatic convention alike in *The Restoration Rake-Hero* (Madison, WI: University of Wisconsin Press 1986), p.168.

4 In *Thomas Southerne* (Boston, MA: Twayne 1981) Robert L. Root, Jr offers a more sedate explanation: no longer a virgin, Lucy will not marry Valentine because she 'completely [accepts] the double standard' (p.48). As I see it, neither the character nor the play is that conventional, and Valentine himself approves her freedom in her new role as sexual adventuress (I.i.520–45).

5 On the pervasiveness of secrecy in the play, see Ian Donaldson, *The World Upside-Down: Comedy from Jonson to Fielding* (Oxford: Clarendon Press 1970), p.29.

6 'He lurched all swords of the garland' (II.ii.101).

7 Edward Burns, *Restoration Comedy: Crises of Desire and Identity* (London: Macmillan 1987), p.55.

8 I am indebted here to a graduate student paper by Colby Linthwaite.

9 Harold Weber finds Horner 'an immensely powerful but essentially solitary figure', and finds significance in his apartment with its 'separate and apparently unconnected rooms' (Weber, op. cit., p.67).

10 On the general harmlessness of the fop, see Susan Staves, 'A Few Kind Words for the Fop', *Studies in English Literature*, 22 (1982), p.421; and Robert B. Heilman, 'Some Fops and Some Versions of Foppery', *ELH*, 49 (1982), p.392.

11 Geoffrey Squire, *Dress Art and Society 1560–1970* (London: Studio Vista 1974), p.99.

12 Derek Hughes, 'Play and Passion in *The Man of Mode*', *Comparative Drama*, 15 (1981), p.238; Wandalie Henshaw, 'Sir Fopling Flutter, or the Key to *The Man of Mode*', *Essays in Theatre*, 3 (1985), p.105.

13 Cibber wrote the part for himself, and the same false modesty is a recurring note in his autobiography, *An Apology for the Life of Mr Colley Cibber, Comedian* (1740).

14 Jules Barbey d'Aurevilly, *Dandyism* (1845), trans. Douglas Ainslie (New York: PAJ Publications 1988 (reprinted edn)), p.71. This translation was originally published as *Of Dandyism and of George Brummell* (London: J.M. Dent & Co., 1897).

15 Boucicault originally intended the speech for Max Harkaway, who has been the play's *raisonneur*. In rehearsal, the actor playing Sir Harcourt (William Farren) claimed the speech for himself and Boucicault after some hesitation agreed. The original effect would have been merely logical; the effect of the text as it stands is more piquant, showing a surprising new development in Sir Harcourt. See *London Assurance*, ed. James L. Smith (London: Adam & Charles Black; New York: W.W. Norton 1984), p.130.

16 See Martin Ingram, 'Ridings, Rough Music and Mocking Rhymes in Early Modern England', *Popular Culture in Seventeenth-Century England*, ed. Barry Reay (London and Sydney: Croom Helm 1985), pp.166–97.

17 Zvi Jagendorf, *The Happy End of Comedy: Jonson, Molière, and Shakespeare* (Newark, DE: University of Delaware Press; London and Toronto, Ont.: Associated University Presses 1984), p.59.
18 There has been some critical debate over whether the text makes it clear that Manly has coupled with Olivia, or allows the possibility that he changes his mind at the last moment; the strongest evidence suggests the former. See Derek Hughes, '*The Plain-Dealer*: A Reappraisal', *Modern Language Quarterly*, 43 (1982), p. 323, n.17; and Robert F. Bode, 'A Rape and No Rape: Olivia's Bedroom Revisited', *Restoration*, 12 (1988), pp. 80–86.
19 Edward Burns, op. cit., p.62.
20 In the New York production the sequence was rearranged so that Betty's masturbation speech followed her scene with Gerry, making Betty's speech the climax. In the American edition (New York: Methuen 1984) Churchill is polite about this change (p.ix) but the text restores the original ending, which she clearly prefers. See Helene Keyssar, 'The Dramas of Caryl Churchill: The Politics of Possibility', *Masssachusetts Review*, 24 (1983), p.215; and Susan Carlson, *Women and Comedy: Rewriting the British Theatrical Tradition* (Ann Arbor, MI: University of Michigan Press 1991), p.238.
21 In 'Comic Collisions: Convention, Rage and Order', *New Theatre Quarterly*, 3 (1987), Susan Carlson notes other reconciliations that take place around this central image: 'a woman embraces herself and her sexuality, a woman embraces a man, the straight embraces the gay, the old embraces the new, the order calms our rage' (p.315).

## 4 OTHER PLACES

1 'The Argument of Comedy', in *Theories of Comedy*, ed. Paul Lauter (Garden City, NY: Doubleday 1964), p.456.
2 François Laroque, *Shakespeare's Festive World*, trans. Janet Lloyd (Cambridge: Cambridge University Press 1991), pp.111–14.
3 See Anne Barton, 'Parks and Ardens', in *Essays, Mainly Shakespearean* (Cambridge: Cambridge University Press 1994), pp.352–79.
4 ibid., pp.377–78.
5 Its first use is in Act One, when Harry asks the black servant Joshua, 'Shall we go in a barn and fuck?' (I.i.p.21). Here, gay sex crosses barriers of race and class; but Harry also seems to be using his power over Joshua, and he hastens to add, 'It's not an order.'
6 As Churchill described this scene in a letter to Richard Seyd, who was preparing a production in San Franciso in 1983: 'Then there's the goddess scene, midsummer or so by now, when the women assert themselves, magic happens, ghosts start to be laid . . . .' *File on Churchill*, compiled by Linda Fitzsimmons (London: Methuen 1989), p.48.
7 There can be a moment of this kind in productions of Shakespeare's *The Merry Wives of Windsor* (c.1600) when at the start of the final scene in Windsor Forest a horned figure appears out of the shadows. When the audience realizes it's Falstaff, duped into wearing a buck's head, its laughter not only recognizes his absurdity but provides relief from a momentary confrontation with the uncanny.
8 Michael Billington, *Alan Ayckbourn*, (London: Macmillan 1990 (2nd edn)), p.21.
9 Robert Pogue Harrison, *Forests: The Shadow of Civilization* (Chicago, IL: and London: University of Chicago Press 1992), p.156.
10 J. Dennis Huston, *Shakespeare's Comedies of Play* (London: Macmillan 1981), p.87.
11 Noël Coward, *Play Parade* (New York: Garden City Publishing 1934), p.xiii.
12 In *Early Stages* (London: Theatre Book Club 1953 (revised edn)) John Gielgud recalls an acting exercise of his youth in which students were asked to express different emotions – hate, fear, disgust, joy – with the words 'Baby's burning' (p.54).
13 In Richard Brome's *The Antipodes* (1638) the hero is transported below the equator to an upside-down world in which the people rule the magistrates, the women rule the men,

and so on. But he never leaves England; the Antipodean world is an illusion created by a troupe of actors.

14 Alan Bennett, *Forty Years On* (London: Faber & Faber 1969), p.29.

15 Anne Wright, *Literature of Crisis 1910–22* (London: Macmillan 1984), p.89.

16 *The Orton Diaries*, ed. John Lahr (London: Methuen 1986), p.125.

17 C.W.E. Bigsby, *Joe Orton* (London and New York: Methuen 1982), p.44.

18 *The Orton Diaries*, op. cit., p.199.

19 See, for example, Maurice Charney, 'What Did the Butler See in Orton's *What the Butler Saw?*' *Modern Drama*, 25 (1982), pp.496–504. Leslie Smith, in *Modern British Farce* (London: Macmillan 1989), sees the play as combining celebration with nightmare (pp.127–35).

20 *The Orton Diaries*, op. cit., p.256.

21 The unnaturally short day of *Butler* is the converse of the unnaturally long nights of some Elizabethan comedies. In *Two Angry Women* Sir Ralph asks, 'O, when will this same year of night have end?' (V.i.p.185). In *A Midsummer Night's Dream* Theseus opens the play by complaining that his wedding is four days off; it then appears to take place the following day. If this is not just Shakespeare being cavalier about time, it could suggest an unnaturally long night in the woods.

22 As in *Cloud 9*, the invocation of a supernatural, orgiastic power has something pedantic about it: Lin gets her invocation of the goddess 'out of a book' (II.iii.p.95).

23 In Elizabethan folk belief it was considered unwise to speak of dealings one had had with the fairies, who were 'jealous of their privacy': Keith Thomas, *Religion and the Decline of Magic* (New York: Charles Scribner's Sons 1971), p.614.

24 In the most frightening story in Ray Bradbury's *The Martian Chronicles* (New York: Bantam 1954 (reprinted edn)), a party of American astronauts find themselves in an ordinary American town, where they are greeted by their families. The trouble is, they are on Mars (pp.32–48).

25 Quoted in Leslie Smith, op. cit., p.141.


## 5 PARENTS AND CHILDREN

1 Northrop Frye, 'The Argument of Comedy', p.450; Ludwig Jeckels, 'On the Psychology of Comedy', p.425; both in *Theories of Comedy*, ed. Paul Lauter (Garden City, NY: Doubleday 1964).

2 Ralph A. Houlbrooke sees this pattern in the seventeenth century: see *The English Family 1450–1700* (London and New York: Longman 1984), pp.70, 72.

3 Michael MacDonald, *Mystical Bedlam: Madness, Anxiety, and Healing in Seventeenth-Century England* (Cambridge: Cambridge University Press 1981), p.93; see also Keith Wrightson, *English Society 1580–1680* (London: Unwin Hyman 1990 (reprinted edn)), pp.71–79; and John R. Gillis, *For Better, For Worse: British Marriages, 1600 to the Present* (New York and Oxford: Oxford University Press 1985), pp.46–47.

4 Alan Macfarlane, *Marriage and Love in England: Modes of Reproduction 1300–1840* (Oxford and New York: Blackwell 1986), pp.136–37; for a fully illustrated discussion, see pp.119–47.

5 John R. Gillis, op. cit., p.140.

6 Ralph A. Houlbrooke, op. cit., p.145; Lawrence Stone, *The Family, Sex and Marriage in England 1500–1800* (New York: Harper & Row 1977), p.171.

7 Keith Wrightson, op. cit., p.115.

8 On Blackacre's disruption of male authority, of which her suppression of Jerry is a part, see Helen Burke, ' "Law-suits", "Love-suits" and the Family Property in Wycherley's *The Plain Dealer*', *Cultural Readings in Restoration and Eighteenth-Century Theater*, ed. J.

Douglas Canfield and Deborah C. Payne (Athens, GA, and London: University of Georgia Press 1995), pp.93–102.

9  John Milton, *Paradise Lost*, VII.171–72.

10  Ralph A. Houlbrooke, op. cit., p.140; Linda A. Pollock, *Forgotten Children: Parent–Child Relations from 1500 to 1900* (Cambridge: Cambridge University Press 1983), pp.155–56.

11  G.J. Barker-Benfield, *The Culture of Sensibility: Sex and Society in Eighteenth-Century Britain* (Chicago, IL, and London: University of Chicago Press 1992), p.102.

12  Linda A. Pollock, op. cit., pp.119–20, 156.

13  The play's run on both sides of the Atlantic established a record that was to be broken only by *Charley's Aunt*; during its London run the bus stop outside the Vaudeville theatre was known as 'Our Boys'. See *Plays by H.J. Byron*, ed. Jim Davis (Cambridge: Cambridge University Press 1984), pp.24–25.

14  In *Private Lives, Public Spirit: A Social History of Britain, 1870–1914* (Oxford: Oxford University Press 1993) Jose Harris notes that historians have been unable to agree on whether the effect of the Victorian family on its members was nurturing or traumatic (pp.61–62). The dilemma is not confined to this period.

15  Inchbald seems uncertain whether her first name is Maria or Elizabeth (I.i.p.17, IV.iii.p.56).

16  There is an early example in Thomas Dekker's *The Honest Whore, Part Two* (1605): Orlando, father of the title character, is stern and unforgiving on the surface, but helps her in secret, and Dekker gives him many opportunities to burst into tears.

17  See nn.3, 10.

18  In his introduction to the New Mermaid edition (London: Ernest Benn 1979), Tom Davis takes quite seriously Mrs Hardcastle's offer to die for Tony in the 'highwayman' scene (p.xvii). Given Goldsmith's general ability to create rounded characters, the reading is worth entertaining; but Mrs Hardcastle's gift for self-dramatization works against it.

19  There was a widespread recognition on the part of parents that the oldest son had a responsibility to his siblings; see Ralph A. Houlbrooke, op. cit., p.41.

20  Lynda E. Boose, 'The Father and the Bride in Shakespeare', *PMLA*, 97 (1982), pp. 327–28; Diane Elizabeth Dreher, *Domination and Defiance: Fathers and Daughters in Shakespeare* (Lexington, KY: University Press of Kentucky 1986), p.119.

21  On the relationship between Portia and Jessica, see Lynda E. Boose, ibid., pp. 335–37.

22  Alexander Leggatt, *Citizen Comedy in the Age of Shakespeare* (Toronto, Ont. and Buffalo, NY: University of Toronto Press 1973), pp.33–53.

23  G.J. Barker-Benfield, op. cit., pp.69–70.

24  Ibid., pp.23–36.

25  The play is a little ambiguous on this point. Nick claims, 'I attempted last night to misbehave myself with her. I didn't succeed' (I.p.396). But the wording of Mrs Prentice's protest at his having photographs of the occasion suggests otherwise: 'When I gave myself to you the contract didn't include cinematic rights' (I.p.370).

## 6  NEGOTIATIONS

1  For a sampling, see Alan Macfarlane, *Marriage and Love in England: Modes of Reproduction 1300–1840* (Oxford and New York: Blackwell 1986), pp.168–73.

2  T.G.A. Nelson, *Comedy: An Introduction to Comedy in Literature, Drama, and Cinema* (Oxford and New York: Oxford University Press 1990), p.46. See also Eric Rothstein and Frances M. Kavenik, *The Designs of Carolean Comedy* (Carbondale and Edwardsville, IL: Southern Illinois University Press 1988), p.9.

3  In *Comedy* (London: Hutchinson 1949), L.J. Potts explains the pervasiveness of what he calls sex (what would now be called gender difference) as a comic subject; it is the only

area where we can '*all* be said to be eccentric . . . . All women appear abnormal to all men, and all men to all women' (pp.49–50).

4  Keith Wrightson, *English Society 1580–1680* (London: Unwin Hyman 1990 (reprinted edn)), p.82; Alan Macfarlane, op. cit., p.165; Martin Ingram, *Church Courts, Sex and Marriage in England, 1570–1640* (Cambridge: Cambridge University Press 1987), p.141.

5  Michael MacDonald, *Mystical Bedlam: Madness, Anxiety, and Healing in Seventeenth-Century England* (Cambridge: Cambridge University Press 1981), pp.88–89.

6  Mary Astell, *Some Reflections Upon Marriage* (New York: Source Book Press 1970), p.20; see also Ralph A. Houlbrooke, *The English Family 1450–1700* (London and New York: Longman 1994), pp.114–15.

7  Jacqueline Pearson sees Amanda as a male fantasy of the perfect woman, faithful and desirable, and a female fantasy of virtue rewarded: *The Prostituted Muse: Images of Women and Women Dramatists 1642–1737* (New York: St Martin's Press 1988), p.61.

8  Leonore Davidoff, *The Best Circles: Society Etiquette and the Season* (London: Croom Helm 1973), p.24.

9  Susan Carlson, *Women and Comedy: Rewriting the British Theatrical Tradition* (Ann Arbor, MI: University of Michigan Press 1991), p.21.

10  Jose Harris, *Private Lives, Public Spirit: A Social History of Britain, 1870–1914* (Oxford: Oxford University Press 1993), p.24. Lawrence Stone notes a growing tendency, beginning in the late seventeenth century, for individual marriage settlements to protect the property rights of the wife: *The Family, Sex and Marriage in England 1500–1800* (New York: Harper & Row 1977), p.244.

11  Ralph A. Houlbrooke, op. cit., p.119; Martin Ingram, op. cit., pp.143–44; Keith Wrightson, op. cit., p.92.

12  Kato's fame spread beyond the play, and he became a bugbear for the suffragettes; see Joel H. Kaplan and Sheila Stowell, *Theatre and Fashion: Oscar Wilde to the Suffragettes* (Cambridge: Cambridge University Press 1994), p.190, n.15.

13  James Thurber, *Men, Women and Dogs* (New York: Harcourt Brace 1943), pp.187–205.

14  Ian Clarke, *Edwardian Drama: A Critical Study* (London and Boston, MA: Faber & Faber 1989), p.114.

15  Camille Wells Slights, *Shakespeare's Comic Commonwealths* (Toronto, Ont.: University of Toronto Press 1993), p.44.

16  Ibid., p.51.

17  Karen Newman, *Fashioning Femininity and English Renaissance Drama* (Chicago, IL, and London: University of Chicago Press 1991), p.42. As Alan Somerset has pointed out to me, Bartholomew's obedience stops short of granting Sly's request for sex – another reminder that this 'wife' is a performance.

18  He is echoing a famous line from Beaumont and Fletcher's *The Maid's Tragedy*: 'A maidenhead, Amintor, / At my years?' (II.i.194–95).

19  Derek Hughes, 'Play and Passion in *The Man of Mode*', *Comparative Drama*, 15 (1981), pp.242–50.

20  Peter Laslett, *The World We Have Lost Further Explored* (London: Methuen 1983), p.78.

21  Cited in Lawrence Stone, op. cit., p.401.

22  Brian Corman, 'Interpreting and Misinterpreting *The Man of Mode*', *Papers on Language and Literature*, 13 (1977), p.53.

23  Mary Astell, op. cit., p.34; Keith Wrightson, op. cit., p.79.

24  Joel B. Altman, *The Tudor Play of Mind* (Berkeley, CA, and London: University of California Press 1978), p.23.

25  Peter Holland, *The Ornament of Action* (Cambridge: Cambridge University Press 1979), p.231.

26  Jacqueline Pearson, op. cit., pp.39–40, 54.

27  Richard Bevis takes a more favourable view, reading Marlow as 'a naturally affable fellow' who with the lower orders can 'relax and be himself': *The Laughing Tradition: Stage Comedy in Garrick's Day* (Athens, GA: University of Georgia Press 1980), p.210.

28  Peter Holland, op. cit., p.240; Jacqueline Pearson, op. cit., p.56.

29  Miriam Slater, *Family Life in the Seventeenth Century: The Verneys of Claydon House* (London: Routledge 1984), p.84.

30  Harriett Hawkins, *Likenesses of Truth in Elizabethan and Restoration Drama* (Oxford: Clarendon Press 1972), p.134. Lawrence Stone, op. cit., p.198, cites a puritan tract of 1622 that makes similar objections to terms of endearment in marriage.

31  Edward Burns, *Restoration Comedy: Crises of Desire and Identity* (London: Macmillan 1987), pp.207–8; Julie Stone Peters, *Congreve, the Drama, and the Printed Word* (Stanford, CA: Stanford University Press 1990), p.186.

32  As Albert Wertheim points out, this scene is unlike the marriage contracts of the actual world, in that it never mentions money: 'Romance and Finance: The Comedies of William Congreve', *Comedy from Shakespeare to Sheridan*, ed. A.R. Braunmuller and J.C. Bulman (Newark, DE: University of Delaware Press 1986), p.270.

33  Sara Heller Mendelson, 'Stuart Women's Diaries and Occasional Memoirs', *Women in English Society 1500–1800*, ed. Mary Prior (London and New York: Methuen 1985), p.196.

34  Richard Braverman sees this as a contrast between the Stuart concept of arbitrary monarchy and the legal authority of parliament that replaced it: 'The Rake's Progress Revisited: Politics and Comedy in the Restoration', *Cultural Readings in Restoration and Eighteenth-Century Theater*, ed. J. Douglas Canfield and Deborah C. Payne (Athens, GA, and London: University of Georgia Press 1995), p.160.

## 7  COMEDY AGAINST ITSELF

1  Adrian Poole, 'Laughter, Forgetting and Shakespeare', *English Comedy*, ed. Michael Cordner, Peter Holland and John Kerrigan (Cambridge: Cambridge University Press 1994), p.85.

2  Quoted in Michael Coveney, *Maggie Smith: A Bright Particular Star* (London: Victor Gollancz 1992), p.118.

3  Stephen Leacock, *My Discovery of England* (Toronto, Ont.: McClelland and Stewart 1961 (reprinted edn)), p.167.

4  *Ben Jonson*, ed. C.H. Herford and Percy and Evelyn Simpson, VIII (Oxford: Clarendon Press 1947), 643; Steele, quoted in Frank H. Ellis, *Sentimental Comedy: Theory and Practice* (Cambridge: Cambridge University Press 1991), p.22.

5  William Hazlitt, *Lectures on the English Comic Writers* (1818), intro. R. Brimley Johnson (London, New York and Toronto, Ont.: Geoffrey Cumberlege, Oxford University Press 1907; repr. 1951), pp.38, 42; Henri Bergson, 'Laughter' (1900), *Comedy*, ed. Wylie Sypher (Garden City, NY: Doubleday 1956), pp.187–88.

6  Richard Bevis, *The Laughing Tradition: Stage Comedy in Garrick's Day* (Athens, GA: University of Georgia Press 1980), p.223.

7  Katharine Worth reports that in the 1990 National Theatre production Lady Sneerwell's defence of malice raise a sympathetic laugh: *Sheridan and Goldsmith* (New York: St Martin's Press 1992), p.142.

8  Stuart M. Tave, *The Amiable Humorist: A Study in the Comic Theory and Criticism of the Eighteenth and Early Nineteenth Centuries* (Chicago, IL: University of Chicago Press 1960), p.51.

9  David B. Paxman, 'The Burden of the Immediate Past: The Early Eighteenth Century and the Shadow of Restoration Comedy', *Essays in Literature*, 17 (1990), p.23.

10  William Hazlitt, op. cit., p.217.

11  Susan Carlson, 'Comic Collisions: Convention, Rage, and Order', *New Theatre Quarterly* 3 (1987), p.303.

12  John Creaser, 'Enigmantic Ben Jonson', *English Comedy*, p.103.

13  Walter Kerr, *Tragedy and Comedy* (New York: Simon & Schuster 1967), p.58.

14  Anne Barton, *Essays, Mainly Shakespearean* (Cambridge: Cambridge University Press 1994), p.101.

15  Robert L. Root, Jr, *Thomas Southerne* (Boston, MA: Twayne 1981), pp.26–27.

16  *Bond on File*, compiled by Philip Roberts (New York and London: Methuen 1985), p.30.

17  Northrop Frye, 'The Argument of Comedy', *Theories of Comedy*, ed. Paul Lauter (Garden City, NY: Doubleday 1964), p.452.

18  George McFadden, *Discovering the Comic* (Princeton: Princeton University Press 1982), p.164; Susan Purdie, *Comedy: The Mastery of Discourse* (Toronto, Ont. and Buffalo, NY: University of Toronto Press 1993), pp.150–67.

19  Ralph A. Houlbrooke, *The English Family 1450–1700* (London and New York: Longman 1984), p.118; Lawrence Stone, *The Family, Sex and Marriage in England 1500–1800* (New York: Harper & Row 1977), p.37.

20  Michael Holroyd, *Bernard Shaw, vol.II, 1898–1918: The Pursuit of Power* (New York: Random House 1989), p.340.

21  Ibid., p.333.

22  The text of the original play is quoted from *Four Plays by Bernard Shaw*, intro. Louis Kronenberger (New York: Modern Library 1953).

23  For a different reading of the revisions, arguing that Shaw's purpose was to exalt Higgins and degrade Eliza, see Arnold Silver, *Bernard Shaw: The Darker Side* (Stanford, CA: Stanford University Press 1982), pp.253–79.

24  Ronald R. Macdonald, '*Measure for Measure*: The Flesh Made Word', *Studies in English Literature*, 30 (1990), pp.268–69.

## CONCLUSION

1  Preface to *The Picture of Dorian Gray*, *Complete Works of Oscar Wilde*, intro. Vyvyan Holland (London and Glasgow: Collins 1948; repr. 1983), p.17.

2  Susan Carlson, *Women and Comedy: Rewriting the British Theatrical Tradition* (Ann Arbor, MI: University of Michigan Press 1991).

# APPENDIX

This appendix lists the editions that have been used for quotations from plays. The following abbreviations refer to multi-author anthologies from which more than one play has been taken.

Bell: *Bell's British Theatre*, London: George Cawthorn, 1797, 34 vols.

Bowers: *The Dramatic Works in the Beaumont and Fletcher Canon*, general editor F. Bowers, Cambridge: Cambridge University Press, 1966–96 (in progress), 10 vols.

Cordner: *Four Restoration Marriage Plays*, ed. M. Cordner, Oxford: Oxford University Press, 1995.

Lyons and Morgan: *Female Playwrights of the Restoration: Five Comedies*, ed. P. Lyons and F. Morgan, London: J.M. Dent, 1991.

Nettleton, Case and Stone: *British Dramatists from Dryden to Sheridan*, ed. G.H. Nettleton and A. Case, revised by G.W. Stone, Carbondale and Edwardsville, IL: Southern Illinois University Press, 1969.

Rowell: *Nineteenth Century Plays*, ed. G. Rowell, London: Oxford University Press, 1953.

Taylor: *Plays by Samuel Foote and Arthur Murphy*, ed. G. Taylor, Cambridge: Cambridge University Press, 1984.

Whitworth: *Three Sixteenth-Century Comedies*, ed. C.W. Whitworth, London: Ernest Benn, New York, W.W. Norton, 1984.

Wood: *Plays by David Garrick and George Colman the Elder*, ed. E.R. Wood, Cambridge: Cambridge University Press, 1982.


Anon., *The London Prodigal*, in *The Shakespeare Apocrypha*, ed. C.F. Tucker Brooke, Oxford: Clarendon Press, 1908.

—— *The Taming of a Shrew*, in *Narrative and Dramatic Sources of Shakespeare*, vol. I, ed. G. Bullough, London: Routledge & Kegan Paul, New York: Columbia University Press, 1966.

Ayckbourn, A. (1977) *The Norman Conquests*, Harmondsworth: Penguin.

—— (1979) *Absent Friends, Absurd Person Singular*, both in *Three Plays*, Harmondsworth: Penguin.

—— (1979) *Relatively Speaking*, London: Evans Plays.

—— (1986) *Woman in Mind*, London: Faber & Faber.

Beaumont, F., *The Knight of the Burning Pestle* in Bowers.

Behn, A. (1967) *The Rover*, ed. F.M. Link, Lincoln, NB: University of Nebraska Press.

—— *The Feigned Courtesans* in Lyons and Morgan.

Bond, E. (1988) *The Sea*, London: Methuen, revised edn.

Boucicault, D. (1984) *London Assurance*, ed. J.L. Smith, London: Adam & Charles Black, New York: W.W. Norton.

—— (1984) *Old Heads and Young Hearts*, in *Plays by Dion Boucicault*, ed. P. Thomson, Cambridge: Cambridge University Press.

Bullwer-Lytton, E., *Money* in Rowell.

Byron, H.J. (1984) *Our Boys*, in *Plays by H.J. Byron*, ed. J. Davis, Cambridge: Cambridge University Press.

Centlivre, S. (1761) *The Beau's Duel*, in *The Works of the Celebrated Mrs Centlivre*, vol. I, London: J. Knapton.

—— (1968) *A Bold Stroke for a Wife*, ed. T. Stathas, Lincoln, NB: University of Nebraska Press.

—— *The Busybody* in Lyons and Morgan.

Churchill, C. (1984) *Cloud 9*, New York: Methuen, revised edn.

Cibber, C. (1973)*Love's Last Shift*, in *Three Sentimental Comedies*, ed. M. Sullivan, London and New Haven, CT: Yale University Press.

Colman, G., the Elder, *The Jealous Wife* in Wood.

Congreve, W. (1985) *The Double Dealer, Love for Love, The Old Bachelor, The Way of the World*, all in *The Comedies of William Congreve*, ed. E.S. Rump, Harmondsworth: Penguin.

Cooper, G. (1963) *Everything in the Garden*, in *New English Dramatists*, vol. VII, intro. J.W. Lambert, Harmondsworth: Penguin.

Coward, N. (1965) *Blithe Spirit, Hay Fever, Private Lives*, all in *Three Plays by Noël Coward*, intro. E. Albee, New York: Delta.

Cowley, H. (1994) *The Belle's Stratagem*, in *The Meridian Anthology of Restoration and Eighteenth-Century Plays by Women*, ed. K.M. Rogers in New York: Penguin.

Crowne, J. (1694) *The Married Beau*, London: Richard Bentley.

—— (1966) *Sir Courtly Nice*, ed. C. Bradford Hughes, The Hague and Paris: Mouton.

Cumberland, R., *The Fashionable Lovers* in Bell.

—— *The West Indian* in Nettleton, Case and Stone.

Dekker, T. (1953–61)*The Honest Whore, Part Two, The Shoemakers' Holiday*, both in *The Dramatic Works of Thomas Dekker*, ed. F. Bowers, Cambridge: Cambridge University Press, 4 vols.

Dryden, J. (1967) *Marriage a-la-Mode, Secret Love*, both in *Four Comedies*, ed. L.A. Beaurline and F. Bowers, London and Chicago, IL: University of Chicago Press.

D'Urfey, T. (1987) *The Richmond Heiress*, ed. R.A. Biswanger, Jr, New York and London: Garland.

Etherege, G. (1966) *The Man of Mode*, ed. W.B. Carnochan, Lincoln, NB: University of Nebraska Press.

Farquhar, G. (1995) *The Beaux' Stratagem, The Recruiting Officer, The Twin Rivals*, all in *The Recruiting Officer and Other Plays*, ed. W. Myers, Oxford and New York: Oxford University Press.

Fielding, H. (1775) *The Modern Husband*, in *The Works of Henry Fielding, Esq.*, vol. II, London: John Bell.

—— (1784) *The Fathers*, in *The Works of Henry Fielding, Esq.*, vol. IV, London: W. Strahan.

Fletcher, J., *Monsieur Thomas, The Woman's Prize* in Bowers.

Foote, S., *The Minor, The Nabob* in Taylor.

Fry, C. (1950) *The Lady's Not for Burning*, London: Oxford University Press, 2nd edn.

Garrick, D. and Colman, G., the Elder, *The Clandestine Marriage* in Wood.

Gilbert, W.S. (1982) *Engaged*, *The Palace of Truth*, both in *Plays by W.S. Gilbert*, ed. G. Rowell, Cambridge: Cambridge University Press.

Goldsmith, O. (1990) *The Good-Natured Man*, in *Poems and Plays*, ed. T. Davis, London: Dent.

—— (1979) *She Stoops to Conquer*, ed. T. Davis, London: Ernest Benn.

Hankin, St John (1962) *The Return of the Prodigal*, in *Edwardian Plays*, ed. G. Weales, New York: Hill & Wang.

Inchbald, E. (1987) *Wives as They Were, and Maids as They Are*, in *Selected Comedies*, intro. R. Manvell, Lanham, New York and London: University Press of America.

—— (1991) *Everyone has his Fault*, in F.H. Ellis, *Sentimental Comedy: Theory and Practice*, Cambridge: Cambridge University Press.

Jones, H.A. (1982) *The Case of Rebellious Susan*, in *Plays by Henry Arthur Jones*, ed. R. Jackson, Cambridge: Cambridge University Press.

Jonson, B. (1925–52) *Bartholomew Fair*, *Epicoene*, *Every Man in his Humour*, *Every Man out of his Humour*, *The New Inn*, *Volpone*, all in *Ben Jonson*, ed. C.H. Herford, P. Simpson and E. Simpson, Oxford: Clarendon Press, 11 vols.

Kelly, H., *False Delicacy*, *The School for Wives*, *A Word to the Wise* in Bell.

Lyly, J. (1969) *Gallathea*, in *Gallathea and Midas*, ed. A. Begor Lancashire, Lincoln, NB: University of Nebraska Press.

Macklin, C., *The Man of the World* in Bell.

Marston, J. (1965) *The Dutch Courtesan*, ed. M.L. Wine, Lincoln, NB: University of Nebraska Press.

Massinger, P. (1978) *A New Way to Pay Old Debts*, in *The Selected Plays of Philip Massinger*, ed. C. Gibson, Cambridge: Cambridge University Press.

Maugham, W.S. (1963) *The Circle*, *The Constant Wife*, both in *Selected Plays*, Harmondsworth: Penguin.

Medwall, H. (1972) *Fulgens and Lucrece*, in *Tudor Plays*, ed. E. Creeth, New York: W.W. Norton.

Middleton, T. (1969) *A Chaste Maid in Cheapside*, ed. R.B. Parker, London: Methuen.

Morton, J.M. (1974) *Box and Cox*, in *The Magistrate and other Nineteenth-Century Plays*, ed. M.R. Booth, London, Oxford and New York: Oxford University Press.

Murphy, A., *The Citizen* in Taylor.

Orton, J. (1976) *Loot*, *What the Butler Saw*, both in *The Complete Plays*, intro. J. Lahr, London: Methuen.

Otway, T. *The Soldiers' Fortune* in Cordner.

Pinero, A.W. (1896) *The Benefit of the Doubt*, London: William Heinemann.

—— (1995) *The Magistrate*, in *Trelawney of the Wells and Other Plays*, ed. J.S. Bratton, Oxford and New York: Oxford University Press.

Porter, H. (1888) *The Two Angry Women of Abingdon*, ed. H. Ellis, in *Nero and Other Plays*, ed. H.P. Horne *et al.*, London: Vizetelly.

Reynolds, F. (1927) *The Dramatist*, in *Lesser English Comedies of the Eighteenth Century*, ed. A. Nicoll, Oxford: Oxford University Press.

Robertson, T.W., *Caste* in Rowell.

—— (1982) *Society*, in *Plays by Tom Robertson*, ed. W. Tydeman, Cambridge: Cambridge University Press.

'S., Mr', *Gammer Gurton's Needle* in Whitworth.

Sedley, C. (1687) *Bellamira*, London: D. Mallett.

—— (1970) *The Mulberry Garden*, in *Restoration Comedies*, ed. D. Davison, London, Oxford and New York: Oxford University Press.

Shadwell, T. (1930) *Epsom Wells*, in *Epsom Wells and The Volunteers*, ed. D.M. Walmsley, Boston, MA: D.C. Heath & Co.

—— (1995) *Bury Fair*, ed. J.C. Ross. New York and London: Garland.

Shaffer, P. (1981) *Black Comedy*, in *Four Plays*, Harmondsworth: Penguin.

Shakespeare, W. (1992) *All's Well That Ends Well, As You Like It, The Comedy of Errors, Love's Labour's Lost, The Merchant of Venice, The Merry Wives of Windsor, Measure for Measure, A Midsummer Night's Dream, Much Ado About Nothing, The Taming of the Shrew, Twelfth Night*, all in *The Complete Works of William Shakespeare*, ed. D. Bevington, New York: HarperCollins, 4th edn.

Shaw, B. (1941) *Pygmalion*, Harmondsworth: Penguin.

—— (1946) *Man and Superman*, Harmondsworth: Penguin.

—— (1964) *Heartbreak House*, Harmondsworth: Penguin.

Sheridan, R.B. (1979) *The Rivals*, ed. E. Duthie, London: Ernest Benn.

—— (1979) *The School for Scandal*, ed. F.W. Bateson, London: Ernest Benn.

Shirley, J. (1976) *Hyde Park*, in *Drama of the English Renaissance, II: the Stuart Period*, ed. R.A. Fraser and N. Rabkin, New York: Macmillan.

Simpson, N.F. (1960) *One-Way Pendulum*, London: Faber & Faber.

Southerne, T. (1988) *Sir Anthony Love*, in *The Works of Thomas Southerne*, vol. I, ed. R. Jordan and H. Love, Oxford: Clarendon Press.

—— *The Wives' Excuse* in Cordner.

Steele, R., *The Conscious Lovers* in Nettleton, Case and Stone.

—— (1967) *The Tender Husband*, ed. C. Wilson, Lincoln, NB: University of Nebraska Press.

Stoppard, T. (1983) *The Real Thing*, London: Faber & Faber, revised edn.

—— (1986) *Jumpers*, London: Faber & Faber, revised edn.

Taylor, T. and Duborg, A.W. (1973) *New Men and Old Acres*, in *English Plays of the Nineteenth Century, III: Comedies*, ed. M.R. Booth, Oxford: Clarendon Press.

Udall, N., *Roister Doister* in Whitworth.

Vanbrugh, J. (1989) *The Provoked Wife, The Relapse*, both in *Sir John Vanbrugh: Four Comedies*, ed. M. Cordner, Harmondsworth: Penguin.

Vanbrugh, J. and Cibber, C. (1975) *The Provoked Husband*, ed. P. Dixon, London: Edward Arnold.

Wilde, O. (1988) *The Importance of Being Earnest*, ed. R. Jackson, London: Adam & Charles Black; New York: W.W. Norton.

Wycherley, W. (1966) *The Country Wife, Love in a Wood, The Plain Dealer*, all in *The Complete Plays of William Wycherley*, ed. G. Weales, Garden City, NY: Doubleday.

# INDEX